Experiments in the Machine Interpretation of Visual Motion

Experiments in the Machine Interpretation of Visual Motion

David W Murray and Bernard F Buxton

The MIT Press
Cambridge, Massachusetts
London, England

Library of Congress Cataloging-in-Publication Data

Murray, David W.

   Experiments in the machine interpretation of visual motion / David W. Murray and Bernard F. Buxton.
         p.   cm. — (Artificial Intelligence)
   Includes bibliographical references and index.
   ISBN 978-0-262-13263-3 (hc. : alk. paper) — 978-0-262-52816-0 (pb)
   1. Computer vision. 2. Motion perception (Vision) I. Buxton, Bernard F. II. Title. III. Series.
TA1635.M87   1990   90-43645
006.3'7—dc20   CIP

The MIT Press is pleased to keep this title available in print by manufacturing single copies, on demand, via digital printing technology.

Contents

Contents

List of Figures

List of Tables

Series Foreword

Artificial intelligence is the study of intelligence using the ideas and methods of computation. Unfortunately, a definition of intelligence seems impossible at the moment because intelligence appears to be an amalgam of so many information-processing and information-representation abilities. Of course psychology, philosophy, linguistics, and related disciplines offer various perspectives and methodologies for studying intelligence. For the most part, however, the theories proposed in these fields are too incomplete and too vaguely stated to be realized in computational terms. Something more is needed, even though valuable ideas, relationships, and constraints can be gleaned from traditional studies of what are, after all, impressive existence proofs that intelligence is in fact possible. Artificial intelligence offers a new perspective and a new methodology. Its central goal is to make computers intelligent, both to make them more useful and to understand the principles that make intelligence possible. That intelligent computers will be extremely useful is obvious. The more profound point is that artificial intelligence aims to understand intelligence using the ideas and methods of computation, thus offering a radically new and different basis for theory formation. Most of the people doing work in artificial intelligence believe that these theories will apply to any intelligent information processor, whether biological or solid state.

There are side effects that deserve attention, too. Any program that will successfully model even a small part of intelligence will be inherently massive and complex. Consequently, artificial intelligence continually confronts the limits of computer-science technology. The problems encountered have been hard enough and interesting enough to seduce artificial intelligence people into working on them with enthusiasm. It is natural, then, that there has been a steady flow of ideas from artificial intelligence to computer science, and the flow shows no sign of abating

The purpose of the Artificial Intelligence series is to provide people in many areas, both professionals and students, with timely, detailed information about what is happening on the frontiers in research centers all over the world.

Patrick Henry Winston
J. Michael Brady
Daniel Bobrow

Preface

The aim of research into computational vision is to perform on a machine that task which our own visual systems appear to achieve quite effortlessly[1]. That task is seeing — taking those two dimensional images that fall on our retinae and from them obtaining percepts of the three dimensional world around us. It is those three dimensional percepts that enable us and, at an infinitely humbler level, our machines to take intelligent actions in the world, actions which most often will involve *motion*.

Motion in our universe is all pervading, on scales ranging from the atomic to the astronomic. It threads through our everyday existence, and is the symptom of change and purpose. It is crucial to have an understanding of motion and an appreciation of its likely consequences at an early stage in our sensory processes. Robots, if they are to act intelligently in our own everyday environment, will have to be similarly endowed.

To those who, while gazing from the window of a moving car, have considered why roadside objects seem to flash by whereas the distant landscape appears to move hardly at all, it comes as no surprise that moving imagery tells us a great deal about the disposition of the world around us. Emulating this ability to recover information about the world around us by processing such *visual motion* has been the aim of the research we describe in this book.

But a moment's comparison of the current state of machine visual intelligence with that of a baby only a few months old will indicate that our understanding of, and ability to solve, such natural processing problems is somewhat restricted. Most problems turn out to be hard — and visual motion interpretation is no exception. In these circumstances, setting anything in print seems an act of pompous futility, like scratching in the sand and hoping that the next wave of progress will leave the scribble legible. And yet it seems to us that the last decade of work in the machine interpretation of visual motion has yielded a key fact: that it is both feasible and computationally practicable to derive visual motion from moving imagery, to compute scene structure from that visual motion and, in simple cases, to use that recovered geometry for the recognition of objects. In other words, visual motion can enable traversal of bottom-up, data-driven paths through the visual processing

---

1) give or take the odd 10^{10} neurons

hierarchy, paths which link images to objects. The computational approach espoused perhaps most forcibly in Marr's writings is (yet again) vindicated. This book evidences that through an experimental exploration of a few of those paths.

*

The organization of the book is covered in more detail in the opening chapter, and here we make only a few asides. First, any description with hindsight of what were heat-of-the-moment endeavours presents the welcome opportunity of enduing the whole with an almost respectable coherence. At one and the same time, it presents the strong temptation to draw a decent veil over some of the heat-of-the-moment nonsenses. We hope that this has been resisted. Secondly, we trust that our visual routines have been presented in sufficient detail for the reader to exploit them if so desired. Finally, we note without trace of apology that we have kept discussion of our results to a minimum, nor do we use our results to support our or anybody else's 'theory of vision'. For the most part the experimental facts can speak for themselves.

*

One of the pleasures of working in a field like computational vision is interacting with people who are in similar awe at how well evolution seems to do have done things but have a similar stubborn urge to get *something* working on rather shorter timescales. It is a pleasure to acknowledge the help of colleagues in the Long Range Research Laboratory at GEC Research over several years. Derek Roberts, Dennis Scotter and Cyril Hilsum provided the research environment; David Castelow not only worked unstintingly on visual motion estimation and integrating our processing chains, but almost by the way provided a civilized computing resource; Steve Maybank, Pavel Grossman, Joachim Rieger and Harit Trivedi were always game for an argument and ready with advice. Elsewhere, extraordinary thanks go to Hilary Buxton and John Mayhew for their early inspiration and continuing enlightening discussion. Christopher Longuet-Higgins and Guy Scott were instrumental in much of the work on planar surfaces. More recently Michael Brady and Andrew Blake have given considerable encouragement. Caroline Murray has done wonders proof-reading. Any bludners are down to wee Laura on the one hand, and Ben and Charlie on the other. Finally, we must acknowledge the tremendous impetus given to machine vision research in the UK by the Alvey programme for information technology: our thanks go to the IKBS Director, David Thomas, for his support and to our colleagues and collaborators for their help and encouragement, especially Chris Harris and John Fox.

*

Experiments in the
Machine Interpretation of Visual Motion

1 Image, Scene and Motion

"The interpretation of visual motion is the process by which a description of the environment in terms of objects, their three dimensional shape, and their motion through space is constructed on the basis of the changing image that reaches the eye."

Shimon Ullman

The practical importance to robotics of the recovery of information about a scene, its motion and disposition or structure, at an early stage in the visual processing hierarchy cannot be overstated. In general terms, if we succeed in making machines capable of understanding the world, we will surely want them to take *action*, and action almost invariably implies *motion*. Simply stated:

- Understanding motion is a principal requirement for a machine or organism to interact meaningfully with its environment.

As we shall see, the two dimensional visual motion derived from a sequence of time-varying imagery turns out to be a potentially valuable source of information about the 3D scene being viewed. At a basic level, visual motion can be used simply to flag motion in the scene. It flags something that demands attention, perhaps alerting a simple creature to something about to eat it or, more promising, to something worth eating. But it has long been appreciated, for example by such luminaries as von Helmholtz (1896) and Mach (1886), that encoded in visual motion is much more detail about the three dimensional geometric structure and motion of the scene. The capacity to exploit this detailed information has been demonstrated to exist in a wide variety of creatures. The common fly, for example, is able to track moving objects and segment targets on the basis of their visual motion (Reichardt and Poggio 1980); the common man has been shown to be capable of recovering 3D scene structure using image motion cues *alone*, especially when the scene can be interpreted as a rigid or hinged object (Wallach and O'Connell 1953;

Johansson 1973; Proffitt and Bertenthal 1984). Understanding visual
motion then holds the promise of enabling tasks covering a broad range
of difficulty, from simple tracking of objects, through passive navigation
and object recognition and ultimately to the understanding of complex
extended temporal events.

Curiously, as Koenderink (1986) points out, von Helmholtz and others late last century did not develop detailed theories of visual motion
processing, though nothing more than Euclidean geometry is required
for much analysis. Perhaps their lack of computing power dulled its
relevance. Indeed, it was not until the middle of this century that substantial attention was again paid to the area, initially from perceptual
psychologists, where Gibson is the outstanding (though later contro-
versial) figure (Gibson 1950, 1966; Gibson, Olum and Rosenblatt 1955;
Gibson and Gibson 1957; Reed 1989), and latterly from researchers in artificial intelligence and robotics, for example, Koenderink and van Doorn
(1975, 1976a), Ullman (1979) and Longuet-Higgins and Prazdny (1980).
Over the last ten years, efforts have grown apace with the emerging
realization of the fundamental importance of motion understanding, a
growing confidence in the computational nature of vision and, of course,
with the inexorable increase in computing resources to do something
about it.

However despite (or perhaps because of) the enormous potential of
visual motion, the opening paragraph of Ullman's *The Interpretation
of Visual Motion* quoted at the chapter's head (Ullman 1979) possesses
for the initiated an almost idyllic simplicity born of understatement —
understatement, in fact no statement at all, of the difficulties of interpreting visual motion in practice.

Perhaps the fundamental reason for the difficulties of the task (and
indeed of the broad sweep of so-called natural tasks — vision, speech
recognition and so on) is that so often the signal processing involved is
ill-posed. That is, one set of raw data permits a large, possibly infinite,
number of solutions. Our own percepts and those much cruder ones
of our machines are constructed from processing over a range of levels
— in the case of vision from low-level detection of intensity features
to high-level interpretation of scenes and events. At most levels some
recourse to experience, memory or embedded knowledge is necessary
to discriminate between available solutions. So reconstructing scenes
from imagery, moving or otherwise, requires the imposition of constraints

— constraints about the way the world works or, more usually and precariously and excitingly, about the way we *expect* the world to work.

On the practical front a difficulty which immediately confronts those researching into visual motion is the enormous data rate ($\approx 25\text{MBs}^{-1}$) which even today means that experimentation is slow and cumbersome, and usually limited to short snapshot processing. A further emergent difficulty, and one to which we return in the final chapter, is how to embed our ability to recover instantaneous scene structure and motion into the broader framework of a time-evolving percept of the viewed surroundings.

Although the emergence of the subtleties and complexities of the interpretation of visual motion has been gradual, and is certainly far from complete, significant progress has been made over the last few years, chiefly in demonstrating the practical feasibility, albeit in restricted domains, of recovering quite detailed descriptions of the scene and its motion from image motion in a data-driven, bottom-up fashion. This book aims to demonstrate at least some of those practical possibilities by exploiting some of the constraints available.

1.1 Exegesis

In this book we develop algorithms to interpret visual motion around four principal constraint themes in three dimensions (Table 1.1). An important aspect is that we only assume partial knowledge of each visual motion vector, thereby accommodating the so-called aperture problem (of which more later) without recourse to insecurely founded operations in the image. First we consider perhaps the simplest constraint regime of all, that where the relative motion between camera and scene is known a priori. The scene structure may be recovered on a pointwise basis. The second regime constrains the scene to comprise a set of connected straight edges moving rigidly but arbitrarily. Later we pursue this representation to the recognition level, where the 3D wireframe percept reconstructed from the imagery is matched to a 3D wireframe model held in memory. The third constraint theme makes the transition between edge and surface representations by demanding that the wireframe recovered is strictly polyhedral. This enables a percept in terms of planar surfaces to be recovered, a percept which is later matched to polyhedral models described in terms of their surfaces. The final constraint assumes that the scene is made up of planar surfaces, and recovers them directly. Early on it had been hoped to pursue this surface scheme to the recognition level but, as we shall describe, the individual algorithms did not knit happily together. The principal difficulty proved to be achieving a satisfactory segmentation of the image and scene into separate surface facets, a problem which is, unfortunately, largely unsolved here and elsewhere. Indeed the broader issues of segmentation remain ones of key concern in machine vision.

In **this chapter** we consider the properties of visual motion and its relationship to the projected motion and thus to the three dimensional structure of the scene and its motion relative to the sensor. We characterize the principal schemes for computing image motion and discuss how the image motion they compute is tied to the scene geometry.

In **Chapter 2** we motivate and describe an algorithm which computes visual motion by matching elements of intensity edge (edgels) as they move from frame to frame. The method draws on an earlier pixel patch matching recipe due to Scott (1987b) which is able to adapt between gradient-based and token tracking schemes according to the data available. By matching edgels which are themselves computed to sub-pixel accuracy the algorithm is capable of producing high quality results for edge-dominated imagery.

Chapter 3 discusses the implications for 3D structure from motion computation of the aperture problem. We show that if it applies, then constraints are not merely desirable but essential for reconstructing the 3D scene structure and motion. We discuss the application of the simplest scene constraint, that of known relative motion, to recover depth on a point by point basis, and introduce the issue of segmentation by considering a scheme for recovering the structure of unlinked straight edges with known motion.

Chapter 4 describes a scheme for the recovery of the 3D structure and 3D motion (up to the inherent depth/speed scaling ambiguity) from visual motion components which suffer the aperture problem, on the assumption that the scene comprises *linked* straight edges. The recovered structure is later matched to models. The chapter opens with the description of a set of 2D rules which segment visual motion components arising from the same straight edge.

Chapter 5 considers a method of progressing from edge-based scene representations towards those based on surfaces. It discusses a modification to the structure from motion algorithm of Chapter 4 by the imposition of polyhedral constraints using the line drawing analysis of Sugihara (1986). This allows the recovery of 3D edges *and* planar surfaces, which are later matched to 3D planar surface object models.

Chapter 6 describes two algorithms for the recovery of 3D scene structure and motion on the assumption that the scene comprises a single planar facet. If the motion is known a priori, the depths in the scene can be computed pointwise, so fitting a surface is particularly straightforward. Both algorithms again function using only *components* of the image motion, and so overcome the aperture problem described in Chapter 1. We analyze the algorithms' behaviour as the camera viewing angle is reduced and explore situations in which they fail entirely. Once a scene is recovered it is, of course, a trivial matter to reconstruct the full image motion, and we briefly compare this sort of motion field reconstruction with that obtained using Hildreth's contour smoothness constraint (Hildreth 1984b).

For the algorithms of Chapter 6 to be useful in a multi-faceted world, a way must be found to segment visual motion into regions arising from different facets. This turns out to be a non-trivial problem and **Chapter 7** explores two rather different approaches, but both based on the scene rather than the image. The first builds a global reconstruction of the scene surfaces, the other detects local changes in surface orientation and motion. We conclude that the segmentation problem for surfaces is largely unsolved by these or other techniques.

The partial wireframes recovered from the structure from motion algorithm of Chapter 4 are matched to complete 3D wireframe models using the constraints described in **Chapter 8**. Our main concern is the development of scaleless matching constraints and the matching space is searched using a variant of the method introduced by Grimson and Lozano-Pérez (1984). The constraints avoid the use of absolute size, which is unknown up to a scaling factor because of the depth/speed scaling ambiguity. We show that the matching process can resolve this ambiguity, enabling absolute depth and motion recovery. This chapter therefore completes a processing chain from moving imagery to recognized, located, moving objects.

A second much briefer chapter on matching, **Chapter 9**, gives a description of the constraints required for scaleless matching to *surfaces*, as

Table 1.1: The four schemes for interpreting motion and where they are discussed.

Task	Scheme I 3D Points	Scheme II 3D Edges	Scheme III 3D Polyhedra	Scheme IV 3D Planar Surfaces
Computing 2D Image Motion ↓	Edgel Correspondence Ch 2 ↓	(as I) ↓	(as I) ↓	(as I) ↓
Motion Segment- ation ↓	Unnecessary ↓	Using 2D Edgels § 4.1 ↓	(as II) ↓	Using Visual Motion Ch 7 ↓
Structure from Motion ↓	Point by Point Ch 3 ↓	3D Straight Edges Ch 4 ↓	Polyhedral Constraints Ch 5 ↓	3D Planar Facets Ch 6 ↓
Matching to Models		Wireframe Models Ch 8	Surface Models Ch 9	(as III)

required for the data from Chapters 5 and 6. The matcher uses a search technique similar to the wireframe method of Chapter 8, and again uses constraints which involve only shape not size. Again this completes a thread from images to objects.

The final chapter, **Chapter 10**, draws together the strands of the work, tries to set them in context, and points to agendas for future research.

1.2   Scene and image motion

Brief details of many specific methods used in visual motion processing were given by Barron (1984). A more general review of the conceptual and computational aspects of motion processing was given by Koenderink (1986) and an excellent review comparing the physiological and computational issues involved in motion processing has been written by Hildreth and Koch (1987). It is evident from the first, and noted in the other two, that there has been much emphasis in machine vision on explicit recovery of discrete image velocities or *visual motion* as the initial step in motion understanding [1].

Notwithstanding this concentration of effort, computing visual motion is still by no means a routine task, and it remains one for which a bewildering battery of different techniques have been and continue to be proposed. Moreover, even when visual motion has been recovered, it may not be immediately obvious how it is related to the *projected motion*, the projection of the motion of the scene onto the image plane — if at all. It is essential to understand this relationship if meaningful scene information is to be extracted from the visual motion. This is the topic of the remainder of our opening chapter.

1.2.1 Projected motion

That the projected motion of the 3D scene in the 2D image plane depends on both scene structure and motion is easily shown.

Consider the camera geometry sketched in Figure 1.1, where the optic axis extends along $\hat{z}$, the lens is equivalent to a pinhole at the origin and where the image plane lies at $z = -l$. Scene points $\mathbf{R} = (X, Y, Z)^T$ are imaged at $\mathbf{r} = (x, y, -l)^T$ under the perspective transformation as

$$\mathbf{r} = -\frac{l\mathbf{R}}{Z} \; . \tag{1.1}$$

The projected motion in the image is simply the time differential of the above, ie

$$\dot{\mathbf{r}} = -\frac{l}{Z}\left(\dot{\mathbf{R}} - \mathbf{R}\frac{\dot{\mathbf{R}} \cdot \hat{z}}{Z} \right) \; . \tag{1.2}$$

Later we will have need to describe the scene motion $\dot{\mathbf{R}}$ in terms of instantaneous rectilinear and angular velocities with respect to the camera:

$$\dot{\mathbf{R}} = \mathbf{V} + \mathbf{\Omega} \times \mathbf{R} \; . \tag{1.3}$$

After some rearrangement, we find the projected motion to be

$$\dot{\mathbf{r}} = -\frac{l\mathbf{V}}{Z} - \mathbf{r}\frac{\mathbf{V} \cdot \hat{z}}{Z} + \mathbf{\Omega} \times \mathbf{r} + \mathbf{r}\frac{\mathbf{\Omega} \times \mathbf{r} \cdot \hat{z}}{l} \tag{1.4}$$

---

1) It is by no means clear to what extent biological systems use this route alone to process motion — certainly, other techniques are available. Indeed, the route is not necessary in computational vision: Negadaripour and Horn (1985) demonstrated recovery of planar surface structure and motion analogous to that of Chapter 6 *directly* from the time-varying image irradiance.

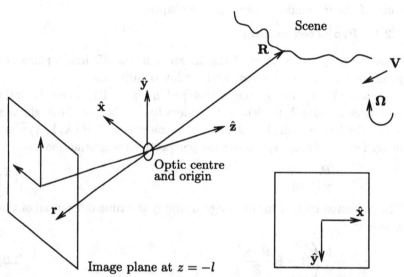

Figure 1.1: The camera geometry used throughout this book. (Note that wherever image properties are displayed in the text, they are rotated by π about $\hat{\mathbf{z}}$ so that they appear the 'right way up', as shown in the inset.)

or, broken into components,

$$
\begin{aligned}
\dot{x} &= -\frac{lV_x}{Z} - x\frac{V_z}{Z} - l\Omega_y - y\Omega_z + x\frac{y\Omega_x - x\Omega_y}{l} \qquad (1.5)\\
\dot{y} &= -\frac{lV_y}{Z} - y\frac{V_z}{Z} + x\Omega_z + l\Omega_x + y\frac{y\Omega_x - x\Omega_y}{l}\,.
\end{aligned}
$$

Two interesting features are immediately apparent. First, only the rectilinear velocity terms contain the scene depth Z. Secondly, Z always appears in ratio with the magnitude of $\mathbf{V}$ — that is, there is a depth/speed scaling ambiguity inherent in monocular motion processing — it is quite impossible to decide whether something is large, far-off and moving quickly, or small, near-to and moving slowly.

On this fact rests the fortune of many a maker of action movies. The ambiguity can only be resolved by introducing extra knowledge, and later we show how such knowledge can be introduced during object recognition (Chapters 8 and 9).

However, the tasks of immediate concern are first the computation of visual motion from the time-varying image irradiance $E(\mathbf{r}, t)$ and secondly exploration of the relationship of that visual motion to the projected motion.

1.3 Paradigms for computing visual motion

It is useful to distinguish two complementary classifications of schemes to compute visual motion. The first classifies according to the spatio-temporal range over which methods are applicable: by analogy with the human visual system (Braddick 1974, 1980) it is convenient to consider short range and long range processes. The other classification distinguishes between the fundamentally different processes involved; on the one hand are gradient-based schemes which use spatio-temporal image irradiance gradients to derive image motion, and on the other are correspondence or similarity matching methods. The former are intrinsically short range, whereas the latter can be short range or long range.

Here we further discuss three schemes, which are:

- "raw" gradient-based schemes,

- "edge" gradient-based schemes and

- token tracking and matching schemes.

1.3.1 Raw gradient schemes

Raw gradient-based schemes compute visual motion directly from the ratios of temporal to spatial image irradiance gradients. Visual motion computed this way is usually called *optical flow*. The idea was first mooted in 1D by Limb and Murphy (1975) and introduced in 2D imagery by Horn and Schunck (1981) who devised the now famous motion constraint equation

$$\frac{\partial E}{\partial t} + \nabla E \cdot \dot{\mathbf{f}} = 0 \tag{1.6}$$

to compute the optical flow field $\dot{\mathbf{f}}$. Their equation is derived from the chain rule on the assumption that the total time differential of the image irradiance, dE/dt, is zero. (The assumption that $dE/dt = 0$ is strictly incorrect — it cannot hold when the sun comes out from behind a cloud nor when the eye is caught by specular reflections, and there are other more complex and widespread effects such as mutual illumination which will confound it. Nonetheless, it must overall be a very reasonable assumption, for without it vision would be an unstable sensing modality. Recently, Girosi, Verri and Torre (1989) have proposed $d(|\nabla E|)/dt = 0$ as a constraint on which to base visual motion computation. This too appears inexact and it is too early to judge whether there is much tangible advantage in its use over the Horn and Schunck formulation.)

The often quoted advantage of a raw gradient-based scheme is that it can be applied uniformly across the image, although where the spatial or temporal gradients are small the results will be sensitive to noise. A more obvious disadvantage of the method is that only the component of image motion along the gradient direction can be derived — the well-known aperture problem (Wallach 1976; Fennema and Thompson 1979; Ullman 1979), which is illustrated in Figure 1.2. Viewing the image locally (here the result of using differentials), one cannot perceive motion perpendicular to the gradient direction, that is, along the local intensity edge direction. The recovered component, $\dot{\mathbf{f}}_\perp$, is often called the *vernier velocity*. We return to the repercussions of the aperture problem in 3D in Chapter 3.

A final point of note is that raw gradient schemes have been successfully implemented in analogue VLSI neural networks (Hutchinson, Koch,

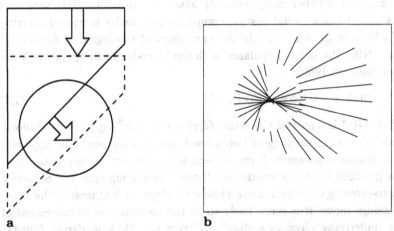

a   b

Figure 1.2: The aperture problem. Although the motion of the area of the image with an intensity gradient is downwards in (a), all that is perceived through the aperture is the motion component along the gradient direction or perpendicular to the edge. A computed example is shown in (b): the headlight of a truck, from Figure 4.11, is moving left to right. (With such a circular feature the ends of the components form a graceful limaçon of Pascal.)

Luo and Mead 1988) though it should be stressed that the physical limitations of such nets impose additional, apparently beneficial, constraints. The hardware does not solve equation (1.6), but a regularized version of it (see §1.4).

1.3.2   Edge gradient schemes

There is a wide consensus that the information rich areas in imagery lie at discontinuities in the irradiance, of which the most common manifestation is the 1D intensity structure, the image edge. (We should though be mindful of other image events!) Marr and Ullman (1981) proposed that the human visual system computes motion by temporal filtering of edge signals found as the zero-crossings of the signal S formed by convolving the image irradiance with the Marr-Hildreth operator (Marr and Hildreth 1980):

$$S(\mathbf{r}) = -\nabla^2 G(\mathbf{r}) * E(\mathbf{r}) , \qquad (1.7)$$

where $G(\mathbf{r})$ is a spatial Gaussian, $G(\mathbf{r}) = \exp[-(x^2 + y^2)/2\sigma^2]$. Hildreth and Ullman (1982) suggest two advantages of using zero-crossings over raw irradiance schemes. First, zero-crossings correspond to points where the gradient is locally maximum, thereby "reducing error"[2]. Secondly, "zero-crossings are tied more closely to physical features; if the zero-crossings move, it is more likely to be the consequence of movement of the underlying physical surface". Witkin (1983), Koenderink (1984a) and Yuille and Poggio (1986) have given more rigorous justification of the use of the Marr-Hildreth operator over continuous scales, but it has become clearer that the mapping of zero-crossings onto physical surface features is more complicated than foreseen (Berzins 1984; Yuille 1984, 1989).

In (Hildreth and Ullman 1982), the $S = 0$ surfaces were interpolated between zero crossings and used to derive the edge-normal component of the optical flow using a motion constraint equation for the signal:

$$\frac{\partial S}{\partial t} + \nabla S \cdot \dot{\mathbf{f}} = 0 , \qquad (1.8)$$

from which

$$\dot{\mathbf{f}}_{\perp} = -\left(\frac{\partial S}{\partial t}\frac{1}{\nabla S \cdot \nabla S}\right)\nabla S \quad (\text{at } S = 0) . \qquad (1.9)$$

---

2) By implication, *random* error.

Clearly, edge gradient schemes suffer from the aperture problem in just the same way that raw gradient schemes do.

An extension of this approach into the temporal domain was proposed by Buxton and Buxton (1983, 1984). They searched for zero-crossings in a signal created by convolving spatio-temporal extensions of the Marr-Hildreth operator with the image irradiance, for example by defining

$$S(\mathbf{r}, t) = -\left(\nabla^2 + \frac{1}{c^2}\frac{\partial^2}{\partial t^2}\right) G(\mathbf{r}, t) * E(\mathbf{r}, t) , \qquad (1.10)$$

where c is some scaling velocity and $G(\mathbf{r}, t) = \exp[-(x^2 + y^2 + c^2 t^2)/2\sigma^2]$ is a spatio-temporal Gaussian smoothing function. The image-wide uniformity of the gradient-based approach was exploited in a parallel implementation of the work on a SIMD architecture, an ICL Distributed Array Processor[3] (Buxton, Buxton, Murray and Williams 1984; Buxton, Murray, Buxton and Williams 1985; Buxton and Williams 1986). Perhaps spurred on by the possibilities of realizable networks to perform such operations, the use of spatio-temporal filters has recently returned to prominence. Indeed Buxton and Buxton's technique appears to have been re-explored and extended by Duncan and Chou (1988), and variants of the scheme are used by Baraldi, De Micheli and Uras (1989) and Tistarelli and Sandini (1990).

The neuro-physiological implications of edge gradient schemes are reviewed by Hildreth and Koch (1987).

1.3.3 Token tracking methods

Token tracking schemes, eg those of Barnard and Thompson (1980), Thompson and Barnard (1981), Dreschler and Nagel (1981), Nagel (1983), Westphal and Nagel (1986) and Harris, Ibison, Sparkes and Stephens (1986), are conceptually much simpler than gradient schemes, though inherently somewhat more involved computationally. In them, distinctive image features are detected and their correspondences tracked from frame to frame in a sequence. The features, such as corners, blobs and straight line segments, are assumed to arise from distinctive scene features. The displacement of a feature from frame to frame, $\Delta\mathbf{r}$, is related to the visual motion by $\Delta\mathbf{r} = \dot{\mathbf{r}}\Delta t$, where Δt is the inter-frame

---

3) The DAP architecture is now manufactured as an attached processor by Active Memory Technology Inc. and similar processor array boards can now be obtained from other manufacturers, eg the Marconi MARADE system.

period. The advantage of such schemes is that by tracking appropriate features they can yield high quality information about two (orthogonal) components of the visual motion, that is, the *full* visual motion. A disadvantage is that as the features become more distinctive they, and the resulting visual motion, become sparser in the image. A further perceived drawback is that the cost of computation per visual motion vector is relatively high.

We noted earlier that correspondence methods could be either short or long range. It is customary (eg Hildreth and Koch (1987)) to illustrate this by contrasting correlation techniques, which are short range, with conventional token-tracking methods, which are long range. In our view a more important distinction is that rotational scene motion involved in short range correspondence can be described using instantaneous infinitesimal rotations, whereas long range (apparent) motions have to be described by finite rotations. The latter approach is exemplified by the work of Faugeras and co-workers (eg Faugeras, Lustman and Toscani (1987)).

1.4   Visual versus projected motion

We now turn to the relationship between visual and projected motions. This might appear of secondary importance, but this is not the case.

First, to demonstrate that there may be a difference between visual and projected motions recall the classic example of a sphere with uniform albedo rotating about its fixed axis under static lighting conditions (for example, see Figure 12.2 of *Robot Vision* by Horn (1986)). It is evident from equation (1.2) that the projected motion is non-zero, but it is equally obvious from the physical situation that $E(\mathbf{r}, t)$ is constant over time and thus that the visual motion must be zero everywhere. The difference between these measures is not a result of noise in the image or inadequate algorithms. The visual motion is simply not necessarily equal to the projected motion.

But in that case, what are the many "successful" algorithmic variants in each of the above "successful" computational paradigms computing? The fact is that visual motion (and optical flow) is not a strictly defined quantity. We can be physically sure when it is zero but, apart from that case, computational methods must necessarily derive their own brand of results, recovering visual motion that neither necessarily equals that from any other method nor equals the projected motion. So we can do no more than to take, for example, equation (1.6) as a *definition* of optical flow, or at least the vernier velocity, à la Horn and Schunck.

This seems to open a Pandora's box[4]. How can one proceed? The only sensible course seems *not* to ask 'Which of these measures or methods is most correct?' but rather 'Which of these measures relates most usefully to the task in hand?' In other words, it becomes important to know the expected relationship of the visual motion to what is happening out there in the scene. For the task of recovering structure from motion, we argue that the most useful relationship between visual and projected motions is *equivalence*, the conditions for which we now examine.

1.4.1 Equivalence of visual and projected motions

Marr and Ullman's intuition that "if zero-crossings move, it is more likely to be the consequence of movement of the underlying physical surface" (Marr and Ullman 1981) points the way to these conditions. Similarly, at an intuitive level, tracking distinctive image features in correspondence schemes seems to present a way of recovering the projected motion. However, recent work by Verri and Poggio (1987) lays a firmer foundation.

Verri and Poggio (1987) studied in detail the conditions for equivalence between the components of the optical flow and projected motion in the direction of the image intensity gradient, evaluating for a number of examples the difference:

$$\Delta = \frac{(\dot{\mathbf{f}} - \dot{\mathbf{r}}) \cdot \nabla E}{|\nabla E|} .$$
(1.11)

For each example they found a result of the form

$$\Delta = \frac{F(\text{scene, lighting})}{|\nabla E|} ,$$
(1.12)

and in several examples they found special conditions of scene structure, scene motion and lighting which made the function F vanish, thus implying equivalence between optical flow and projected motion. However, in the most general case examined, F could not be made zero, and so it was concluded that for equivalence at a point in the image

---

4) Does even hope remain for the Epimetheus of visual motion processing?

$$|\nabla E| \to \infty \tag{1.13}$$

at that point. Verri and Poggio went on to consider the uses of optical flow, $\dot{\mathbf{f}}$, when the conditions for equivalence were *not* satisfied. However, by concentrating on cases where the function F could be made zero, they obfuscated the consistency in their results — that the difference *always* disappears as $|\nabla E| \to \infty$. It is this consistency which points to an underlying information processing argument about equivalence, based on the observation that the projected motion field is locally unambiguous.

To develop this further, consider a smooth surface $S(a, b, t)$ moving in front of a camera as depicted in Figure 1.3. At time t a patch $p_1(t) = p(a, b, t)$ is imaged at $\mathbf{r}(p_1, t)$, and a neighbouring patch at $\mathbf{r}(p_2, t)$. When the surface moves over time Δt, patch p_2 becomes responsible for the irradiance at the first image position: ie, $\mathbf{r}(p_1, t) = \mathbf{r}(p_2, t + \Delta t)$.

Let the scene be illuminated by any number of sources, with the proviso that the lighting is unstructured and that there are no shadow or mutual illumination effects. (These can only make the situation more complex.) Whichever sources are visible from any patch at any time are visible from all patches at all times. Let too a coordinate system be attached to each patch so that the normal is the polar direction, and directions into space are defined by (θ, ϕ).

In such conditions, the source radiance $L_i(\theta_i, \phi_i, p)$ is a smoothly varying function of angle and intrinsic surface coordinates (a, b), as is the scene irradiance

$$E(p) = \int_{\omega_i} L_i(\theta_i, \phi_i, p) \cos \theta_i d\omega_i \tag{1.14}$$

where $d\omega_i$ is an element of solid angle in the (θ_i, ϕ_i) direction.

The scene *radiance* is related to the source radiance by the bi-directional reflection function (BDRF), $f(\theta_i, \phi_i; \theta_r, \phi_r; p)$ (Horn and Sjoberg 1979):

$$L_r(\theta_r, \phi_r, p) = \int_{\omega_i} f(\theta_i, \phi_i; \theta_r, \phi_r; p) L_i(\theta_i, \phi_i, p) \cos \theta_i d\omega_i \ . \tag{1.15}$$

If the BDRF changes smoothly with respect both to angles and to the intrinsic coordinates (a, b) then the scene radiance will be similarly smoothly varying. We note here that the BDRF is typically made up of arguments that depend solely on the intrinsic coordinates (eg albedo)

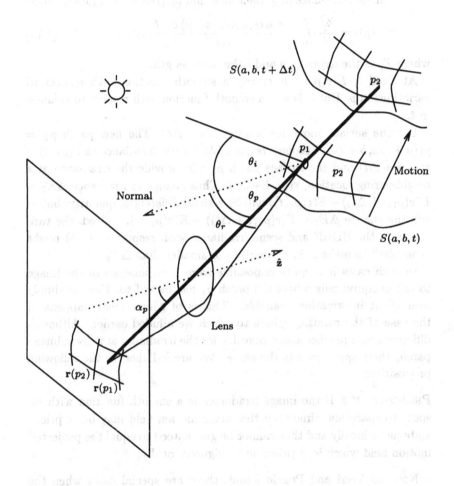

Figure 1.3: Patches lying on a moving object illuminated with static unstructured light and imaged by the camera.

and those that depend also on viewpoint and lighting directions (eg if the surface is specular).

The image *irradiance* may then be found as (Horn and Sjoberg 1979)

$$E(\mathbf{r}(p)) = \frac{Z_p^2}{l^2} \int_{\text{lens}} \frac{\cos \alpha_p L_r(\theta_r, \phi_r, p) \cos \theta_r}{\cos \theta_p} d\omega_r \,, \qquad (1.16)$$

where Z_p is the depth of p and l the focal length.

At fixed t, $E(\mathbf{r}(p,t))$ is clearly a smooth function with respect to variations in p. But it is also a smooth function with respect to changes in t.

Let the surface move for a short time Δt. The new patch $p_2 = p_1(a + \Delta a, b + \Delta b)$ becomes responsible for the irradiance at $\mathbf{r}(p_1, t) = \mathbf{r}(p_2, t + \Delta t)$ and the surface patch p_1 will provide the irradiance at a neighbouring location, $\mathbf{r}(p_1, t + \Delta t)$. Thus change in irradiance $\Delta E_\mathbf{r} = E(\mathbf{r}(p_1, t + \Delta t)) - E(\mathbf{r}(p_1, t))$ will be a small differential quantity; but so will the change $\Delta E_t = E(\mathbf{r}(p_2, t + \Delta t)) - E(\mathbf{r}(p_1, t))$. Indeed, the variations in the BDRF and scene irradiance with respect to (a, b) might "conspire" to make ΔE_t as small as or smaller than $\Delta E_\mathbf{r}$.

In such cases it is quite impossible from local analysis of the image to tell unequivocally where the patch p_1 has moved to: there is simply insufficient information available. This is of course what happens in the case of the rotating sphere to which we alluded earlier. Although different scene patches are responsible for the irradiance at a given image patch, their *appearance* is the same. We are led then to the following proposition:

PROPOSITION 1 If the image irradiance is a smooth function with respect to space and time then the image motion field may be, a priori, ambiguous locally and thus cannot be guaranteed to equal the projected motion field which is, a priori, unambiguous locally.

Now, as Verri and Poggio found, there are special cases when the local ambiguity "conspiracy" cannot occur, but in general such benign conditions will not apply. The only general remedy is to demand that patches p_1 and p_2 give rise to *finitely* different irradiances in the image. Thus, echoing the result of Verri and Poggio:

PROPOSITION 2 To determine image motion in a particular direction locally and unambiguously, there must be an infinite spatial irradiance gradient in that direction.

But looking at the equations describing the irradiance in the image, it is clear that for the image irradiance discontinuity to be connected with scene alone, it must arise from a discontinuity in a quantity that depends only on the intrinsic properties (a, b). Thus:

PROPOSITION 3 For the locally disambiguated component of visual motion to equal a component of projected motion at a point, the discontinuity in spatial gradient along the component direction at that point should arise from a discontinuity in intrinsic surface properties.

Given the stated lighting conditions, this can be guaranteed if the image irradiance discontinuities arise from discontinuities in surface orientation or from discontinuities in an intrinsic argument of the BDRF, such as the albedo. In general of course this intrinsic source of discontinuity cannot be guaranteed. Structured lighting, shadow effects, mutual illumination (Forsyth and Zisserman 1990) and the non-intrinsic parts of the BDRF will yield confounding discontinuities. In practice, all one can say is that computing visual motion at image irradiance discontinuities gives the best chance that the visual motion will equate to the projected motion.

There are several corollaries which are worth highlighting.

COROLLARY 1 Because the image irradiance cannot everywhere be discontinuous, it is impossible to compute everywhere in the image a visual motion field that is guaranteed to equate to the projected motion field.

COROLLARY 2 To recover the full visual motion at a point, one requires infinite image irradiance gradients in two orthogonal directions, and thus in all directions.

COROLLARY 3 Along a curve of irradiance discontinuities, the recovered full visual motion can only be guaranteed to equate to the full projected motion at points of infinite two-dimensional curvature.

The first corollary raises fundamental questions about the underlying motive in efforts to recover dense flow fields using, for example, smoothness constraints. The last deserves a little discussion too. Given that the aperture problem exists for locally straight edges, one could argue, as Gong (1989a) does, that it is possible to break the aperture problem by examining points of *finite* curvature. This is an attractive notion,

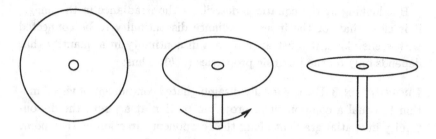

Figure 1.4: A spinning disc shows that points of high curvature do not necessarily overcome the aperture problem.

but a simple counter example shows that this is not guaranteed to be so.

Consider a background in front of which there is a uniformly painted disc spinning on a fixed axis coincident with the optic axis of the camera, (Figure 1.4). The visual motion is zero, whereas the projected motion is not. Suppose the axis is tilted and again fixed. The projected edge curve is now an ellipse, but the visual motion is still zero. We can keep on tilting the disk until the curvature at two points on the ellipse become arbitrarily high, but the visual motion is still zero, and not equal to the projected motion.

The use of points of merely high curvature *must* involve an assumption about the scene and image: in essence, that the contour is not slipping along itself. Thus, the argument that high (but not infinite) curvature points can yield more information about visual motion components than straight edges must be treated with caution. In absolute terms the information at these points is no greater: it is rather that the scene conditions required to confound our expectations of the motion of such points are more degenerate and unlikely. The only points at which we can be sure that a contour cannot slip along itself are ones of infinite curvature.

1.5   Remarks

In choosing a method for computing visual motion, one seems faced with the need to compromise. Raw gradient methods are highly effective at yielding dense flow fields and giving an overall view of the motion. In our experience, their deficiency lies in the difficulty of mapping their output precisely onto the underlying image geometry and hence onto the scene geometry. This mapping appears important for the successful recovery of structure from motion. (Certainly *our* experiments earlier this decade trying to recover structure from motion computed using raw gradient-based techniques met with mixed success.)

Much more successful in terms of structure from motion recovery are the token matching techniques where quite high level, geometrically unambiguous features are matched — features, such as straight lines, which already involve implicit perceptual grouping. However, such distinctive features are sparse, and their use seems to reduce motion processing to yet another photogrammetric tour de force.

What is clear is that there is a need for both types of processing, analogous to our own visual systems. However, in machine vision we have at least one luxury — that of being able, or at least attempting, to design a single process with an element of compromise, and it is in this spirit that in the next chapter we describe a method for computing visual motion that combines elements of an edge gradient-based scheme with elements of token matching. Its virtue is that it can yield dense visual motion along contours that, as our structure from motion computations show later, are well tied to the underlying scene geometry.

When interpreting visual motion in the remainder of this book we assume that the visual motion we recover equates to the projected motion or, more strictly, that components of the visual motion equate to components of the projected motion. The method described in Chapter 2 to compute visual motion is an edge gradient-based method which, as we have shown, increases the likelihood of these two measures being equivalent.

2 Computing Image Motion

In the previous chapter we argued that motion computed at edges of anything less than infinite curvature inevitably suffers the aperture problem.

Even the skeptical might agree that this *would* be the case using, say, Marr-Hildreth zero-crossings, simply because such edge tokens are described only by their positions. There is nothing to indicate that a zero-crossing in one image is more or less similar to any zero-crossing in another image. However — to continue as devil's advocate — image edges do have further attributes, such as orientation, strength or grey-level difference and curvature, which can be made explicit (for example, using Spacek's edge detector (Spacek 1986)) and which surely might help to resolve the aperture problem.

To show that this is not the case *locally*, consider an extended intensity edge comprising several edge elements or *edgels* — elements of edge occupying one pixel. First, consider orientation as an attribute for disambiguating a match. Similar orientation between an edgel in one image and an edgel in the next might indicate that they are likely to match. This, however, is a constraint on what one expects the motion of the scene relative to the camera to be, and thus cannot resolve the aperture problem. (In particular, use of this constraint suggests that perceived rotation about the optic axis, $\hat{z}$, should be small.) Secondly, consider strength. Similarity of strength between an edgel in one image and an edgel in the next might indicate that they are likely to match. This would certainly distinguish between two distinct contours, but it cannot distinguish between edgels on a single contour. This is because infinitesimally separated portions of a single contour cannot have finitely different strengths. If they were to, there would exist an infinite intensity gradient along the contour at that point, and the 'edge' at that position would be a feature of higher rank. Finally, we again call on the example of the spinning disc (§1.4.1) to show that merely finite edge curvature cannot be relied on completely to disambiguate matches.

2.1 Edgels as weak tokens

However, provided we understand the assumptions made and constraints imposed by the above, all three measures on the edge are useful and can

be thought of as turning edge elements into "weak tokens", which may
help to indicate which edge elements are most likely to match from frame
to frame in an image sequence. This chapter describes a method which
achieves this matching. The richer the description obtained from weak
tokens, say with higher curvature edges, the smaller is the likelihood that
the underlying scene motion will confound the assumptions embodied in
the constraints.

2.1.1 Matching weak tokens

For weak tokens which may be indistinguishable or only mildly distin-
guishable from one another, one-to-one matching is quite unthinkable.
Instead we must consider one-to-many matching and try to determine
whether one out of the many matches is more likely than the rest.

An elegant process for matching weak tokens was proposed by Scott
(1987a,b). He putatively matched a pixel patch from one image to all
patches around it in the next image, assigning to each potential match a
probability of occurring, and building up thereby a probability matching
surface around each patch. This probability surface was then analyzed,
using a standard principal axis decomposition (Ballard and Brown 1982)
to yield the two orthogonal components of the image motion which had
maximum and minimum confidences. Where the patches were distinctive his algorithm behaved like a token matcher, where they were not
his algorithm behaved more like a gradient scheme.

Although the skeleton of Scott's algorithm is elegant, it was found
to have two drawbacks (Castelow, Murray, Scott and Buxton 1988).
First, significant errors were introduced by auto-correlation effects when
matching between only two frames. The solution to this problem was
found to be to symmetrize the matching by using three frames and
matching from the temporally central to both the forward and backward frames, then time-reversing the backward results. We return to
this later. The second problem was that the pixel patch sampling produced coarse-grained results. It was clear that in edge-dominated imagery Scott's pixel patch matcher was trying to perform edge detection,
something to which it was ill-suited. A remedy for this class of imagery is
to incorporate a purpose-built edge detector, for example, that of Canny
(1983, 1986), which is able to deliver the edge orientation, strength and
positions to sub-pixel acuity.

Scott's process is somewhat is similar to that of Ananden and Weiss

(1985) and Ananden (1987) (though the main thrust of Ananden's work was towards a hierarchical coarse-to-fine framework for recovering dense smoothed flow fields). However, Ananden and Weiss searched for the largest peak in the probability surface and performed a principal axis decomposition about the peak to determine the confidences. While this will produce sensible results for corners and for straight edges, the process must fail, as Scott argued, whenever the probability surface has more than one peak. This can occur whenever there are a pair of nearby edges as in Figure 2.3. More troublesome is Ananden and Weiss's scheme does not indicate it may have failed: ie, it returns an incorrect result with a high confidence. Because of the frequent repetition of structure in nature, pairs of such edges occur in many of our images, eg Figures 2.6, 2.8 and especially 2.12 and 2.13. Scott's scheme itself will be biased at a corner since it computes the centre of mass of the probability surface, and that must be inside the corner. As we are matching using orientation, the matching strengths either side of a sharp corner will be insignificant and the bias small. At the other extreme for straight edges there is of course zero bias, indicating that the bias is maximum for an intermediate value of curvature.

2.2 An edgel matching algorithm outlined

Suppose for now that the matching probability between an edgel in one frame and edgels close to it in the next frame is assessed on similarity of orientation, a similar orientation yielding a high probability of matching. In Figure 2.1(a) and (b) we consider the possible matches from a particular edge element to edgels in its vicinity in the next image for two different edgel configurations. For the edgel in the extended edge, case (a), the probability distribution is similarly extended. The principal axis analysis will yield orthogonal axes along and tangential to the line of matches. The centre of mass of the probability distribution is the position to which the edgel has most likely moved, so that we obtain a most probable motion vector, but the different extents of the distribution along the principal axes yield different confidences in the components of that vector projected onto the principal axes. Clearly for the extended edge only the edge-normal component is returned with certainty. In case (b) on the other hand, the probability distribution

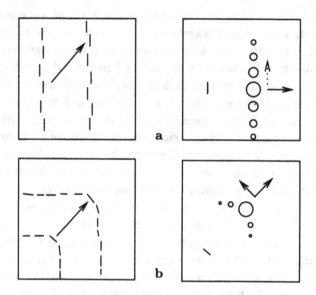

Figure 2.1: Examples of two different edgel matching probability distributions. In (a) the displacement in the direction of the solid arrow is recovered with much higher confidence than that along the direction of the dashed arrow. In (b), displacements in both directions are similarly well determined.

is tightly clustered and both components of visual motion are returned with similar confidence.

Thus the confidences returned by the principal axis decomposition indicate to what extent the aperture problem applies for the particular edgel. Although individual edgels viewed locally do not encode any shape information, by taking the broader non-local view, both components of the motion may be obtained reliably at a distinctive shape such as a corner, under the assumption that the contour is not sliding along itself.

2.3   The algorithm in detail

The information supplied to the algorithm are the positions, r, of intensity edgels computed to sub-pixel acuity, their orientations, a, and grey-level differences or strengths, s, in each image of the sequence. In all the examples in this book edgels have been computed using the edge detector of Canny followed by a thresholding operation involving a bi-state threshold with hysteresis. Frames are processed in groups of three, with the visual motion computed at the temporally central frame, so that it lags behind the most recently acquired edgel map by one inter-frame period.

2.3.1   Setting initial matching probabilities

Consider now an edgel i computed at r_i in the temporally central frame. In the forward frame (ie, that captured one period later in time) we suppose it will appear somewhere in a *locale*, $\mathcal{F}_i$, centred around r_i, with radius ρ_L as shown in Figure 2.2. The locale may contain several edgels j, each of which is a possible match. We therefore assign an initial probability of matching to each edgel on the basis of similarity of orientation and strength:

$$p_{ij}^{(0)}{}_{(j:j\in\mathcal{F}_i)} = \exp\left(-\frac{1}{2}\left(\frac{\Delta a_{ij}^2}{\sigma_a^2} + \frac{\Delta s_{ij}^2}{\sigma_s^2}\right)\right) , \qquad (2.1)$$

where $\Delta a_{ij} = (a_i - a_j)_{\mathrm{mod}2\pi}$ and $\Delta s_{ij} = s_i - s_j$ are, respectively, the differences in orientation and strength between edgels i and j. The ranges of edge strengths and orientations which lead to high initial match strengths are specified by the widths σ_s and σ_a respectively.

We repeat the search in the locale $\mathcal{B}_i$, also of radius ρ_L, in the previous (backward) frame, looking for edgels from which the current edgel might have originated. The matching probabilities are computed similarly and can be combined with the forward matches simply by reversing the displacement vectors. That is, a backward match from i to an edgel j' at $r_{j'}$ involving a displacement $(r_{j'} - r_i)$ is equivalent to a forward match to a position $2r_i - r_{j'}$ involving a displacement of $-(r_{j'} - r_i)$. Thus we obtain a spatial matching probability distribution comprised of several delta functions within the locale.

There are several advantages in using three frames to compute motion. First, the matching is symmetrical and the visual motion computed can be attributed unequivocally to the edgels in the central frame. Secondly, it provides a degree of noise suppression. Thirdly and most importantly it overcomes auto-correlation problems which occur in two frame matching, as we show now.

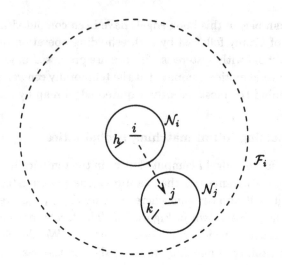

Figure 2.2: Edgels involved in matching i to j. Edgel i is in the central frame, edgel j in i's forward locale, $\mathcal{F}_i$. Edgel $h \in \mathcal{N}_i$, is a neighbour of i, and $k \in \mathcal{N}_j$ is a neighbour of j in the forward frame.

Consider the pair of edgels e and f of Figure 2.3 initially at $x = 0$ and $x = c$ respectively and moving along the positive x-axis at v units per frame. Consider two frame matching from edgel e, as shown on the left. There will be two possible forward matches to the new position of e (let this be e^+) at $x = v$ and the new position of f (f^+) at $x = c + v$. The average matching strength will be placed incorrectly at $x = (v + v + c)/2 = v + c/2$. Now consider the symmetrized matching shown on the right. The backward match to e^- at $x = -v$ will produce a time-reversed probability distribution at $x = v$, and that to f^- will produce a distribution at $x = -(c - v)$. The average displacement distribution will be at $x = (v + v + c + v - (c - v))/4 = v$; that is, correctly placed.

2.3.2   Introducing neighbourhood support

The initial probability distribution around an edgel i can be modified by introducing support from neighbours within a relaxation scheme. Each edgel (in whatever frame) is notionally surrounded by a neighbourhood $\mathcal{N}$ of radius ρ_N (Figure 2.2). If the edgels within the neighbourhood

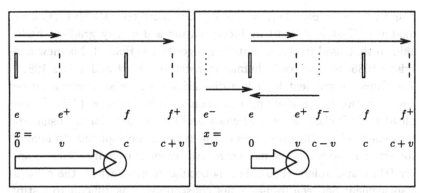

Figure 2.3: On the left is the two-frame matching, where the average match is wrongly placed. On the right is the three-frame matching, where the average distribution is correctly placed at $x = v$.

have mutual high probability of moving in a certain direction then the probability that the individual edgel moves in that direction is increased, and vice versa.

Matching probabilities are updated using a typical relaxation formula (Rosenfeld and Kak 1982). For matches to the forward frame,

$$p_{ij}^{(t+1)} = \frac{1}{n(\mathcal{N}_i)+1} \left[p_{ij}^{(t)} + \sum_{h \in \mathcal{N}_i} \max_{k \in \mathcal{N}_j \cap \mathcal{F}_h} \left[c(i,j;h,k) p_{hk}^{(t)} \right] \right] \quad , \quad (2.2)$$

where $\mathcal{N}_j$ is the neighbourhood of j, $j \in \mathcal{F}_i$ and $n(\mathcal{N}_i)$ is the number of edgels in $\mathcal{N}_i$, the neighbourhood of i. A similar expression holds for matches to the backward frame.

In practice, we find that one iterative update using the relaxation formula brings tangible improvement to the visual motion computed. More than one becomes hard to justify on the basis of the heavy computational load involved.

One of the advantages of relaxation schemes is that neither the initial probabilities nor the compatibility function c have to be "correct". All that is required is that the compatibility function embody the spirit of the scheme. The earliest compatibility function used by us was based solely on differences in relative displacement

$$c(i,j;h,k) = \frac{(\Delta \mathbf{r}_{ih})^2}{(\Delta \mathbf{r}_{ih})^2 + (\Delta \mathbf{r}_{ij} - \Delta \mathbf{r}_{hk})^2} \qquad (2.3)$$

(where, for example, $\Delta \mathbf{r}_{ij} = \mathbf{r}_j - \mathbf{r}_i$), but more recently this has been modified (Castelow 1989) by incorporating a disparity gradient limit, akin to that used in stereo matching algorithms (Pollard, Mayhew and Frisby 1985) and active in human stereovision (Burt and Julesz 1980). The disparity gradient limit is a dimensionless number which must be less than two if the visibility condition is to be satisfied (Trivedi and Lloyd 1985; Pollard, Porrill, Mayhew and Frisby 1986) for the usual arrangement where the optic axes of the cameras are coplanar. In human stereovision, however, the more conservative value of unity seems to apply (Burt and Julesz 1980). For monocular motion, where the camera displacement between frames is not constrained, it is difficult to justify choosing one value of the disparity gradient limit over any other, except that it should not be two. However, one assumption of our entire matching procedure is that similarity of orientation is a cue for matching, which implies that no large rotations may occur in the image plane about the $\hat{\mathbf{z}}$ axis. Thus, regarding the relative motion as due to a moving camera in a static scene, we see that a pair of successive camera positions ought not to deviate much from the typical stereo-camera geometry. Without any other indication of how to choose a value it seems appropriate, and is certainly expedient, to choose one similar to the value of unity used successfully in machine stereo-processing (Pollard, Mayhew and Frisby 1985).

2.3.3   Analyzing the probability distributions

As we noted earlier, the more elegant part of the algorithm to compute visual motion is adapted from Scott (1987a,b). It analyzes the probability distributions using a principal axis decomposition, which determines to what extent a distribution is elongated or clustered.

The mean displacement of the edgel i is computed from the sum of the displacements computed in each locale, weighted by their probabilities, where again we note that displacements to the backward locale are reversed. Thus, after the t-th iteration of equation (2.2), where t is usually just one, the mean displacement of edgel i is found as:

$$\langle \Delta \mathbf{r}_i \rangle = \frac{\sum_{j \in \mathcal{F}_i} p_{ij}^{(t)} \Delta \mathbf{r}_{ij} - \sum_{j' \in \mathcal{B}_i} p_{ij'}^{(t)} \Delta \mathbf{r}_{ij'}}{\sum_{j \in \mathcal{F}_i} p_{ij}^{(t)} + \sum_{j' \in \mathcal{B}_i} p_{ij'}^{(t)}} . \tag{2.4}$$

Deviations from the mean, $\delta \mathbf{r}_{ij} = \Delta \mathbf{r}_{ij} - \langle \Delta \mathbf{r}_i \rangle$, are then used to construct a scatter matrix for edgel i:

$$[\mathbf{M}]_i = \sum_{j \in \mathcal{F}_i} p_{ij}^{(t)} \delta \mathbf{r}_{ij} \delta \mathbf{r}_{ij}^T + \sum_{j' \in \mathcal{B}_i} p_{ij'}^{(t)} (-\delta \mathbf{r}_{ij'})(-\delta \mathbf{r}_{ij'}^T) . \qquad (2.5)$$

The visual motion components $\mathbf{v}_i$ at i are found by minimizing the error term

$$\epsilon_i^2 = \hat{\mathbf{n}}^T [\mathbf{M}]_i \hat{\mathbf{n}} \qquad (2.6)$$

with respect to the unit vector $\hat{\mathbf{n}}$. This yields the direction $\hat{\mathbf{n}}_1$ along which we have *maximum* confidence in our estimate of the visual motion at edgel i. In fact, $\hat{\mathbf{n}}_1$ is the eigenvector of $[\mathbf{M}]_i$ corresponding to the smaller eigenvalue $\lambda^{(1)}$, which itself provides a measure of the uncertainty in that component of the visual motion. We will refer to this axis as the *major* axis. The orthogonal eigenvector $\hat{\mathbf{n}}_2$ is the direction along which we have least confidence in the visual motion, and this will be called the *minor* axis.

We resolve the estimated visual motion into two orthogonal components along the major and minor axes such that

$$\mathbf{v}_i^{major} = (\langle \Delta \mathbf{r}_i \rangle \cdot \hat{\mathbf{n}}_1) \hat{\mathbf{n}}_1 \qquad (2.7)$$
$$\mathbf{v}_i^{minor} = (\langle \Delta \mathbf{r}_i \rangle \cdot \hat{\mathbf{n}}_2) \hat{\mathbf{n}}_2 \qquad (2.8)$$

The confidence measures, $w_i^{major,minor}$, in these components are the inverses of the corresponding eigenvalues:

$$w_i^{major,minor} = 1/\lambda_i^{(1,2)} . \qquad (2.9)$$

As we outlined earlier, if $w_i^{major} \gg w_i^{minor}$ then the edgel i is likely to be part of an extended edge, where the aperture problem prevails and where only the edge-normal component of motion is obtained reliably. At a distinctive feature, however, $w_i^{major} \approx w_i^{minor}$: both components are estimated with similar confidence and so the *full* visual motion estimate is recovered reliably.

The eigenvalue notation, though concise, might for some hide the simplicity of the principal axis decomposition. It is no more than a weighted least squares fit to a straight line when neither of the two variables is dependent. That is, referring to Figure 2.4, we seek to minimize $\sum_i w_i \delta_i^2$ with respect to the parameters (f, θ). For $\mathbf{r}_i = (x_i, y_i)^T$ this is

$$\min_{(f,\theta)} \sum_i w_i (x_i \cos \theta + y_i \sin \theta - f)^2 . \qquad (2.10)$$

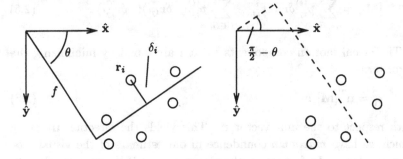

Figure 2.4: A principal axis decomposition effectively fits a straight line to data which are not dependent. On the left is the minimum solution, on the right is the saddle solution.

By setting the partial differentials with respect to f and θ to zero one finds the solution

$$\tan 2\theta = 2 \left[\frac{\overline{x}.\overline{y} - \overline{xy}}{(\overline{x}^2 - \overline{x^2}) - (\overline{y}^2 - \overline{y^2})} \right] \qquad (2.11)$$

$$f = \overline{x}\cos\theta + \overline{y}\sin\theta , \qquad (2.12)$$

where $\overline{x} = \sum w_i x_i / \sum w_i$ and so on. There are two solutions for θ, separated by $\pi/2$ as shown in Figure 2.4, corresponding on the left to a minimum, which is equivalent to the *minor* axis, and on the right to a saddle, which is the *major* axis.

2.4 Computer experiments

We first show a test using a controlled image sequence which illustrates the recovery of both components of motion with different confidence and the algorithm's ability to adapt from a gradient-based scheme to a token matcher.

2.4.1 The moving Mondrian

The Mondrian in Figure 2.5(a) is moving towards the top left of the image at $(-1, -1)$ pixels per frame. The visual motion computed at

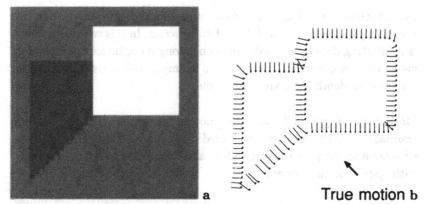

a   True motion b

Figure 2.5: The Mondrian in (a) moves to the top left. Only at corners in (b) are both components of visual motion computed with confidence, yielding full visual motion vectors.

edges is shown in Figure 2.5(b). More precisely, where both components of visual motion were recovered with similar confidence ($w^{major} \approx w^{minor}$) we show the full vector, the vector sum of the two components, and where the major component had significantly higher confidence ($w^{major}/w^{minor} > 10$) we show just one component. At most of the corners, the full visual motion has been recovered with certainty, whereas along the extended edges only the component perpendicular to edge direction has been recovered with confidence.

2.4.2 On real imagery

We continue with several examples of the algorithm at work on a variety of real images. In addition there are several more examples of the algorithm being run on imagery used for structure from motion computations in Figures 4.1, 4.8, 4.10, 4.11, 6.7, 6.8. In most examples we show only two images from the sequence of three used to compute the visual motion. These are always the central and forward frames.

VDU on a trolley. Figure 2.6 shows visual motion computed for a scene containing a display unit on a trolley moving against a static background. Notice the motion of the shadow on the wall.

1st Office scene.   Figure 2.7 shows visual motion computed when the camera moves relative to a cluttered office scene. In this case the camera is translating directly towards the scene along its optic axis and the full visual motion is pure expansion. This example will be used in Chapter 3 to recover depth from known motion.

Desk top.   Figure 2.8 shows the motion computed when the camera translates directly towards a cluttered desktop. We use this example in Chapter 6 to compute the orientation and disposition of the desk surface with respect to the camera.

Eyes.   Figure 2.9 shows an example of a different sort of visual motion! The subject's gaze moved from frame to frame, and his face fell slightly. Notice that the highlights in the eyes are all but stationary.

2nd Office scene.   Figure 2.10 shows another office scene used in Chapter 3 to recover depth from known motion. The camera is translating past the static scene along the +x-axis.

Toy truck.   Figure 2.11 shows results from a sequence where the camera moves directly towards a toy truck. These data are used later in Chapters 4 and 5 to recover structure from motion.

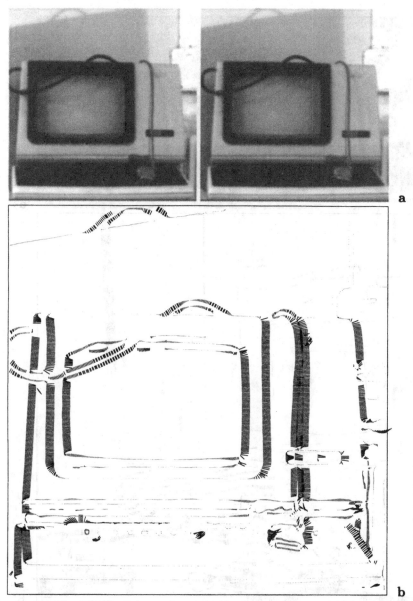

Figure 2.6: Two consecutive frames (the current and forward frames) from a simple motion sequence (a), and the computed major visual motion components (b).

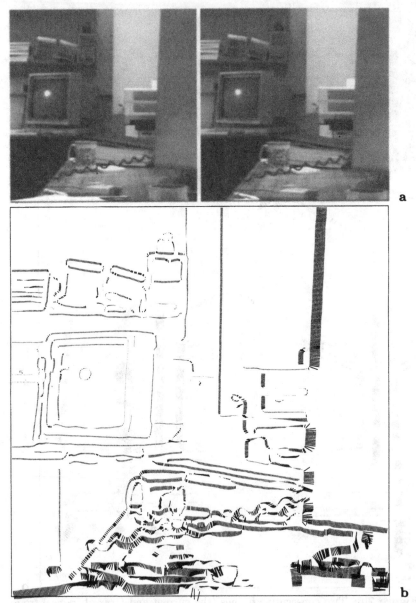

Figure 2.7: The current and forward frames from a sequence of a more complex scene (a), and the computed major visual motion components (b).

Figure 2.8: Current and forward frames from a motion sequence of a desk
(a) where the camera translates directly towards the desk, and the computed
major visual motion components (b).

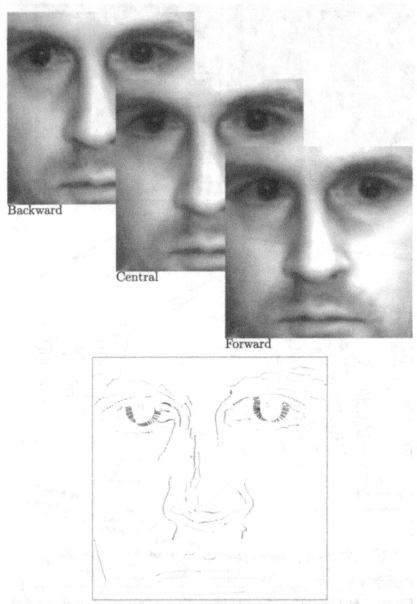

Figure 2.9: Frames from a motion sequence where a subject moves his eyes and the computed visual motion. The face is moving downwards slightly.

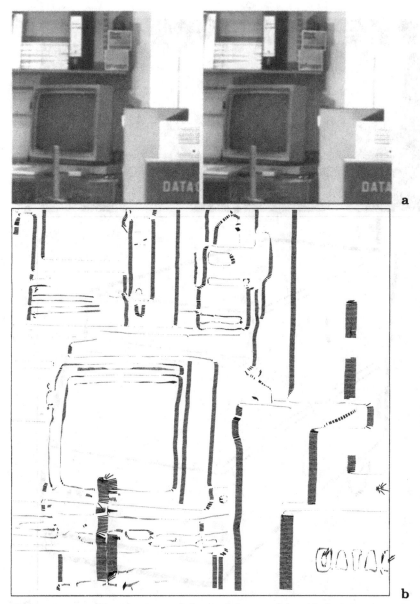

Figure 2.10: The current and forward frames (a) and the visual motion components (b) for a camera translating in a second office scene. The motion relative to the camera is along the $-\hat{x}$-axis.

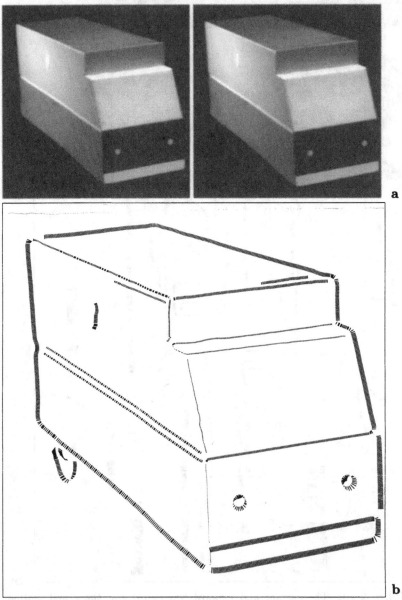

a

b

Figure 2.11: The central and forward images (a) and visual motion (b) computed when the camera moved directly towards a toy truck.

2.4.3   Tests of the output in 2D

We have argued that the algorithm described combines the benefits of
the method of Scott with the measurement precision afforded by a good
edge detector. To give an indication of the quality of output, and to
illustrate where the algorithm tends to fail we consider experiments using
natural imagery where the *image* is displaced by a known amount from
frame to frame, so that $\dot{\mathbf{r}}^{actual}$ is the same throughout the image and
is known. For each edgel e we compare the size of the computed major
component, $|\mathbf{v}_e^{major}|$, with the expected component $\dot{\mathbf{r}}^{actual} \cdot \hat{\mathbf{v}}_e^{major}$ and
plot a histogram of the frequency of occurrence of the deviations

$$\Delta = \dot{\mathbf{r}}^{actual} \cdot \hat{\mathbf{v}}_e^{major} - |\mathbf{v}_e^{major}| \;. \tag{2.13}$$

In Figure 2.12(a) we show one frame from an outdoor sequence where
the image was displaced in the $\hat{\mathbf{x}}$-direction (left to right) at 2 pixels per
frame. In (b) we show the computed visual motion components (over
7000 in all) and in Figure 2.12(c) we show the histogram of errors, Δ,
in pixels. The distribution is symmetrically disposed about zero, with
a spread (HWHM) of about ± 0.1 pixels. These results are typical for
situations where there is low chance of grossly erroneous matching.

Erroneous matching is obviously more likely to occur as the characteristic texture scale becomes smaller than the visual motion itself. To
illustrate this, first consider Figure 2.13(a) where we show one frame of
a sequence where the image of a hand was displaced in the $-\hat{\mathbf{y}}$-direction
at 4 pixels per frame. The outline is clean but there is a good deal of
texture around the palm. In (b) we show the computed visual motion
components and in Figure 2.13(c) we show the histogram of errors, Δ,
in pixels. The peak is again at zero deviation, with, again, a HWHM
on the negative side of about 0.1 pixels, but there is a large tail on the
positive side. This is caused by predominance of components which are
found to be shorter than they should be.

Two more extreme cases are shown in Figure 2.14. A 64×64 image
of a textured carpet is moved first at six pixels per frame (a), and then
at nine pixels per frame (d). The progressive degradation in results is
shown in the histograms at (c) and (f) respectively.

Another indication that this algorithm is not well-suited to texture
comes from a consideration of computational cost. The amount of computation per edgel depends on the product of the number of edgels in

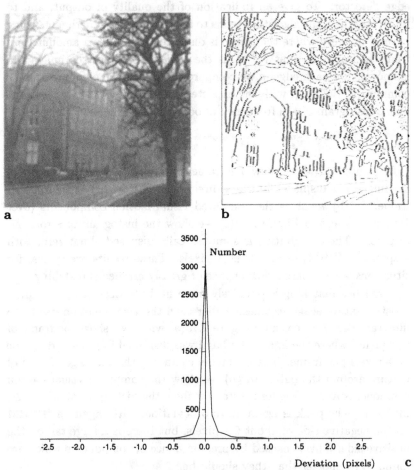

Figure 2.12: An image from the outdoor sequence (a), the visual motion components (b) and a histogram of the error in those components (c).

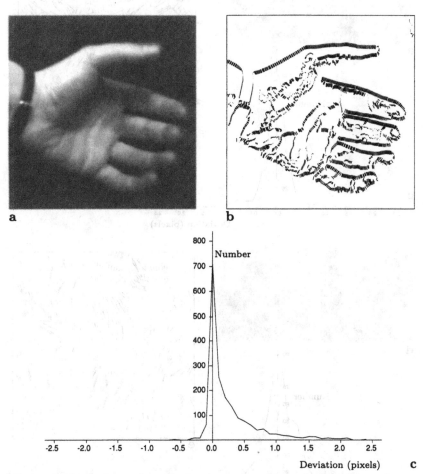

Figure 2.13: An image from the hand sequence where the hand moves downwards (a), the visual motion components (b) and a histogram of the error in those components (c).

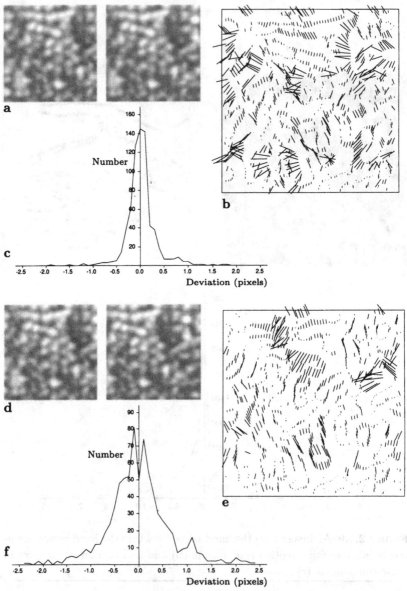

Figure 2.14: The current and forward frames from a sequence where the textured carpet moves to the left at 6 pixels per frame (a). The visual motion (b) has the error histogram (c). In (d), (e) and (f) the carpet is moving by 9 pixels per frame.

the locale and the number in both neighbourhoods. In the best case situation, the image will be dominated by linear rather than textural features. Then we can estimate the number of the edgels in the locale as $2\rho_L$ and in each neighbourhood as $2\rho_N$. Thus the computation per pixel varies as $8\rho_N^2\rho_L$. The overall area density of edgels to maintain the linear regime must be $1/\rho_N$, so that the total computation is

$$C_{best} \propto 8 \left(\frac{D^2}{\rho_N}\right) \rho_N^2\rho_L = 8D^2\rho_N\rho_L \ . \tag{2.14}$$

where D is the linear dimension of the image. By contrast, for an image dominated by texture with density d_T, the amount of computation per edgel depends on $\pi^3 d_T^3 \rho_N^4 \rho_L^2$. Then the total computation is

$$C_{worst} \propto \pi^3 D^2 d_T^4 \rho_N^4 \rho_L^2 \ . \tag{2.15}$$

There are several palliatives for the heavy computation required, though none has been thoroughly explored to date. First, the method is inherently parallel. Secondly, if the edges do possess line or contour structure, searches for neighbours can be much reduced by making the contour neighbourhoods explicit. Gong (1989b) has recently explored a parallel method of propagating information along contours of visual motion combining both wave and diffusion processes. Finally, a contour typically possesses a history of motion, which can be used to restrict search in subsequent frames. McIvor (1988) has worked through many of the necessary procedures required to implement such a restricted search using Kalman Filters. In addition, when working with a sequence of frames with the present algorithm, the preceding forward match provides the matches, matching strengths and displacements for many (but not all) of the current frame's backward matches. Since the relaxation is performed separately in the forward and backward match probabilities, this potential saving applies to the improved as well as to the initial matches.

3 Structure from Motion of Points

In this chapter we introduce the simplest form of algorithm to compute structure from visual motion, in which the relative 3D motion between the scene and the camera is known. Before that however, we indicate the issues raised in 3D scene reconstruction by the aperture problem.

3.1 The aperture problem: the need for constraints

In Chapter 1 we discussed the manifestation of the aperture problem in the image. It turns out that the aperture problem is no mere trivial inconvenience when it comes to reconstructing the structure and motion of the 3D scene from the visual motion in the image. Whereas using full visual motion vectors it is possible to recover the structure and motion of an arbitrary set of points in the scene provided they are moving rigidly (eg Longuet-Higgins (1981)), using just components of visual motion this is *impossible*. At first, such a fundamental difference seems unreasonable. One might think that by combining many components measured at different image positions and pointing in different directions, around a contour say, it would be possible to "make up" a full vector. We can demonstrate that this is not the case using a simple argument based on counting the number of items of information available and the number of parameters to be determined.

Suppose we measure the full visual motion at m points in the image, all of which arise from a single rigid moving object in space. The information we appear to need is

- the m coordinates $\mathbf{R}$ ($3m$ items in all) and

- the six motion components $\mathbf{V}, \boldsymbol{\Omega}$

totalling $3m + 6$ items in all. In fact, as we observed in §1.2.1, there is an inherent depth/speed scaling ambiguity in monocular motion processing. We cannot solve for this scaling parameter and so the number of parameters is reduced by one to $3m + 5$. The number of pieces of information per visual motion vector is four — the components of $\mathbf{r}$ and $\dot{\mathbf{r}}$ — and so there are $4m$ data items in all. Thus to solve this problem, we need $m \geq 5$ points of data.

Suppose now that we suffer the aperture problem and can measure only edge-normal components, $\mathbf{v}$, of visual motion at m points in the image, all of which arise from m edge entities lying on a rigid object in space. To specify the scene, as well as $\mathbf{R}$ for each datum it appears at first that we need two parameters (Θ, Φ) to describe the orientation of the edge. In fact though, the orientation of the edge within the plane that contains the edge and the optic centre (see Figure 3.1) has no effect on the visual motion from the point $\mathbf{R}$, and thus is irrecoverable a priori. So we need only one angle Θ to specify orientation, and in total the information we require to specify the scene is

- the $\mathbf{R}$ for each of these m edge entities ($3m$ items),

- m angles Θ to specify the edge orientations, and

- the motion of the object relative to the sensor, $\mathbf{V}$ and $\boldsymbol{\Omega}$.

Thus we have $4m + 6 - 1$ scene parameters. Now, each visual motion component carries four pieces of information so we still have $4m$ pieces of data. Since

$$\forall m > 0 : \quad 4m < 4m + 5 , \tag{3.1}$$

the problem is insoluble unless one imposes some further constraints or assumptions *in addition* to the usual one that the scene is made up of rigid bodies. (The rigidity assumption is taken as read throughout this book.)

3.2   3D constraints on the aperture problem

Most structure from motion algorithms proposed in the early 1980's assumed that the *full* visual motion field was available as input. Those working on gradient-based algorithms to compute visual motion therefore felt that an important step in the motion processing chain was to reconstruct the full visual motion field *in the image* at an early stage, before any attempt was made to recover 3D structure or motion. Consequently, there was considerable interest in deriving 2D image constraints to facilitate this. Horn and Schunck (1981) introduced the notion of the smoothest motion field, using an area-based smoothness constraint to

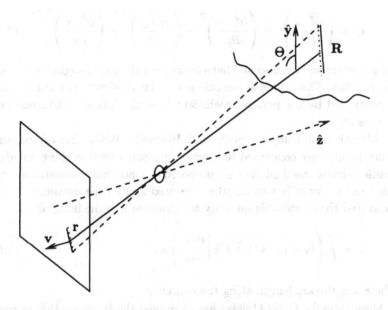

Figure 3.1: The orientation of the scene edge feature within the plane containing the edge and the optic centre does not affect the visual motion and is irrecoverable. Thus only one angle Θ is needed to specify edge orientation.

recover the full visual motion from their raw gradient-based scheme. They minimized

$$I = \int \int \left(\left(\nabla E \cdot \dot{\mathbf{f}} + \frac{\partial E}{\partial t} \right)^2 + k\epsilon_c^2 \right) dx dy \tag{3.2}$$

where the first term measures fidelity to the image data through the motion constraint equation (equation 1.6); and where

$$\epsilon_c^2 = \left(\frac{\partial \dot{\mathbf{f}} \cdot \hat{\mathbf{x}}}{\partial x} \right)^2 + \left(\frac{\partial \dot{\mathbf{f}} \cdot \hat{\mathbf{x}}}{\partial y} \right)^2 + \left(\frac{\partial \dot{\mathbf{f}} \cdot \hat{\mathbf{y}}}{\partial x} \right)^2 + \left(\frac{\partial \dot{\mathbf{f}} \cdot \hat{\mathbf{y}}}{\partial y} \right)^2 \tag{3.3}$$

measures the smoothness and behaves as a regularizer (Poggio, Torre and Koch 1985). The degree of smoothness versus fidelity to the image data is controlled by the positive coefficient k — the larger k the smoother the result.

Hildreth and Ullman (1982) and Hildreth (1984a, 1984b) on the other hand, were concerned to recover full visual motion using an edge gradient-based method and so proposed a smoothness constraint applied not to areas but to lengths measured along edge contours. They suggested that a suitable quantity to minimize was the integral:

$$I = \int \left(|\mathbf{v} - (\dot{\mathbf{r}} \cdot \hat{\mathbf{v}})\hat{\mathbf{v}}|^2 + k \left| \frac{\partial \dot{\mathbf{r}}}{\partial s} \right|^2 \right) ds \tag{3.4}$$

where s is the arc length along the contour.

More recently, Gong (1989a) has examined the incorporation of constraints based on contour curvature within the framework of Hildreth's smoothness technique. His curve motion constraint equation gives greater weight to components of tangential motion which are computed at "seed" points of high contour curvature. Gong also considered a parallel process to disseminate information from seeds, using a mixture of diffusion and wave-like processes.

These three constraint techniques for reconstructing the full visual motion are based in the image, though their respective authors motivate them, to various extents, from conditions in the 3D scene. However, Buxton, Buxton, Murray and Williams (1984) pointed out that if an image constraint is deemed to be "good" when it is based on a good assumption about the scene, then, if one is concerned with the recovery of scene structure, one might as well try to enforce that scene assumption directly — that is, *during* the structure from motion computation, and not as a precursor to it. Once the 3D scene is recovered, it is of course a trivial matter to reconstruct the expected full visual motion, if in fact this remains of any interest[1].

Our book takes this second approach, and the emphasis is on *three dimensional* solutions to the aperture problem. Most interesting of course are structural constraints, which enable reconstruction of the scene structure *and* motion. We present algorithms which solve the aperture problem and recover structure from motion based on 3D edge, 3D polyhedral and 3D planar facet constraints. Somewhat less interesting but still very useful, as we explore now, are reconstructions based on the constraint of known relative motion between scene and camera.

3.3 Point structure from known motion

Using the counting argument of §3.1, we see immediately that if the motion V and Ω is known, then we have $4m$ pieces of data, but now just $4m$ pieces of information to recover. In other words, if the scene motion is known then depth can be recovered on a point by point basis *despite* the aperture problem.

With pointwise depths available to us, we are free to fit to them whatever higher level geometrical constructs seem appropriate. In Chapter 6 we fit the orientations and positions of planar surfaces in the scene to the depths, but here we briefly demonstrate the use of known motion constraints in two simpler ways: first, by recovering pointwise depths and, secondly, by fitting the depths to extended straight lines in 3D. This latter exercise will in turn introduce the issue of segmentation.

3.4 Pointwise depths

Our starting point is equation (1.4), which derives the full projected motion at a point in terms of the corresponding scene depth Z and scene motion V and Ω:

---

1) In Chapter 6 we give some comparisons between reconstructions of the full flow field via a 3D structure from motion algorithm and those via the contour smoothness equation of Hildreth.

$$\dot{\mathbf{r}} = -\frac{l\mathbf{V}}{Z} - \mathbf{r}\frac{\mathbf{V} \cdot \hat{\mathbf{z}}}{Z} + \mathbf{\Omega} \times \mathbf{r} + \mathbf{r}\frac{\mathbf{\Omega} \times \mathbf{r} \cdot \hat{\mathbf{z}}}{l} \, .$$

Following our discussion in Chapter 1, we first make the important assumption that the visual motion components computed using the method described in Chapter 2 are equal to components of the projected motion. Let us denote a measured component of visual motion by $\mathbf{v}$ and a unit vector in its direction by $\hat{\mathbf{v}}$, so that

$$\hat{\mathbf{v}} \cdot \dot{\mathbf{r}} = |\mathbf{v}| = v \, . \tag{3.5}$$

Taking the scalar product of both sides of equation (1.4) with $\hat{\mathbf{v}}$ leads to

$$v = -\frac{l\hat{\mathbf{v}} \cdot \mathbf{V}}{Z} - \hat{\mathbf{v}} \cdot \mathbf{r}\frac{\mathbf{V} \cdot \hat{\mathbf{z}}}{Z} + \hat{\mathbf{v}} \cdot \mathbf{\Omega} \times \mathbf{r} + \hat{\mathbf{v}} \cdot \mathbf{r}\frac{\mathbf{\Omega} \times \mathbf{r} \cdot \hat{\mathbf{z}}}{l} \, . \tag{3.6}$$

If the relative motion is known, equation (3.6) is easily rearranged to give an equation for Z, or rather for the *reciprocal depth*:

$$\begin{aligned}
\zeta &= 1/Z \\
&= \frac{\hat{\mathbf{v}} \cdot [\mathbf{\Omega} \times \mathbf{r} + \mathbf{r}(\mathbf{\Omega} \times \mathbf{r}) \cdot \hat{\mathbf{z}}/l] - v}{\hat{\mathbf{v}} \cdot [\mathbf{V}l + \mathbf{r}(\mathbf{V} \cdot \hat{\mathbf{z}})]} \, .
\end{aligned} \tag{3.7}$$

Clearly, the reciprocal depth can be recovered on a point by point basis.

3.4.1   Experiments

In Figure 3.2(c) we show a pointwise depth map recovered from the visual motion of an office sequence, shown previously as Figure 2.7, where the camera translates towards the scene. Darker points are further away and lighter ones nearer to. The points have been overlaid onto the image grey-levels which are themselves "ghosted" by compressing them into the mid-grey range.

In a second example, Figure 3.3, where the visual motion was displayed previously as Figure 2.10, we show the results when the camera platform is translating sideways.

a

b

c

Figure 3.2: The image (a), visual motion (b) and the depth (c) computed at each visual motion component. Light is near to, dark far off. (The motion was shown more clearly in Figure 2.7).

a

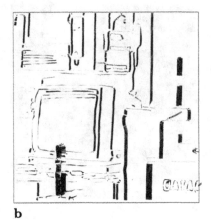

b

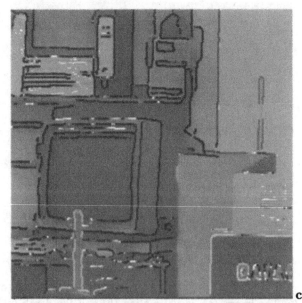

c

Figure 3.3: Point by point depths (c) derived from the visual motion (b) of a second office sequence (a).

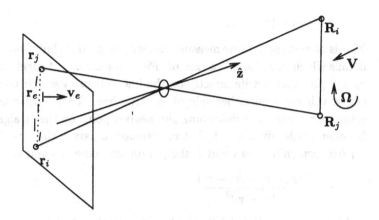

Figure 3.4: A straight edge in the scene and its image.

3.5 Straight edges with known motion

Earlier in the chapter, we noted that if pointwise depths — and hence scene positions, $\mathbf{R}$ — are available, then one may fit them to any 3D scene structure that seems appropriate. As an example here, we consider fitting straight edges. However, rather than doing this in 3D, we can just as well exploit the fact that straight edges in the scene project onto straight edges in the image and solve for the 3D depths of the two endpoints of a line in the image directly.

Figure 3.4 sketches the scene and image geometries under consideration. The image endpoint i at $\mathbf{r}_i$ is related to the corresponding scene point $\mathbf{R}_i$ by the perspective transformation, equation (1.1).

On the assumption that the visual motion components recovered by the method of Chapter 2 are equal to components of the projected motion field we can express the full visual motion at $\mathbf{r}_i$ as

$$\dot{\mathbf{r}}_i = -\zeta_i l \mathbf{V} - \zeta_i (\mathbf{V} \cdot \hat{\mathbf{z}}) \mathbf{r}_i + \mathbf{\Omega} \times \mathbf{r}_i + (\mathbf{\Omega} \times \mathbf{r}_i) \cdot \hat{\mathbf{z}} \frac{\mathbf{r}_i}{l} \tag{3.8}$$

and similarly for $\mathbf{r}_j$. Now consider a point $\mathbf{r}$ on the straight line between endpoints $\mathbf{r}_i$ and $\mathbf{r}_j$ which is defined parametrically as

$$\mathbf{r} = \gamma \mathbf{r}_j + (1 - \gamma) \mathbf{r}_i \quad : 0 \le \gamma \le 1 . \tag{3.9}$$

The visual motion at this point must be a similar linear combination of $\dot{\mathbf{r}}_i$ and $\dot{\mathbf{r}}_j$: that is,

$$\dot{\mathbf{r}} = \gamma \dot{\mathbf{r}}_j + (1 - \gamma) \dot{\mathbf{r}}_i . \tag{3.10}$$

This is *almost* the data we measure and wish to predict, but there are two details which must be taken care of. First, the measured edgel positions $\mathbf{r}_e$ will probably not lie directly on the line between i and j: computed edgels will meander either side of the true line. To overcome this, we estimate γ to be that describing the *nearest* point on the straight line. In other words, given an edgel at $\mathbf{r}_e$, deemed to part of the straight edge $\mathcal{E}_{ij}$ between endpoints i and j, the parameter value is found as

$$\gamma_e = \frac{(\mathbf{r}_e - \mathbf{r}_i) \cdot (\mathbf{r}_j - \mathbf{r}_i)}{|\mathbf{r}_j - \mathbf{r}_i|^2} \tag{3.11}$$

and hence the predicted full visual motion at the edgel is

$$\dot{\mathbf{r}}_e^{pred} = \gamma_e \dot{\mathbf{r}}_j + (1 - \gamma_e) \dot{\mathbf{r}}_i . \tag{3.12}$$

Secondly, we require a *component* of $\dot{\mathbf{r}}_e^{pred}$ to compare with the computed *component* of visual motion. This is found straightforwardly by vector projection onto the measured component $\mathbf{v}_e$. In other words, our predicted value of the component is

$$\mathbf{v}_e^{pred} = (\dot{\mathbf{r}}_e^{pred} \cdot \hat{\mathbf{v}}_e) \hat{\mathbf{v}}_e . \tag{3.13}$$

After some routine working, the magnitude of the predicted component is found to be

$$
\begin{aligned}
|\mathbf{v}_e^{pred}| \;=\; & \mathbf{V} \cdot \hat{\mathbf{x}}[\zeta_i(\gamma_e - 1) - \zeta_j \gamma_e] l \cos\theta + \\
& \mathbf{V} \cdot \hat{\mathbf{y}}[\zeta_i(\gamma_e - 1) - \zeta_j \gamma_e] l \sin\theta + \\
& \mathbf{V} \cdot \hat{\mathbf{z}}[\zeta_i(\gamma_e - 1) f_i - \zeta_j \gamma_e f_j] + \\
& \mathbf{\Omega} \cdot \hat{\mathbf{x}}[(1 - \gamma_e) f_i y_i + \gamma_e f_j y_j + l^2 \sin\theta]/l + \\
& \mathbf{\Omega} \cdot \hat{\mathbf{y}}[(\gamma_e - 1) f_i x_i - \gamma_e f_j x_j - l^2 \cos\theta]/l + \\
& \mathbf{\Omega} \cdot \hat{\mathbf{z}}[(\gamma_e - 1) g_i - \gamma_e g_j],
\end{aligned}
\tag{3.14}
$$

where

$$
\begin{aligned}
\cos\theta &= (\hat{\mathbf{x}} \cdot \mathbf{v}_e)/|\mathbf{v}_e| \\
\sin\theta &= (\hat{\mathbf{y}} \cdot \mathbf{v}_e)/|\mathbf{v}_e|
\end{aligned}
\tag{3.15}
$$

and

$$f_i = x_i \cos\theta + y_i \sin\theta \tag{3.16}$$

$$g_i = y_i \cos\theta - x_i \sin\theta$$
$$f_j = x_j \cos\theta + y_j \sin\theta$$
$$g_j = y_j \cos\theta - x_j \sin\theta \ .$$

The only unknowns are the reciprocal depths of the two endpoints, ζ_i and ζ_j. These can be recovered using any standard linear least-squares technique, by minimizing for straight edge $\mathcal{E}_{ij}$

$$D_{\mathcal{E}_{ij}} = \sum_{e \in \mathcal{E}_{ij}} w_e(|\mathbf{v}_e| - |\mathbf{v}_e^{pred}|)^2 \qquad (3.17)$$

where w_e is the confidence associated with the measurement at edgel e.

3.5.1 Segmentation

There is one more thing to do before we can perform this straight line fitting to the visual motion components, and that is to *segment* the visual motion.

Motion segmentation is concerned with grouping together those motion vectors in the image which arise from a single moving entity in the scene. Visual motion itself is a demonstrably powerful cue for scene and image segmentation in many visual systems as we will explore in Chapter 7. However, as we shall see there, segmentation using motion properties alone proves to be a difficult and, we suggest, largely unsolved problem in computational vision. Working within the bounds of our present impoverished understanding, it is much more straightforward to use some simpler image property such as texture or colour to segment the image, and then to apply a structure from motion computation to the visual motion found for each segment.

This simple approach is the one we have taken in this example. We are concerned to group visual motion arising from moving straight edges in the scene and therefore lying along straight edges in the image. As we have computed visual motion at edgels using the method of the previous chapter, segmentation is achieved by grouping the edgels into those lying on straight lines. The details of the segmentation are given in the next chapter. For our immediate task we require only the early stages of the process described there. Edgels are linked to their neighbours to form strings, which are then broken into sub-strings at points where the string curvature is high. An attempt is made to fit a straight line to each sub-string using the positions of the edgels e in the string and, if successful, the sub-string is deemed to be a straight edge, $\mathcal{E}_{ij}$, say. The fitting yields estimates of the endpoints of $\mathcal{E}_{ij}$, $\mathbf{r}_i$ and $\mathbf{r}_j$.

3.5.2 Experiment

The segmentation was applied to the edge map of the current image of the second office sequence, most recently shown in Figure 3.3(a), and the 3D edge fitting was then performed as described. The recovered depth map is shown in Figure 3.5(a) and in (b) is shown a plan view of the recovered midpoint depths overlaid on the prominent items in the office. The registration of recovered and actual geometry is good to better than $\pm10\%$, although problems are experienced with the near horizontal lines; because the motion is horizontal the edge-normal component of motion is small and the reconstruction is consequently sensitive to noise.

3.6 Remarks

In this chapter we have discussed the impact that the aperture problem has on 3D structure and motion recovery, and have discussed the first and simplest scene constraint that can be introduced to finesse it, prior knowledge of the 3D scene motion.

In the next three chapters we will examine more interesting structural constraints that can be used to recover both scene structure *and* motion.

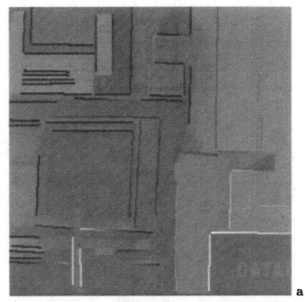

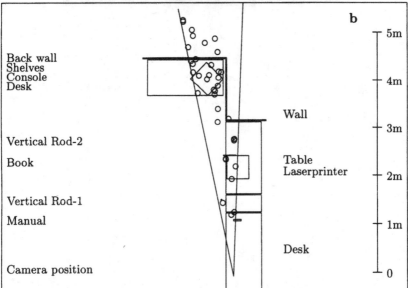

Figure 3.5: (a) The depths of the recovered straight lines coded in grey and overlaid on the image. (Light near, dark far.) (b) A plan view of the office scene with the depths of the midpoints of the lines projected onto it.

4 The Structure and Motion of Edges

In the previous chapter we indicated the need for constraints when recovering the structure and motion of a 3D scene using visual motion components and demonstrated that the constraint of known motion between camera and scene is sufficient to recover the structure. In this chapter we examine our first structure from motion algorithm to recover the motion of the scene in addition to its structure. It again utilizes visual motion components that arise from points lying on straight edges in the image, but here those edges are linked together into a higher structure, a vertex-edge graph. We shall consider this segmentation of edgels into groups forming straight edges first.

4.1 Motion segmentation using edges

To segment the edgel positions we build a vertex-edge graph in the image using a recipe which borrows much from techniques described in standard texts such as (Ballard and Brown 1982). Although the recipe contains mostly reasoned principles, it also uses helpful expedients such as 'delete short edges'. Such heuristics in computer vision are at once deplorable and seemingly — at least at present — inevitable. (Haralick (1986) has written a pointed article on the subject.) Fortunately, there are indications that there are more principled methods of extracting lines from images, eg Burns, Hanson and Riseman (1986), locating kinks, eg Blake, Zisserman and Papoulias (1986) and Blake and Zisserman (1987), and so on, which one could exploit were this the sole raison d'être of this work.

4.1.1 The edgel segmentation in detail

The starting point for the construction of the vertex-edge graph is the set of edgels in the central frame of the sequence in which visual motion is to be obtained. In Figure 4.1(a) we show the central image from a synthetic sequence of a house, constructed using a Constructive Solid Geometry (CSG) modeller, translating relative to the camera along the $-\hat{x}$ axis. The edge map computed using Canny's edge detector is shown in Figure 4.1(b). Although this is a very simple image it indicates some of the problems inherent in raw edgel output. The more routine difficulties are apparent from the enlarged region of the edge map shown in

Figure 4.1(d): the edgels are pointillist, unconnected and meandering, and there are breaks at corners. These are of similar size to the mask width used in the convolutions in Canny's method, and are a result of the non-maximal suppression stage of his algorithm (Canny 1983, 1986). His edge detector is designed to preserve geometry not topology.

The principal tasks then are to find edgels and link them into continuous strings, to determine which strings comprise straight edges, and then to extend edges into vertices. We begin by linking edgels into extended strings as follows:

1. Starting at the strongest unvisited edgel i, links are made to edgels on the left until a break occurs. The leftmost edgel becomes the left end of a new string. (Left and right are defined by looking from the dark to the light side of an edgel.)

2. Links are made to the right from i until a break occurs. The rightmost edgel becomes the right end of the string.

3. If there are unvisited edgels, continue from (1).

The linking process, similar to that in Ramer (1975), is illustrated in Figure 4.2. Suppose for example that linking is travelling leftwards from an edgel i. The orientation a_i of the edge is used to determine which of the eight pixel neighbours is directly to the left of it, and this neighbour is labelled C. The two pixels on the dark and light sides of C are labelled D and L. A search is first made for an edgel j_C in C and if successful i and j_C are linked, provided the orientation difference between i and j_C is less than some threshold angle. If the threshold angle is exceeded the string terminates at i. If there is no edgel in C, a search is made in both D and L and potential links established if edgels j_D and/or j_L exist and the orientation difference threshold is not exceeded. If only one potential link is found this is confirmed immediately, but if two exist then the one with the smaller orientation difference is chosen. Naturally, if no potential link exists, the string is terminated.

The next step, Figure 4.3, is to find points of high curvature along the strings. A signal S is derived by convolving the edge orientation a (now including winding number) as a function of length l along the string with the derivative of a Gaussian, G, whose width is a few edgels (Asada and Brady 1984). That is, for each string we derive

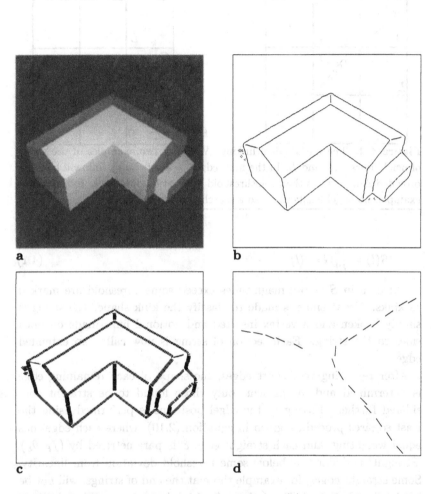

Figure 4.1: The central image (a), the edge map (b) and the visual motion (c) from a synthetic sequence where the camera translates past the CSG house. In (d) is an enlargement of the edge map at the leftmost roof gable showing a corner break typical of the output of the Canny edge detector.

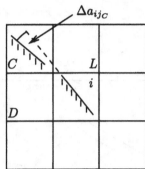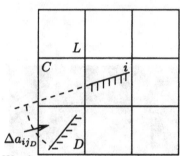

Figure 4.2: The initial edgel linking. We show two examples of the choice of neighbours C,D and L. In the first, edgel j_C exists and a link will be made provided Δa_{ij_C} is less than the threshold orientation difference. In the second example, no edgel exists in C, so a search is made in L and D.

$$S(l) = \frac{\partial}{\partial l} G * a(l) \ . \tag{4.1}$$

Extrema in S whose magnitudes exceed some threshold are marked as kinks. No attempt is made to classify the kink shape: the string is simply broken and a vertex inserted and notional links made on both sides to the string. Each section of string is now called an extended edge.

After removing very short edges, the shape of each remaining edge is determined and, at present, only those found to be straight considered further. Fitting to the edgel positions is performed using the least squares procedure given in equation (2.10), where each edgel has equal weighting, and each straight edge $\mathcal{E}$ is parametrized by $(f_\mathcal{E}, \theta_\mathcal{E})$. 'Straight' is defined as below some threshold deviation from linearity. Some straight edges, for example those at the end of strings, will not be bounded at both ends by vertices. A search is made around each 'loose end' to find a vertex, or other loose end, to which to link, as illustrated in Figure 4.4.

The final steps in constructing the vertex-edge graph are to coalesce collinear linked edges (by recursively testing pairs of linked straight edges for overall linearity) and to refine the position of every vertex which has three or more edges entering it. The vertex position is taken to be that giving the least sum of the squared perpendicular distances to each edge attached to the vertex. That is, we vary a vertex's position in the image,

Edgels

Orientation vs. length

Signal vs. length

Vertices inserted

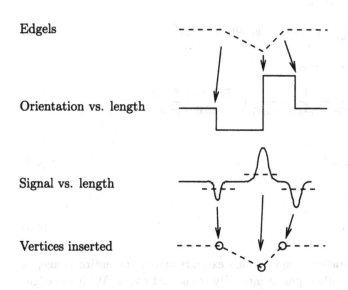

Figure 4.3: The stages in locating substantial kinks in predominantly straight edgel strings. The strings are broken and vertices inserted.

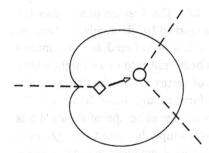

Figure 4.4: Linking of a 'loose end' (marked as a diamond) to a nearby vertex. The contour is one of constant linking likelihood: forward growth is favoured, but backward growth not prohibited.

(x_V, y_V), so as to find

$$\min_{(x_V, y_V)} \sum_{\mathcal{E}} (x_V \cos\theta_{\mathcal{E}} + y_V \sin\theta_{\mathcal{E}} - f_{\mathcal{E}})^2 \ . \tag{4.2}$$

The refined position is

$$\mathbf{r}_V = \frac{1}{2(\overline{sc}^2 + \overline{c^2}(\overline{c^2} - n))} \left(\begin{array}{c} \overline{sc}.\overline{s} + \overline{c}(\overline{c^2} - n) \\ \overline{sc}.\overline{c} - \overline{c^2}.\overline{s} \end{array} \right) \tag{4.3}$$

where

$$\overline{c} = \sum_{\mathcal{E}} \cos\theta_{\mathcal{E}} \tag{4.4}$$

and so on, and

$$n = \sum_{\mathcal{E}} 1 \ . \tag{4.5}$$

The segmentation graph, which extends across the entire image, is then split into subgraphs of mutually connected edges. With the edgel segmentation complete, it is now a trivial matter to import the visual motion at the edgels and attach it to the graph data structure.

4.1.2   Experimental example

The edgel map from the central frame of the CSG house sequence was supplied to the segmentation algorithm, with the results at various stages in the segmentation shown in Figure 4.5. The first graphic shows the creation of strings. The loose ends are marked by diamonds. Notice, for example, that the front edge of the roof has been found as a continuous string. By the second graphic this has been split into two straight edges, labelled 34 and 35, with the insertion of vertex 17. In the final graphic, edge 56, for example, has been grown forward and linked to vertex 17.

It is worth noting now that the vertex-edge subgraph of Figure 4.5 is not a complete line drawing of the object, simply because two edges were extremely weak in the original image and were removed by the hysteresis thresholding stage of edge detection. Any such loss of information must of course degrade the structure from motion computation described in the next section. However, as we shall see, the success of the structure from motion stage does not rely critically upon completeness of the linedrawing from the 2D segmentation, only on there being a sufficient amount of structural linkage. We indicate the sufficient conditions later.

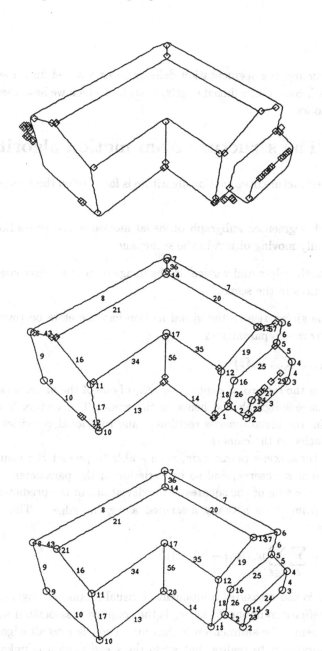

Figure 4.5: Stages in creating the vertex-edge graph segmentation for the CSG house.

In summary, the segmentation delivers to us a set of linked straight edges, each comprising linked edgels, at each of which we have measured visual motion.

4.2   The structure from motion algorithm

The edge structure from motion algorithm is founded on the assumptions that

1. each segmented subgraph of visual motion is the projection of a rigidly moving object in the scene; and

2. straight edges and vertices in the image map to straight edges and vertices in the scene.

The scene giving rise to the visual motion can therefore be (over-) described by $m + 6$ parameters

$$\{\zeta_1, \ldots, \zeta_m, \mathbf{V}, \mathbf{\Omega}\}$$

where ζ_i is the reciprocal depth $\zeta_i = 1/Z_i$ of one of the m vertices found in the image subgraph and hence in the scene. The vectors $\mathbf{V}$ and $\mathbf{\Omega}$ are, again, the instantaneous rectilinear and rotational velocities of the scene relative to the camera.

Given these scene parameters, we are able to predict the visual motion we should observe, and so by variation of the parameters we can minimize the sum of the squares of the deviations of the predicted components from those actually measured along the edges. That is, we minimize

$$D = \sum_{\mathcal{E}} \sum_{e \in \mathcal{E}} w_e (|\mathbf{v}_e| - |\mathbf{v}_e^{pred}|)^2 \qquad (4.6)$$

where $\mathbf{v}_e$ is the *measured* component of visual motion at edgel e, $\mathbf{v}_e^{pred}$ is the *predicted* component and w_e is the confidence associated with the measurement. The summation is thus for all edgels e on all edges $\mathcal{E}$.

It is important to realize that when the scene motion is unknown it is impossible to compute more than $m + 5$ of the parameters because of the depth/speed scaling ambiguity in monocular motion processing, discussed in §1.2.1. We could multiply the rectilinear velocity components and divide the reciprocal depths by any scalar value without affecting the minimization. There are two obvious ways of reducing the dimensionality of the parametrization: (i) by arbitrarily fixing one of the reciprocal depth values or (ii) by arbitrarily fixing the magnitude of the rectilinear velocity. Here we use the former method.

4.2.1 The algorithm in detail

Almost all of the detail for the edge algorithm has already been explored in the previous chapter.

Recall that the geometry involved is that of Figure 3.4, and that for an edgel lying approximately on the straight edge $\mathcal{E}_{ij}$ between $\mathbf{r}_i$ and $\mathbf{r}_j$ the magnitude of the predicted component of visual motion is (to reiterate equation 3.14)

$$
\begin{aligned}
|\mathbf{v}_e^{pred}| = \; & \mathbf{V} \cdot \hat{\mathbf{x}}[\zeta_i(\gamma_e - 1) - \zeta_j \gamma_e]l \cos\theta + && (4.7) \\
& \mathbf{V} \cdot \hat{\mathbf{y}}[\zeta_i(\gamma_e - 1) - \zeta_j \gamma_e]l \sin\theta + \\
& \mathbf{V} \cdot \hat{\mathbf{z}}[\zeta_i(\gamma_e - 1)f_i - \zeta_j \gamma_e f_j] + \\
& \mathbf{\Omega} \cdot \hat{\mathbf{x}}[(1 - \gamma_e)f_i y_i + \gamma_e f_j y_j + l^2 \sin\theta]/l + \\
& \mathbf{\Omega} \cdot \hat{\mathbf{y}}[(\gamma_e - 1)f_i x_i - \gamma_e f_j x_j - l^2 \cos\theta]/l + \\
& \mathbf{\Omega} \cdot \hat{\mathbf{z}}[(\gamma_e - 1)g_i - \gamma_e g_j],
\end{aligned}
$$

where

$$
\begin{aligned}
\cos\theta &= (\hat{\mathbf{x}} \cdot \mathbf{v}_e)/|\mathbf{v}_e| && (4.8) \\
\sin\theta &= (\hat{\mathbf{y}} \cdot \mathbf{v}_e)/|\mathbf{v}_e|
\end{aligned}
$$

and

$$
\begin{aligned}
f_i &= x_i \cos\theta + y_i \sin\theta && (4.9) \\
g_i &= y_i \cos\theta - x_i \sin\theta \\
f_j &= x_j \cos\theta + y_j \sin\theta \\
g_j &= y_j \cos\theta - x_j \sin\theta
\end{aligned}
$$

Unlike the known motion case, the minimization of the cost term D is a nonlinear problem as there are product terms $\mathbf{V}\zeta$. We employ a general nonlinear least-squares technique due to Marquardt (1963), which gradually changes its method of search from a decoupled gradient search to a linearization of the fitting function as it approaches convergence. (The algorithm turns out to be a near rediscovery of an earlier method due to Levenberg (1944) and is often described by both authors' names. The method is described by Bevington (1969).) The minimization requires specification of the partial derivatives of $|\mathbf{v}_e^{pred}|$ at each edgel e with respect to each of the $m+5$ parameters. At first this seems computationally onerous, but in fact, of the $m-1$ partial derivatives with respect to the reciprocal depth parameters[1], all but two are identically zero. For an edgel between vertices i and j, the two non-zero partial derivatives with respect to the reciprocal depths are those with respect to ζ_i and ζ_j:

$$\frac{\partial |\mathbf{v}_e^{pred}|}{\partial \zeta_i} = l(\gamma_e - 1)(\mathbf{V} \cdot \hat{\mathbf{x}} \cos \theta + \mathbf{V} \cdot \hat{\mathbf{y}} \sin \theta + \mathbf{V} \cdot \hat{\mathbf{z}} f_i / l) \qquad (4.10)$$

and

$$\frac{\partial |\mathbf{v}_e^{pred}|}{\partial \zeta_j} = -l\gamma_e(\mathbf{V} \cdot \hat{\mathbf{x}} \cos \theta + \mathbf{V} \cdot \hat{\mathbf{y}} \sin \theta + \mathbf{V} \cdot \hat{\mathbf{z}} f_j / l) . \qquad (4.11)$$

The partial derivatives with respect to the six motion parameters are easily found from equation (4.7) as

$$\frac{\partial |\mathbf{v}_e^{pred}|}{\partial (\mathbf{V} \cdot \hat{\mathbf{x}})} = [\zeta_i(\gamma_e - 1) - \zeta_j \gamma_e] l \cos \theta \qquad (4.12)$$

and similarly for $\partial |\mathbf{v}_e^{pred}| / \partial (\mathbf{V} \cdot \hat{\mathbf{y}})$, $\partial |\mathbf{v}_e^{pred}| / \partial (\mathbf{V} \cdot \hat{\mathbf{z}})$, $\partial |\mathbf{v}_e^{pred}| / \partial (\boldsymbol{\Omega} \cdot \hat{\mathbf{x}})$, $\partial |\mathbf{v}_e^{pred}| / \partial (\boldsymbol{\Omega} \cdot \hat{\mathbf{y}})$ and $\partial |\mathbf{v}_e^{pred}| / \partial (\boldsymbol{\Omega} \cdot \hat{\mathbf{z}})$.

4.3   Computer experiments

The output of the structure from motion algorithm is a reconstruction of the disposition and motion of a collection of linked 3D edges in the scene. We shall refer to this as a *partial wireframe*.

As we have indicated before, the depths and rectilinear motion recovered contain a depth/speed scaling ambiguity. Whilst this makes no difference to the appearance of the 3D structure, it makes difficult discussion of the recovered structure and motion in quantitative terms. However, the matching processes described in Chapter 8 are able to resolve the ambiguity, by determining the overall length scale of the reconstructed data compared with that of a database model. Thus here we will assume the matching, thereby enabling a detailed quantitative

---

1) Why $m - 1$? Recall that one reciprocal depth, ζ_1 say, is fixed arbitrarily.

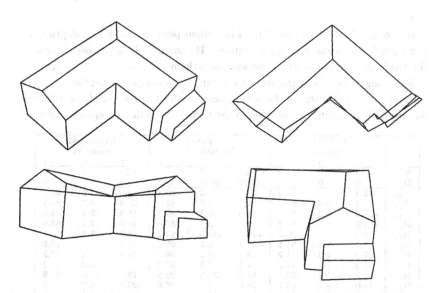

Figure 4.6: Several views around the reconstructed wireframe of the house.

comparison of recovered values with veridical values of the scene variables.

4.3.1 Synthesized scene with well-known geometry

The visual motion of the CSG house, Figure 4.1(c), and the segmentation of Figure 4.5 were supplied to the structure from motion algorithm. Even without resolving the depth/speed scaling ambiguity we can see the quality of reconstruction by moving the reader's eye around the 3D partial wireframe, as in Figure 4.6. The reader's own ability to interpret images and wireframes will indicate that the recovered structure is sound.

Because in this case the scene has been produced by a CSG modeller, the veridical values of the scene coordinates and motion are known accurately and can be compared, after matching, with the reconstruction. The comparison is given in detail in the first two columns of Table 4.1.

Although at first glance the motion and depth values presented in Table 4.1 show reasonable agreement with the veridical values, closer scrutiny reveals a systematic discrepancy between the reconstructed and veridical depths. The source of this is the apparently innocuous, but

Table 4.1: The veridical motion (Ω in radians per frame and $\mathbf{V}$ in depth units per frame) and scene vertex coordinates ($\mathbf{R}$) compared with those computed for the house sequence when the angular velocity is allowed to vary (central column) and when fixed (rightmost column). The computed depths $Z = \mathbf{R} \cdot \hat{\mathbf{z}}$ have errors of $\pm 5\%$ and all lie within one standard deviation of the veridical values. The subscripts to $\mathbf{R}$ refer to the vertex index in the segmentation.

	Veridical Values			Computed Variable Ω			Computed Fixed Ω		
	x	y	z	x	y	z	x	y	z
$\mathbf{V}$	-1.25	0	0	-1.54	0	0	-1.25	0	0
Ω	0	0	0	.0002	.0024	-.0003	0	0	0
$\mathbf{R}_{10}$	12.9	-7.8	81.2	13.8	-8.4	86.9	13.0	-7.9	81.3
$\mathbf{R}_{15}$	20.0	0.0	83.3	21.3	0.8	87.9	20.4	0.7	84.3
$\mathbf{R}_{12}$	-11.8	-5.3	83.7	-12.6	-5.7	89.1	-11.9	-5.4	84.6
$\mathbf{R}_{17}$	-18.9	2.5	85.8	-19.8	3.3	88.9	-18.6	3.1	83.8
$\mathbf{R}_{18}$	-18.9	-11.7	90.0	-19.8	-12.3	94.3	-18.9	-11.8	90.1
$\mathbf{R}_{21}$	-15.4	-7.8	91.1	-16.2	-8.2	95.0	-15.4	-7.8	90.5
$\mathbf{R}_9$	27.0	2.2	91.2	28.7	2.3	96.3	27.8	2.2	93.2
$\mathbf{R}_{11}$	-1.2	2.2	91.2	-1.3	2.3	97.7	-1.2	2.2	93.2
$\mathbf{R}_2$	12.9	-19.1	92.5	13.8	-20.5	98.3	13.1	-19.6	93.9
$\mathbf{R}_{13}$	-26.0	4.7	93.7	-26.6	4.8	95.6	-25.7	4.7	92.2
$\mathbf{R}_4$	-11.8	-16.6	95.0	-12.3	-17.3	98.5	-11.7	-16.4	93.3
$\mathbf{R}_6$	-18.9	-16.6	95.0	-19.7	-17.4	98.6	-19.0	-16.7	94.9
$\mathbf{R}_{19}$	-29.5	-4.2	97.5	-30.4	-4.3	100.2	-29.6	-4.2	97.8
$\mathbf{R}_5$	-15.4	-14.1	97.5	-16.0	-14.8	101.1	-15.5	-14.3	97.8
$\mathbf{R}_{16}$	-1.2	15.0	98.3	-1.4	16.4	102.0	-1.3	15.8	98.3
$\mathbf{R}_{20}$	-26.0	-0.3	98.6	-26.6	-0.3	100.3	-25.9	-0.3	97.7
$\mathbf{R}_1$	27.0	-9.1	102.5	27.3	-9.3	103.2	27.1	-9.3	102.2
$\mathbf{R}_3$	-1.2	-9.1	102.5	-1.3	-9.3	103.6	-1.2	-9.0	99.5
$\mathbf{R}_7$	-29.5	-9.1	102.5	-30.2	-9.1	103.4	-29.9	-9.0	102.6
$\mathbf{R}_{14}$	-1.2	22.2	111.2	-1.3	22.3	110.7	-1.3	21.7	107.8

actually significant value of the angular velocity component Ω_y. Examination of the components of the projected motion (equation 1.5)

$$\dot{x} = -\frac{l V_x}{Z} - x\frac{V_z}{Z} - l\Omega_y - y\Omega_z + x\frac{y\Omega_x - x\Omega_y}{l}$$

$$\dot{y} = -\frac{l V_y}{Z} - y\frac{V_z}{Z} + x\Omega_z + l\Omega_x + y\frac{y\Omega_x - x\Omega_y}{l}$$

shows immediately that the Ω_y term can give rise to visual motion in the x-direction which could be confused with that arising from the V_x term. Indeed, it is possible to contrive purely rectilinear and purely rotational motion fields which differ only in second order (ie, in x^2, xy or y^2). This makes it difficult to decide whether the scene motion is rectilinear or rotational, the more so when the camera's angle of view is small and when the sequence is short, spanning only a small displacement. In this experiment the full cone of view from the camera was $36°$, but in our

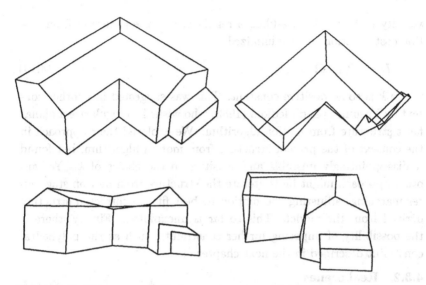

Figure 4.7: Views around the house reconstructed using constrained angular velocity.

experiments on real imagery discussed below the effect is more serious because the full cone angle of view is only 16°. As we discuss there, the effect is not as pronounced if the motion field is dilating.

In practice, it is often possible to measure the angular velocity of the camera, say using gyroscopic sensing, or indeed to constrain it to be some known value, possibly zero. For such cases a simple modification of the structure from motion algorithm is possible; the last three terms of equation (4.7) become a known constant and the three variables Ω are removed from the fitting process. When this is done for the CSG house example, the systematic discrepancy between recovered and veridical values disappears and there is better overall agreement. The recovered partial wireframe is that of Figure 4.7 and the absolute depths and motion recovered after matching are detailed in the rightmost column of Table 4.1.

If it is not possible to measure the angular velocity directly, there are several potential alternatives. The most obvious is to wait for more frames, and integrate the structure using, for example, an extended Kalman filter. A second approach would be to constrain the angular velocity to be small by adding a regularizer to the structure from motion cost function to be minimized:

$$D' = D + k\Omega \cdot \Omega , \tag{4.13}$$

where k is some positive constant. This was suggested in another context by Yasumoto and Medioni (1985) who wished to regularize a planar facet structure from motion algorithm. We explored their approach in the context of the present structure from motion algorithm, but found it disappointingly unstable and sensitive to the choice of k. Yet another approach might be to iterate the structure from motion stage *after* matching, adjusting the motion to best fit the corrected structure derived from the model. This so far is unexplored. Finally, there is the possibility of imposing further constraints, such as the polyhedral constraint described in the next chapter.

4.3.2   Real scenes

A chipped block undergoing lateral translation. The chipped block used in the first experimental sequence, one frame of which is shown in Figure 4.8(a), is approximately $164 \times 75 \times 58$mm. The image sequence was captured off a Panasonic CCD camera with 512×512 rectangular pixels which were resampled in software to produce 512×384 images with square pixels, from which the central 384×384 section was used for experiment. No special calibration of the camera was performed. It was assumed that the optic axis passed through the centre of the captured image, that the pixel width was given by the nominal width of the CCD chip of 8.8mm divided into 512 pixels, that the focal length of the lens was the quoted 24mm and that the optics gave perfect perspective images. The full cone angle subtended by the object to the camera was only $16°$. The chipped block was positioned at a mean distance of about 415mm in front of the camera and translated upwards along the $\hat{y}$-axis at 3mm per frame.

The segmentation and computed visual motion are shown in Figure 4.8(b) and (c). It can be seen that the somewhat rounded physical edges of the object have combined with lighting and reflectance effects to produce rather meandering edges, highlighting the importance of not assuming that edgels lie directly on the straight line between the endpoints of an edge.

The visual motion and segmentation were supplied to the structure

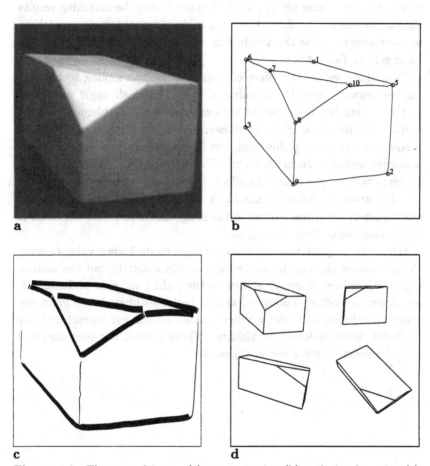

Figure 4.8: The central image (a), segmentation (b) and visual motion (c) for the sequence of the block moving along $\hat{y}$. Views of the reconstructed 3D wireframe are shown in (d). The angular velocity was unconstrained.

from motion algorithm; firstly to the version in which angular velocity is unconstrained. In Figure 4.8(d) we show views around the 3D partial wireframe recovered by the algorithm. This wireframe was then supplied to the edge matching algorithm of Chapter 8 with the matching results shown later as Figure 8.11. From the scale computed during matching we were able to derive the absolute motion and depths shown on the left hand side of Table 4.2.

Here again we see the effect of angular velocity coupling to the rectilinear velocity (now Ω_x coupling to V_y). The small angle subtended to the camera by the scene further exacerbates the problem in this example. The direction of the rectilinear velocity is found correctly to be predominantly in the $\hat{y}$ direction, but its magnitude (that is, the speed) is overestimated as 7mm per frame. The discrepancy is made up of $\Omega_x \overline{Z}$ which is $\approx$ 3mm per frame. In effect, the system believes the camera is panning upwards, following the block to some extent, and so to recreate the observed visual motion in the image calculates that the block is translating faster than it really is.

When the angular velocity is constrained to its known value of zero, the processing through to matching proceeds similarly, but the motion and depth values obtained, shown on the right hand side of Table 4.2, are closer to reality. The speed is now better estimated as 2.9mm per frame (compared with the veridical value of 3mm per frame) and the midpoint depth is found as 420mm. Views around the reconstructed partial wireframe are given in Figure 4.9.

Table 4.2: The motion (Ω and V) and scene vertex coordinates (R) computed by the system for the block translating along $+\hat{y}$ at 3mm per frame. On the left the angular velocity is unconstrained. On the right it has been fixed, and the recovered values are close to reality. The depths $Z = R \cdot \hat{z}$ and speed have computed errors of $\pm 12\%$ (variable Ω) and $\pm 3\%$ (fixed Ω).

Quantity	Variable Ω			Fixed Ω (near veridical)		
	x	y	z	x	y	z
V in mm per frame	.45	7.20	-0.30	0.07	2.88	-0.12
Ω in rad per frame	5e-03	-6e-04	-9e-05	0	0	0
R_5 in mm	19	-6	514	12	-4	321
R_1	21	-61	521	14	-39	332
R_4	-31	27	528	-20	17	335
R_3	-73	29	544	-47	18	352
R_2	-69	-55	552	-46	-36	365
R_6	48	45	580	32	30	394
R_7	83	-13	659	62	-10	495
R_{10}	83	63	660	63	48	500
R_9	41	62	678	3	48	520

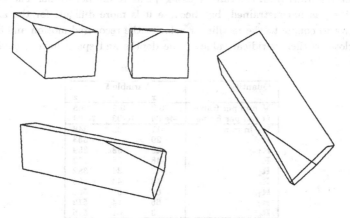

Figure 4.9: Views of the reconstructed partial 3D wireframe for the block when the angular velocity was fixed to its known value.

Block translating along optic axis. In a further experiment the block was placed in a similar position, but moved directly away from the camera at 10mm per frame. An image from the sequence, the computed segmentation and visual motion are shown in Figure 4.10.

Examination of the equations for projected motion, equation (1.5), shows that it is not possible to simulate a purely expanding or contracting visual motion field to any order using rotational terms, and so we expect here that the structure from motion algorithm will be able to discriminate between rotational and rectilinear motion. This is indeed the case. In Figure 4.10(d) we show the partial wireframe reconstructed from the visual motion of Figure 4.10(c) and, after matching, we obtain the absolute depth and motion values of Table 4.3. The rectilinear velocity is now within two standard deviations of its veridical value and the midpoint depth found as 430mm. Note however that there is distortion at the vertex nearest the image centre. This lies close to the focus of expansion (in this case near the image centre), where the visual motion vectors are small and inevitably more prone to noise. This effect is more pronounced in the next example.

Table 4.3: The motion and scene vertex coordinates computed for the block translating away from the camera along $+\hat{z}$ at 10mm per frame. The angular velocity was unconstrained, but because it is more difficult for the angular velocity to couple to the rectilinear velocity the recovered motion and depths are close to their veridical values. The depths and speed have a computed error of $\pm 12\%$.

Quantity	Variable Ω		
	x	y	z
V mm per frame	-0.2	0.2	13.5
Ω rad per frame	-4e-04	1e-03	7e-04
R_4 in mm	-11	33	348
R_5	29	7	353
R_1	29	-38	359
R_3	-48	35	372
R_2	-47	-34	382
R_6	43	44	405
R_{10}	66	61	507
R_7	65	-4	512
R_9	-3	61	516

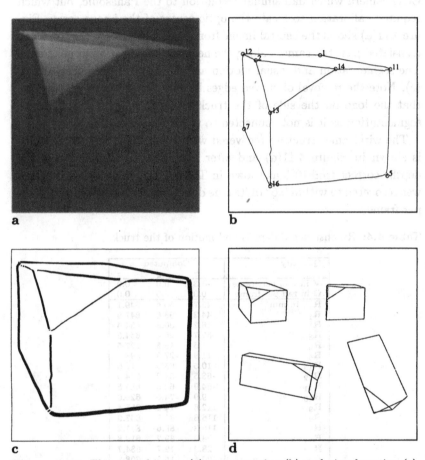

Figure 4.10: The central image (a), segmentation (b) and visual motion (c) from the sequence of the block moving along $\hat{z}$. The reconstructed partial wireframe is shown in (d).

A toy truck translating laterally. We now demonstrate the results of processing a sequence of a somewhat more complicated object, a toy truck. These experiments were performed with an EEV Photon CCD camera which had similar resolution to the Panasonic, but which required calibration to locate the optic centre of the image array. Figure 4.11(a) shows the central image from a sequence where the toy truck translated past the camera along the negative $\hat{x}$-axis at 5mm per frame. The segmentation and visual motion are shown in Figures 4.11(b) and (c). Note the removal of curved edges by the segmentation process and that the logo on the side of the truck forms a separate graph in the segmentation as it is not connected to truck's main outline.

The wireframe structure recovered with constrained angular velocity is shown in Figure 4.11(d) and after matching we obtained absolute depths correct to ±10% as shown in Table 4.4. The velocity direction was recovered to within 0.6° of its true direction, and the speed as 5.3mm per frame.

Table 4.4: Reconstructed depths and motion of the truck.

Quantity	Computed		
	x	y	z
V in mm per frame	-5.3	0.0	0.0
Ω in rad per frame	0.0	0.0	0.0
R_{15} in mm	-45.7	50.4	649.1
R_1	44.2	98.6	847.9
R_4	-46.2	30.8	654.4
R_3	-52.7	26.4	644.3
R_6	-61.5	-16.5	627.5
R_5	11.9	-27.3	598.6
R_{13}	10.6	-63.9	612.6
R_{12}	-63.5	-51.9	634.9
R_{11}	-64.9	-63.0	654.5
R_{10}	9.9	-74.0	620.6
R_9	112.6	-14.2	853.4
R_8	116.8	31.9	867.9
R_7	116.8	88.6	831.2
R_{14}	28.0	39.2	619.8
R_{16}	28.9	19.7	634.7
R_2	20.4	15.2	608.3

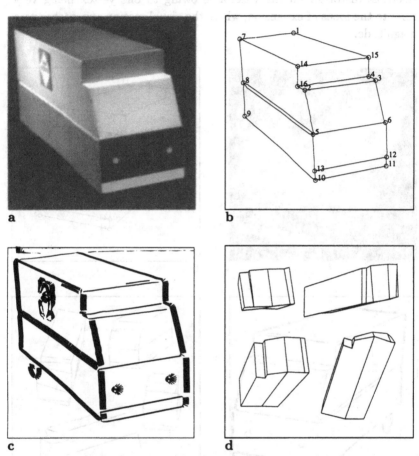

Figure 4.11: The central image (a), the segmentation (b) and the visual motion (c) from a sequence where the truck moves along the $\hat{x}$-axis relative to the camera. The reconstructed partial wireframe is shown in (d).

Camera translating towards truck.   Figure 4.12 illustrates the visual motion and 3D partial wireframe recovered when the camera moved directly towards the truck. Compared with Figure 4.11(d) there is considerable distortion in the wireframe owing to one vertex being very close to the focus of expansion, where the visual motion approaches zero magnitude.

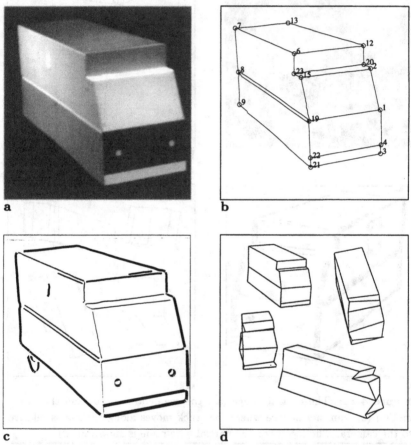

Figure 4.12: The central image (a), segmentation (b), visual motion (c) and views of the wireframe (d) computed when the camera moved directly towards the truck.

4.4 How many edges?

We noted earlier that the line drawing supplied to the algorithm does not have to be complete, but that it must possess *sufficient* connectivity. The CSG house, for example, had two edges missing. The reconstruction was not greatly affected, but if further edges were removed at what point would the method collapse entirely?

Suppose we regard the many measurements along the straight edges as enabling estimates, indeed very accurate estimates, to be made of edge-normal components of motion at both ends of the edge. By assuming that edges meet at vertices in the image and scene, we are able therefore to estimate two components of visual motion, pointing in different directions, and thus recover the *full* visual motion at these vertices. In Chapter 3 we showed that, given full visual motion at m points, we had $4m$ pieces of data and $3m + 5$ pieces of information to recover. Thus we need at least $m = 5$ connected vertex points in the linedrawing at the segmentation stage.

5 From Edges to Surfaces: the Structure and Motion of Polyhedra

This chapter describes the use of algebraic polyhedral constraints in the computation of 3D structure and motion from 2D visual motion. The method, which works when complete 2D linedrawing information is available, guarantees the recovery of planar faces. The normals to these faces are used for matching to models. Several examples are given to illustrate the scope of the method.

We modify the structure from motion computation of Chapter 4 using algebraic constraints to force the reconstructed partial wireframe in 3D to be *strictly* polyhedral. The motivation is to make surfaces explicit at an earlier stage of the processing, in particular, before model matching.

One heuristic way of achieving this would be, say, to fit planes through the 3D edges and vertices computed by the existing, unconstrained, algorithm. If sets of edges were ajudged coplanar, it would then be possible to re-apply the algorithm including these additional constraints. However, such a method neglects the structural information contained in a single image of a polyhedral scene. In this chapter we utilize the information from linedrawing analysis to supply a priori constraints to the structure from motion computation, using the techniques described by Sugihara (1982, 1984, 1986).

Later, in Chapter 9, we demonstrate that the recovered planar faces enable matching to models similarly described in terms of planar surfaces.

5.1 Imposing polyhedral constraints

Although there is an implicit polyhedral assumption in the structure from motion algorithm of Chapter 4, in that we consider a 3D scene to be made up of straight edges linked by vertices, nowhere is this assumption converted into an explicit constraint. To impose polyhedral planarity, we obviously have to discover and specify which edges comprise the border of a face. This can be achieved by analyzing the 2D linedrawing, at least providing it is *complete*.

Two important methods of reconstructing polyhedra from 2D linedrawings are due to Kanade (1981), who recovered shape from linedrawings using a gradient space approach, and Sugihara (1986), who developed linear algebraic constraints imposed in real space. Sugihara's technique claims advantages over that of Kanade. First, the former's constraints impose necessary and sufficient conditions that the object is a polyhedron, where the latter's apply only a necessary condition. Secondly, gradient space techniques appear more sensitive to errors in 2D vertex positions than the algebraic constraints. We utilize Sugihara's method but, unlike previous experimental work, here we apply the constraints under perspective projection.

5.1.1 Sugihara's algebraic constraints

The starting point is the information implicit in the 2D graph derived for segmentation purposes. This is no more than a 2D linedrawing, and can be labelled using the well-known techniques pioneered by Huffmann (1971), Clowes (1971) and Waltz (1975) using a '+' to denote lines corresponding to convex edges, a '−' to denote those corresponding to concave edges, and a '>' to denote occluding edges, where the arrow points such that the area to the right of the arrow is the occluding face.

Following Sugihara (1986), let $\mathcal{V}$ be the set of visible vertices, so that $|\mathcal{V}| = m$, and let $\mathcal{F}$ be the set of (partially or wholly) visible faces, with $|\mathcal{F}| = n$. Now define the set $\mathcal{R}$ as $\mathcal{R} \subseteq \mathcal{V} \times \mathcal{F} : (v, f) \in \mathcal{R}$ iff $v \in \mathcal{V}$ lies on $f \in \mathcal{F}$. Each pair $(v, f) \in \mathcal{R}$ is called an *incidence pair* and the triple $S = (\mathcal{V}, \mathcal{F}, \mathcal{R})$ is an *incidence structure*. This is easily computed from the linedrawing.

To derive the constraints, consider scene points $\mathbf{R}_i = (X_i, Y_i, Z_i)^T$ lying on the face f_j. They can be described by

$$\mathbf{R}_i \cdot \mathbf{N}_j = -1 \qquad\qquad (5.1)$$

where $\mathbf{N}_j$ is the normal to the face, and sticks *out* of the surface into free space. (Note that $\mathbf{N}_j$ is not a unit normal: the perpendicular distance to the plane is $|\mathbf{N}_j|^{-1}$.)

Using the perspective projection (equation (1.1)) each $(v_i, f_j) \in \mathcal{R}$ gives rise to a constraint

$$-\mathbf{r}_i \cdot \mathbf{N}_j + l\zeta_i = 0 \qquad\qquad (5.2)$$

where we recall that ζ is the reciprocal depth, $\zeta = 1/Z$. Collecting these together for every incidence pair in $\mathcal{R}$ results in the homogeneous constraint system:

$$[\mathbf{A}]\mathbf{s} = \mathbf{0} \qquad\qquad (5.3)$$

where

$$\mathbf{s} = (\mathbf{N}_1^T, \mathbf{N}_2^T, \ldots, \mathbf{N}_n^T, \boldsymbol{\zeta}^T)^T \qquad (5.4)$$

is an unknown column vector of length $(3n+m)$ in which $\boldsymbol{\zeta} = (\zeta_1 \ldots \zeta_m)^T$ is a vector of reciprocal depths, and where $[\mathbf{A}]$ is a known $|\mathcal{R}| \times (3n+m)$ matrix involving $\mathbf{r}$ coordinates and l.

Any face f_j bisects space. If a point $\mathbf{R}'$ is such that

$$\mathbf{R}' \cdot \mathbf{N}_j + 1 > 0$$

then the point lies in front of the plane of face f_j, and if

$$\mathbf{R}' \cdot \mathbf{N}_j + 1 < 0$$

it lies behind the plane. Now consider two faces f_j and f_k sharing a concave edge, as illustrated in Figure 5.1(a). Consider the vertex v_i such that $(v_i, f_k) \in \mathcal{R}$ but $(v_i, f_j) \notin \mathcal{R}$. Clearly,

$$- \mathbf{r}_i \cdot \mathbf{N}_j + l\zeta_i > 0 . \qquad (5.5)$$

But suppose these faces share a convex edge as in Figure 5.1(b). Then we can write the constraint

$$- \mathbf{r}_i \cdot \mathbf{N}_j + l\zeta_i < 0 . \qquad (5.6)$$

(In fact the situation is a little more complicated. The analysis above is only straightforwardly applicable when the joining edge is not a reentrant edge on a non-convex face. In practice a test is made (in 2D) as to whether all the vertices of at least one face lie to one side of the line created by extending the shared edge. If they do, then the correct inequality can be chosen. For example in Figure 5.1(c), all the vertices of face f_j lie to one side, so we can easily decide that vertices v_a and v_b lie in front of and behind the plane of f_j, respectively.)

Then consider Figure 5.1(d) where f_k occludes f_j. Let v_p, v_q, v_r be the initial, end and mid point of the occluding edge, following along the label direction. (Note that v_r is not an obvious member of $\mathcal{V}$. Sugihara explains that such pseudo-vertices are added to $\mathcal{V}$ and the pseudo-incidence pair (v_r, f_k) to $\mathcal{R}$ during creation of the incidence structure. They are then treated just like any other members.)

Either none or one of v_q or v_p could touch f_j (but not both, because then the occluding object is deemed part of the occluded and the edge is concave). Thus three constraints become available:

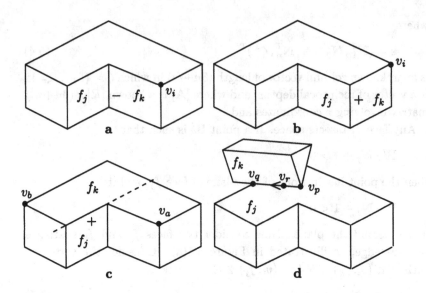

Figure 5.1: Edge labels for the non-occluding (a–c) and occluding (d) configurations. Care must be taken if the shared edge is the re-entrant edge of a non-convex face (c) because points on f_k can lie either side of face f_j.

$$-\mathbf{r}_p \cdot \mathbf{N}_j + l\zeta_p \geq 0 \,, \tag{5.7}$$

$$-\mathbf{r}_q \cdot \mathbf{N}_j + l\zeta_q \geq 0 \tag{5.8}$$

and

$$-\mathbf{r}_r \cdot \mathbf{N}_j + l\zeta_r > 0 \,. \tag{5.9}$$

Unfortunately, we cannot apply these constraints within a single structure from motion computation, because of the possibility that the occluding and occluded objects *move* differently, although they can of course be used to constrain depths between separate applications of the structure from motion algorithm.

Constraints of the type (5.5) and (5.6) (and indeed the occlusion constraints, if used) can be expressed as

$$[\mathbf{B}]\mathbf{s} > \mathbf{0} \tag{5.10}$$

(where, for occlusions, the inequality sometimes permits equality).

Hence, given that we wish to recover a polyhedral object, we could modify the structure from motion optimization of Chapter 4, equation (4.6), and pose it as:

Minimize

$$D = \sum_{\mathcal{E}} \sum_{e \in \mathcal{E}} w_e (|\mathbf{v}_e| - |\mathbf{v}_e^{pred}|)^2 \qquad (5.11)$$

subject to the conditions

$$[\mathbf{A}]\mathbf{s} = \mathbf{0} \qquad (5.12)$$
$$[\mathbf{B}]\mathbf{s} > \mathbf{0},$$

where we would vary all the reciprocal depths ζ and the motion parameters $\mathbf{V}$, $\mathbf{\Omega}$ (less one for the depth/speed scaling ambiguity).

However, Sugihara highlights several difficulties in applying the constraint system naïvely. The principal one is that not all the equations in the equality constraint $[\mathbf{A}]\mathbf{s} = \mathbf{0}$ are linearly independent. In other words, not all the 3D vertex positions in the structure from motion computation are independent. We outline here the steps proposed by Sugihara (1984) to determine a set of independent constraints and vertices.

5.1.2   Eliminating dependent constraints

Because only a few of the vertex positions in a polyhedron are independent, some of the constraints expressed by the set $\mathcal{R}$ depend on others. It is necessary both to eliminate these dependent constraints and to elicit the set of independent vertices.

First, it is necessary for the image vertices $(\mathbf{r}_1 \ldots \mathbf{r}_m)$ to be in *general position*, that is, they must be algebraically independent over the rational field so that there are no special relationships between their positions (eg three vertices must not always be collinear, nor three edges concurrent). Given this condition, we seek a *position-free* incidence structure S, one where the constraint system has a non-trivial solution when the vertices are in general position. Sugihara proves the following:

THEOREM 1 If $S = (\mathcal{V}, \mathcal{F}, \mathcal{R})$ is an incidence structure in which no three faces sharing a vertex have a common line of intersection (restrictions satisfied by all trihedral and convex objects) then S is position-free if and only if for all $\mathcal{X} \subseteq \mathcal{F} : |\mathcal{X}| \geq 2$,

$$|\mathcal{V}(\mathcal{X})| + 3|\mathcal{X}| \geq |\mathcal{R}(\mathcal{X})| + 4$$

where $\mathcal{V}(\mathcal{X})$ is the set of vertices that are on some faces in $\mathcal{X}$ and $\mathcal{R}(\mathcal{X})$ is the set of incidence pairs involving elements of $\mathcal{X}$.

THEOREM 2 If S as described in Theorem 1 is position-free and the vertices are in general position, then the system $[\mathbf{A}]\mathbf{s} = \mathbf{0}$ is linearly independent.

Given some set of incidence pairs $\mathcal{R}$, we can use Theorem 1 to test whether S is position-free. If it is not, we search for a maximal set $\mathcal{R}^* \subset \mathcal{R}$ for which the reduced incidence structure $S^* = (\mathcal{V}, \mathcal{F}, \mathcal{R}^*)$ is position-free by testing that for all $\mathcal{X} \subseteq \mathcal{F} : |\mathcal{X}| \geq 2$,

$$|\mathcal{V}^*(\mathcal{X})| + 3|\mathcal{X}| \geq |\mathcal{R}^*(\mathcal{X})| + 4 \qquad (5.13)$$

where $\mathcal{R}^*(\mathcal{X})$ is the subset of $\mathcal{R}^*$ involving elements of $\mathcal{X}$ and

$$\mathcal{V}^*(\mathcal{X}) = \{v | v \in \mathcal{V}, (\{v\} \times \mathcal{X}) \cap \mathcal{R}^* \neq \emptyset\} . \qquad (5.14)$$

The subset $\mathcal{R}^* \subset \mathcal{R}$ is associated with a subset of the original equality constraints, a subset which we can now express as $[\mathbf{A}^*]\mathbf{s} = \mathbf{0}$. But Theorem 2 shows that it must be possible to permute columns in $[\mathbf{A}^*]$ so that $[\mathbf{A}^*] \rightarrow [\mathbf{A}']$ and $\mathbf{s} \rightarrow \mathbf{s}'$ such that $[\mathbf{A}']$ can be partitioned

$$[\mathbf{A}']\mathbf{s}' = [[\mathbf{A}_1]|[\mathbf{A}_2]]\,\mathbf{s}' = \mathbf{0} \qquad (5.15)$$

where $[\mathbf{A}_1]$ is a non-singular $|\mathcal{R}^*| \times |\mathcal{R}^*|$ matrix whose inverse therefore exists and $[\mathbf{A}_2]$ is a $|\mathcal{R}^*| \times (3n + m - |\mathcal{R}^*|)$ matrix.

The vector $\mathbf{s}'$ has the same members as $\mathbf{s}$ but within it certain of the ζ values will have been permuted. Let us suppose that $\zeta \rightarrow \zeta'$, so that

$$\mathbf{s}' = (\mathbf{N}_1^T, \ldots, \mathbf{N}_n^T, \zeta'^T)^T. \qquad (5.16)$$

We may split $\mathbf{s}'$ into two vectors $\boldsymbol{\eta}$ and $\boldsymbol{\xi}$

$$\mathbf{s}' = (\boldsymbol{\eta}^T, \boldsymbol{\xi}^T)^T , \qquad (5.17)$$

and because the inverse of $[\mathbf{A}_1]$ exists we can use equation (5.15) to find

$$\boldsymbol{\eta} = -[\mathbf{A}_1]^{-1}[\mathbf{A}_2]\boldsymbol{\xi} . \qquad (5.18)$$

It is clear that we may associate the vector $\boldsymbol{\xi}$ with the reciprocal depths of the independent vertices, and $\boldsymbol{\eta}$ with the other, dependent, reciprocal depths and plane parameters. The number of independent vertex parameters is $|\boldsymbol{\xi}| = 3n + m - \text{rank}([\mathbf{A}_1])$.

5.1.3 Finding the independent set of vertices

Section 5.1.2 shows that a set of independent vertices must exist, though
in fact there may be several possible sets. Here we briefly indicate the
method proposed by Sugihara to find a set of independent vertices, and
thus in turn how to find the permutation that transforms $[\mathbf{A}^*]$ to $[\mathbf{A}'] = [[\mathbf{A}_1]|[\mathbf{A}_2]]$, $\mathbf{s}$ to $\mathbf{s}'$, and $[\mathbf{B}]$ to $[\mathbf{B}']$ (used in §5.2).

It is possible to define the degree of freedom $\sigma_D(\mathcal{Y})$ of a set of vertices
$\mathcal{Y} \subseteq \mathcal{V}$ such that the pair $(\mathcal{V}, \sigma_D)$ is a matroid. The subset of vertices we
require is that which is the maximal independent subset of $\mathcal{V}$, that is, a
base of the matroid (Welsh 1976). Sugihara (1982) proves the following:

THEOREM 3 If $S^* = (\mathcal{V}, \mathcal{F}, \mathcal{R}^*)$ is a position-free incidence structure
then $\mathcal{Y} \subseteq \mathcal{V} - \mathcal{V}(\mathcal{R} - \mathcal{R}^*)$ is an independent set of the matroid $(\mathcal{V}, \sigma_D)$
if and only if for all $\mathcal{X} \subseteq \mathcal{F}$

$$|\mathcal{V}^*(\mathcal{X})| + 3|\mathcal{X}| \geq |\mathcal{R}^*(\mathcal{X})| + |\mathcal{V}^*(\mathcal{X}) \cap \mathcal{Y}|.$$

Using this, and the fact that for any $\mathcal{Y} \subseteq \mathcal{V}$:

$$\sigma_D(\mathcal{Y}) = \max\{|\mathcal{Y}'|\} \tag{5.19}$$

such that $\mathcal{Y}' \subseteq \mathcal{Y}$ and $\mathcal{Y}'$ is an independent set of matroid $(\mathcal{V}, \sigma_D)$, we
can build an independent set $\mathcal{Y}$ of vertices by choosing vertices $\{v\}$ one
by one from $\mathcal{V} - \mathcal{V}(\mathcal{R} - \mathcal{R}^*)$. Starting with $\mathcal{Y} = \emptyset$ we test whether $\{v\} \cup \mathcal{Y}$
is independent using Theorem 1. If it is, $\mathcal{Y} \leftarrow \{v\} \cup \mathcal{Y}$, otherwise $\{v\}$ is
discarded. As soon as $|\mathcal{Y}| = \sigma_D(\mathcal{V}) = |\xi|$, $\mathcal{Y}$ must be the required base.

5.1.4 Summary of linear relationships

Before introducing the structure from motion algorithm it is worth sum-
marizing briefly the linear relationships implicit in the above. In particular, we indicate how, given the independent vertices ξ, we can find our
original unknown vector $\mathbf{s}$.

Recall that we eliminate constraints from $[\mathbf{A}]\mathbf{s} = \mathbf{0}$ until the reduced
incidence structure is position-free. The reduced set of constraints is
$[\mathbf{A}^*]\mathbf{s} = \mathbf{0}$. Using the algorithm of §5.1.3 we find a set of independent
vertices, whose reciprocal depths are represented by ξ. We shuffle ζ into
ζ' such that ξ supplies the last elements of ζ'.

This shuffling is represented by

$$\zeta = [\mathbf{T}]\zeta' \tag{5.20}$$

where $[\mathbf{T}]$ is an $m \times m$ permutation matrix with one value in each column and row of unity and the rest zero. Then

$$\mathbf{s} = [\mathbf{G}]\mathbf{s}' = \begin{bmatrix} \mathbf{I_1} & \mathbf{0_1} \\ \mathbf{0_2} & \mathbf{T} \end{bmatrix} \mathbf{s}' , \tag{5.21}$$

where $\mathbf{I_1}$ is a $3n \times 3n$ identity matrix, and $\mathbf{0_1}$ and $\mathbf{0_2}$ are $3n \times m$ and $m \times 3n$ zero matrices. Thus from $[\mathbf{A}^*]$ we find

$$[\mathbf{A}'] = [\mathbf{A}^*][\mathbf{G}] \tag{5.22}$$

which in turn yields $[\mathbf{A}_1]$ and $[\mathbf{A}_2]$ by partitioning.

Given values of $\boldsymbol{\xi}$ we find $\mathbf{s}'$ as

$$\mathbf{s}' = [\mathbf{H}]\boldsymbol{\xi} = \begin{bmatrix} -[\mathbf{A}_1]^{-1}[\mathbf{A}_2] \\ \mathbf{I_2} \end{bmatrix} \boldsymbol{\xi} , \tag{5.23}$$

where $\mathbf{I_2}$ is a $|\boldsymbol{\xi}| \times |\boldsymbol{\xi}|$ identity matrix.

Thus finally:

$$\mathbf{s} = [\mathbf{G}][\mathbf{H}]\boldsymbol{\xi} = \begin{bmatrix} \mathbf{I_1} & \mathbf{0_1} \\ \mathbf{0_2} & \mathbf{T} \end{bmatrix} \begin{bmatrix} -[\mathbf{A}_1]^{-1}[\mathbf{A}_2] \\ \mathbf{I_2} \end{bmatrix} \boldsymbol{\xi} . \tag{5.24}$$

5.2   The polyhedral motion algorithm

Under the constraints, the structure and motion of the 3D wireframe is fully described by the depths or reciprocal depths of the vertices in the base $\mathcal{Y}$, that is, by $\boldsymbol{\xi}$, and by the six motion parameters $\mathbf{V}$ and $\boldsymbol{\Omega}$. However, the constraints have done nothing to resolve the depth/speed scaling ambiguity, and so we must still reduce the number of the parameters by one to $|\boldsymbol{\xi}| + 5$. Here we fix the reciprocal depth of one of the independent vertices, say ξ_1, at unity.

The structure from motion problem becomes one of minimizing

$$D(\mathbf{p}) = \sum_{\mathcal{E}} \sum_{e \in \mathcal{E}} w_e (|\mathbf{v}_e| - |\mathbf{v}_e^{pred}|)^2 \tag{5.25}$$

subject now only to the inequality conditions

$$[\mathbf{B}']\mathbf{s}' = [\mathbf{B}'][\mathbf{H}]\boldsymbol{\xi} > 0 . \tag{5.26}$$

Here, the parameter vector is

$$\mathbf{p} = (\xi_2 \ldots \xi_{|\boldsymbol{\xi}|}, \mathbf{V}^T, \boldsymbol{\Omega}^T)^T , \tag{5.27}$$

[**B'**] is [**B**] after column permutation, and [**H**] is the linear transformation derived earlier.

The complete procedure to obtain structure from motion is then:

1. Label the linedrawing or 2D vertex-edge graph.

2. Find the maximal position-free incidence structure S^* using Theorem 1.

3. Find the maximal independent set of vertices and thereby which vertices are associated with ξ.

4. Set $\xi_1 = 1$ and guess initial values for the parameters $(\xi_2 \ldots \xi_{|\xi|})$ that satisfy $[\mathbf{B'}][\mathbf{H}]\xi > 0$ and guess initial values for the six motion parameters $\mathbf{V}$ and Ω.

5. Starting with these initial values, minimize D with respect to the parameters. If D_{min} is below some threshold, and the ξ at the minimum satisfies the inequalities, go to Step 6. Otherwise go to Step 4.

6. If $\mathcal{R}^* = \mathcal{R}$, end. Otherwise if $\mathcal{R}^* \neq \mathcal{R}$ the scene positions might not satisfy the constraints in $\mathcal{R} - \mathcal{R}^*$ because these were discarded in Step 2. Correct the positions of the vertices involved with elements in $\mathcal{R} - \mathcal{R}^*$ by finding the intersections of the surfaces already computed. Then finish.

Again, the structure from motion minimization is performed using the nonlinear routine of Marquardt (1963). To predict values of $|v_e^{pred}|$ we again use expression (3.14), but now we need to relate the current parameter values $\mathbf{p}$ to the motion $\mathbf{V}$, Ω and the structure ζ. The former is straightforward from equation (5.27), but the latter involves some linear transformations which for clarity we give now. Using $\mathbf{s'} = [\mathbf{H}]\xi$ (equation 5.23) we have

$$\zeta = [\mathbf{T}][\mathbf{0_3}|\mathbf{I_3}][\mathbf{H}]\xi = [\mathbf{C}]\xi \tag{5.28}$$

where $\mathbf{0_3}$ is a $m \times 3n$ zero matrix and $\mathbf{I_3}$ an $m \times m$ identity matrix. Denoting the first column of [**C**] by the vector $\mathbf{c_1}$, and the rest by [**C**₂] we can write

$$[\mathbf{C}] = [\mathbf{c_1}|[\mathbf{C_2}]] \tag{5.29}$$

whence, because $\xi_1 \equiv 1$,

$$\zeta = c_1 + [C_2] \begin{bmatrix} p_1 \\ \vdots \\ p_{|\xi|-1} \end{bmatrix}. \qquad (5.30)$$

The method also requires the specification of the partial derivative of $|v_e^{pred}|$ at each edgel e with respect to each parameter. The derivatives with respect to the motion parameters are, as in §4.2, straightforward to derive from equation (3.14), and those with respect to the reciprocal depth parameters can be found from equation (5.30) using the chain rule. For an edgel between vertices i and j, only two partial derivatives with respect to the reciprocal depths, ie those with respect to ζ_i and ζ_j, are non-zero. Thus the derivatives with respect to the reciprocal depth parameters p_k $(k = 1, ..., |\xi| - 1)$ are:

$$\frac{\partial}{\partial p_k}|v_e^{pred}| = [C_2]_{ik}\frac{\partial}{\partial \zeta_i}|v_e^{pred}| + [C_2]_{jk}\frac{\partial}{\partial \zeta_j}|v_e^{pred}|. \qquad (5.31)$$

5.3   Computer experiments

In this section we compare the results from running the structure from motion algorithms with and without polyhedral constraints on real and synthetic image sequences.

A chipped block. The first experiment uses the chipped block moving directly away from the camera, introduced in the previous chapter at Figure 4.10. Figure 5.2 shows the labelled linedrawing, where the vertex and edge indices are those given by the segmentation process described in Chapter 4. The full incidence structure S comprises

$$\begin{aligned}
\mathcal{V} = \quad & \{v_1\, v_2\, v_5\, v_7\, v_{11}\, v_{12}\, v_{13}\, v_{14}\, v_{16}\}, \\
\mathcal{F} = \quad & \{f_1\, f_2\, f_3\, f_4\}, \\
\mathcal{R} = \quad & \{(v_2, f_1)\, (v_{13}, f_1)\, (v_{14}, f_1)\, (v_1, f_2)\, (v_{11}, f_2)\, (v_{14}, f_2) \\
& (v_2, f_2)\, (v_{12}, f_2)\, (v_{16}, f_3)\, (v_5, f_3)\, (v_{11}, f_3)\, (v_{14}, f_3) \\
& (v_{13}, f_3)\, (v_7, f_4)\, (v_{12}, f_4)\, (v_2, f_4)\, (v_{13}, f_4)\, (v_{16}, f_4)\}.
\end{aligned}$$

This is not position-free, but the removal of, for example, the pair (v_{13}, f_3) from $\mathcal{R}$ (that is, setting $\mathcal{R}^* = \mathcal{R} - \{(v_{13}, f_3)\}$) makes S^* so.

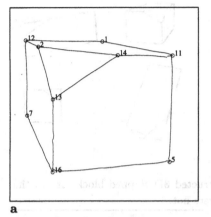
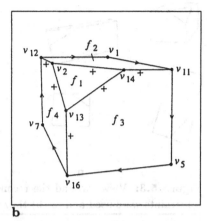

a   b

Figure 5.2: The segmentation for the chipped block and the line labelling derived from it.

Using Theorem 3, a base set of independent vertices is found as

$$\mathcal{Y} = \{v_2\, v_1\, v_{14}\, v_{16}\},$$

thus reducing the size of the parameter space from fourteen (nine reciprocal depths plus six motion parameters less one for the depth/speed ambiguity) to nine.

In the structure from motion minimization, the reciprocal depth of vertex v_2 is fixed at unity and the reciprocal depths of the remaining members of the base are varied together with the rectilinear and angular velocities. After convergence, because the pair (v_{13}, f_3) was not included in the constraints, its scene position is recomputed as the intersection of faces f_1, f_3 and f_4.

Figure 5.3(a) shows views around the reconstruction derived using the polyhedral constraints. There is a clear improvement in the quality of the recovered structure when compared with the reconstruction without the constraints, Figure 5.3(b).

In a second experiment, the same object is translated vertically past the camera. The visual motion was given in Figure 4.8. The structures obtained with and without constraints, Figure 5.4(a) and (b), are of similar quality. In both cases, though, there is a foreshortening of the recovered depth. This is again the result of coupling between the angular velocity and rectilinear velocity terms in equation (3.14), as discussed in

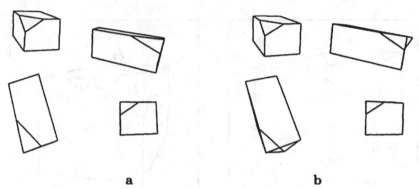

a   b

Figure 5.3: Views around the reconstructed 3D chipped block. In (a) the constraints were used and in (b) they were not.

Chapter 4. If we fix the angular velocity to its known value during the structure from motion minimization, the depth values recovered, both with and without constraints, are improved as shown in Figure 5.4(c) and (d).

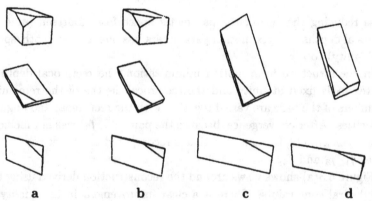

a   b   c   d

Figure 5.4: The 3D reconstruction (a) with and (b) without constraints for the block translating vertically past the camera. The depth distortion, a result of coupling between angular and rectilinear velocities, is removed when the angular velocity is fixed. The reconstructions in this case are shown in (c) with constraints and (d) without constraints.

CSG building. The third experiment uses images from a synthetic sequence where a CSG building translates from left to right past the camera. An image from the sequence, the visual motion and the line labelling are given in Figure 5.5(a-c). In this case the entire incidence structure is position-free and there are five independent vertices in the base which reduces the dimensionality of the minimization from 22 to 10. The reconstruction with constraints is shown in Figure 5.5(d), which can be compared with the wireframe computed without constraints, Figure 5.5(e). Again there is an improvement using the constraints.

The toy truck. This experiment uses the real image sequence of the camera approaching the toy truck first introduced at Figure 4.12. The current image, visual motion and line labelling are shown in Figure 5.6(a-c). The entire incidence structure is again position-free, and the base contains five independent vertices. The reconstruction with constraints is shown in Figure 5.6(d) and that without in (e). Again, there is a substantial improvement in the recovered structure with the extra constraints.

5.3.1 Limitations

In the experiments described thus far the restrictions which are placed on the derivation of the independent vertices in Sugihara's method (Theorem 1) have been satisfied. However, a slight modification to the building shows that they can easily be broken.

Figure 5.7(a) and (b) shows the central image and visual motion of the CSG house used previously in Chapter 4. It is similar to the building in Figure 5.5, but has a pitched roof. If we attempt to find an independent set of vertices from the line labelling in (c) and supply noise-free values of their 3D positions, only half the object can be successfully analyzed. If we give the object the same motion as the flat-roofed building and attempt to recover structure from motion subject to the constraints, the reconstruction, Figure 5.7(d), is rather poor compared with the unconstrained reconstruction in (e).

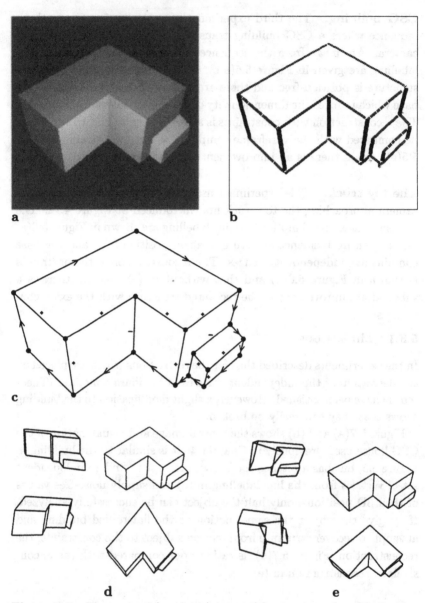

Figure 5.5: The current (synthetic) image (a), visual motion (b), line labelling (c) for a CSG building translating past the camera. The reconstructions with and without constraints are shown in (d) and (e).

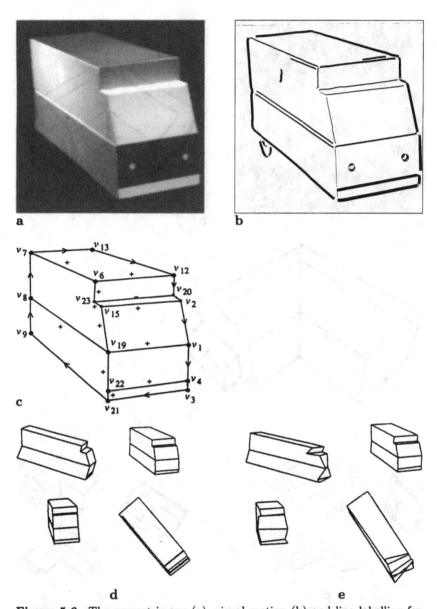

Figure 5.6: The current image (a), visual motion (b) and line labelling for the truck (c). The reconstruction (d) with and (e) without constraints. (Both rectilinear and angular velocities were allowed to vary.)

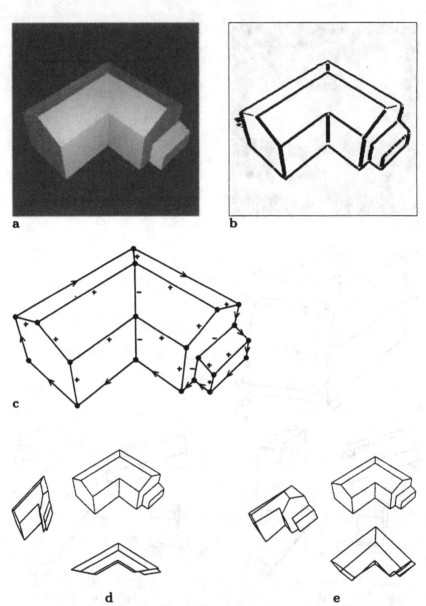

Figure 5.7: The CSG house model exposes the limitations of the method of recovering independent vertices: the reconstruction with constraints (d) is poor compared with that without constraints (e).

5.4   Remarks

We have demonstrated that the polyhedral constraints developed by Sugihara can be used successfully within the framework of a structure from motion algorithm. Later we will show that the surface information recovered is of sufficient quality to match to simple CAD models, enabling absolute depths and motion to be recovered. Matching to surfaces rather than edges has the advantage that the search space for matching is considerably reduced because, as one of Euler's many theorems tells us, faces are always fewer in number than edges. By way of empirical illustration, to obtain the feasible matches using 8 data surface patches and 9 model faces took around 2 cpu-seconds on a 3Mips processor. Using edges, even when restricting the match to only 8 of the 22 data edges, it took 54 cpu-seconds to match to a model of 26 edges. (The code for each compatibility test is of similar complexity in the two cases.)

In most cases explored, the recovered structure was improved over that obtained by the unconstrained algorithm. However, it is clear that by adding extra constraints or expectations about the scene there is a risk of failure because those expectations may not be realized, perhaps because of noise or, more fundamentally, if the quite strict requirements of Sugihara's method are not met. Perhaps the most alarming requirement is that the 2D linedrawing be complete. Given that most existing edge detectors are not designed to preserve topology, this is almost impossible to guarantee.

There are other drawbacks which dampen enthusiasm for the method. Firstly, the computational cost is quite high, requiring in the case of finding the base set of vertices multiple passes through the power set of the faces. Secondly, apart from checking the initial and final reciprocal depths for consistency, the inequality constraints, which yield clues about relative depth, do not actively guide the structure from motion minimization. Although standard techniques exist for active use of inequality constraints in the minimization of linear and quadratic functions, the present minimization function cannot be set into such forms.

6 The Structure and Motion of Planes

In this chapter we consider yet another structure from motion algorithm. We have seen that it is possible to recover the scene structure of points, the scene structure and motion of edges and, in the previous chapter, to recover coplanar sets of edges by imposing quite specialized polyhedral constraints. Our aim now is to constrain surfaces in the scene to be planar a priori, and to reconstruct them directly from the visual motion they give rise to.

6.1 Planar scenes

In Chapter 3 we saw that m edge-normal components of visual motion supplied $4m$ pieces of data, which were insufficient to recover the $4m + 5$ pieces of scene information required for pointwise depth recovery even on a rigidly moving object. Recall that the information required was: the 3D coordinates $\mathbf{R}$ of each of these m edge entities; one angle, Θ, to account for the orientation of each of the m edge entities; and the motion of the object relative to the sensor, $\mathbf{V}$ and $\mathbf{\Omega}$ up to the depth/speed scaling ambiguity.

To solve for the 3D structure and motion under the aperture problem we need to introduce extra constraints. We have already shown that a number of linked straight edges can provide sufficient constraint, but another obvious three dimensional constraint that springs to mind is that the scene points should lie on a single smooth surface — of which the simplest of course is a planar surface facet. This constrains the scene points by

$$\mathbf{R} \cdot \mathbf{N} = -1 , \tag{6.1}$$

where, as in the previous chapter, the normal to the plane, $\mathbf{N}$, points out of the surface and has magnitude $|\mathbf{N}| = 1/d$, where d is the perpendicular distance from the origin to the plane. The geometry under consideration is sketched in Figure 6.1.

Now, rather than specifying (X, Y, Z) and one edge orientation angle Θ to define each point in the scene, we need only (X, Y) and Θ at each point, together with the disposition of the plane, $\mathbf{N}$. The number of unknowns is now $3m + 9$ less one for the depth/speed scaling ambiguity. To solve for these we require

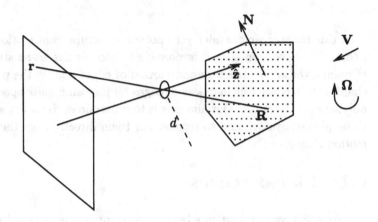

Figure 6.1: The camera and planar facet geometry.

$$4m \geq 3m + 8 \ . \tag{6.2}$$

Thus the minimum number of components of visual motion we require is eight. An algorithm that formally solves this problem will be given in the next section.

As we indicated in Chapter 3, however, it is often the case that the camera is transported through a static environment with accurately known motion. In such circumstances depth is recoverable on a point by point basis despite the aperture problem, and it is then possible to fit whatever kind of geometrical entity is required — at least when given enough points. Obviously, with three or more points we can consider a planar surface, and a simpler '3 point' algorithm will be described. This is useful in itself, but is also of use in examining the behaviour of the '8 point' algorithm used for unknown scene motion.

6.2 Recovering planar structure and motion

To construct the '8 point' algorithm we start in a similar fashion to Chapter 3. Equation (1.4) gives the full projected motion at a point in terms of the corresponding scene depth Z and scene motion $\mathbf{V}$ and $\mathbf{\Omega}$:

$$\dot{\mathbf{r}} = -\frac{l\mathbf{V}}{Z} - \mathbf{r}\frac{\mathbf{V} \cdot \hat{\mathbf{z}}}{Z} + \mathbf{\Omega} \times \mathbf{r} + \mathbf{r}\frac{\mathbf{\Omega} \times \mathbf{r} \cdot \hat{\mathbf{z}}}{l} \ .$$

(Recall that we assume that the projected motion and visual motion computed using the method of Chapter 2 are equal.)

Let us again denote a measured component of visual motion by $\mathbf{v}$ and a unit vector in its direction by $\hat{\mathbf{v}}$, so that

$$\hat{\mathbf{v}} \cdot \dot{\mathbf{r}} = v . \tag{6.3}$$

Taking the scalar product of both sides of equation (1.4) with $\hat{\mathbf{v}}$ leads to equation (3.6):

$$v = -\frac{l\hat{\mathbf{v}} \cdot \mathbf{V}}{Z} - \hat{\mathbf{v}} \cdot \mathbf{r}\frac{\mathbf{V} \cdot \hat{\mathbf{z}}}{Z} + \hat{\mathbf{v}} \cdot \mathbf{\Omega} \times \mathbf{r} + \hat{\mathbf{v}} \cdot \mathbf{r}\frac{\mathbf{\Omega} \times \mathbf{r} \cdot \hat{\mathbf{z}}}{l}$$

in which the unknowns are the depth Z and, if the motion is unknown, $\mathbf{V}$ and $\mathbf{\Omega}$. We now demand that the scene points $\mathbf{R}$ lie on the plane described by $\mathbf{R} \cdot \mathbf{N} = -1$. Using the perspective projection (equation (1.1)) we can write

$$\mathbf{r} \cdot \mathbf{N} = l/Z , \tag{6.4}$$

which allows Z to be eliminated in equation (3.6):

$$\begin{aligned} v = & -(\hat{\mathbf{v}} \cdot \mathbf{V})(\mathbf{r} \cdot \mathbf{N}) + -(\hat{\mathbf{v}} \cdot \mathbf{r})(\mathbf{V} \cdot \hat{\mathbf{z}})(\mathbf{r} \cdot \mathbf{N})/l + \\ & \hat{\mathbf{v}} \cdot (\mathbf{\Omega} \times \mathbf{r}) + (\hat{\mathbf{v}} \cdot \mathbf{r})(\mathbf{\Omega} \times \mathbf{r}) \cdot \hat{\mathbf{z}}/l . \end{aligned} \tag{6.5}$$

This is the fundamental equation which is used to obtain 3D planar solutions to the aperture problem. It is applied to several components of the visual motion $\mathbf{v}_i$ at positions $\mathbf{r}_i$, which in turn gives rise to a number of nonlinear simultaneous equations for the motion $\mathbf{V}$, $\mathbf{\Omega}$ and disposition $\mathbf{N}$ of the planar facet.

6.2.1 Recovering the scene parameters

For each datum i, equation (6.5) can be rewritten to separate the known image quantities from the unknown scene quantities:

$$v_i = \sum_{k=1}^{8} J_{ik}\beta_k \tag{6.6}$$

where, written out in full, the known image-related quantities J_{ik} are

$$\begin{aligned} J_{i1} &= x_i \cos\theta_i \\ J_{i2} &= y_i \cos\theta_i \end{aligned} \tag{6.7}$$

$$J_{i3} = -l\cos\theta_i$$
$$J_{i4} = x_i\sin\theta_i$$
$$J_{i5} = y_i\sin\theta_i$$
$$J_{i6} = -l\sin\theta_i$$
$$J_{i7} = x_i(J_{i1} + J_{i2})/l$$
$$J_{i8} = y_i(J_{i1} + J_{i2})/l$$

where $\cos\theta_i = \hat{\mathbf{v}}_i \cdot \hat{\mathbf{x}}$ and $\sin\theta_i = \hat{\mathbf{v}}_i \cdot \hat{\mathbf{y}}$. The unknown scene-related quantities β_k are

$$\beta_1 = -V_x N_x + V_z N_z \qquad\qquad (6.8)$$
$$\beta_2 = -V_x N_y - \Omega_z$$
$$\beta_3 = -V_x N_z + \Omega_y$$
$$\beta_4 = -V_y N_x + \Omega_z$$
$$\beta_5 = -V_y N_y + V_z N_z$$
$$\beta_6 = -V_y N_z - \Omega_x$$
$$\beta_7 = -V_z N_x - \Omega_y$$
$$\beta_8 = -V_z N_y + \Omega_x .$$

Collecting together all m data we can write equation (6.6) in matrix form:

$$\tilde{\mathbf{v}} = [\mathbf{J}]\boldsymbol{\beta} , \qquad\qquad (6.9)$$

where $\tilde{\mathbf{v}}$ is an $m \times 1$ vector of visual motion magnitudes (*not* a visual motion vector), $[\mathbf{J}]$ is an $m \times 8$ matrix and $\boldsymbol{\beta}$ is the 8×1 vector given above. As there are eight members in $\boldsymbol{\beta}$ we need m to be at least eight, confirming the equation counting argument. We discuss methods of solving for $\boldsymbol{\beta}$ using a least squares technique later, but for now we concentrate on the problem of recovering $\mathbf{V}$, $\boldsymbol{\Omega}$ and $\mathbf{N}$ from $\boldsymbol{\beta}$ (although of course only eight of these nine are recoverable). Solving the eight nonlinear simultaneous equations is a formidable task, but one which has been addressed by Longuet-Higgins (1984) in related work in which he recovers the structure and motion of planes assuming the full visual motion is available.

The solution proceeds by eliminating the quantities that appear linearly in $\boldsymbol{\beta}$, ie the Ω_k, and then constructing a cubic equation for the odd-man-out in the remaining five equations, ie $V_z N_z$. According to Longuet-Higgins, the *middle* root of the cubic is the required value of $V_z N_z$, from which the remaining $V_j N_k$ can be found. That we can only hope to recover eight independent quantities is due to the depth/speed scaling ambiguity, which in turn is the reason that only $V_j N_k$ products occur. (N, we recall, has dimensions of inverse distance.) The independent quantities recoverable are the directions of V and N, ie $\hat{V}$ and $\hat{N}$, (VN) and Ω. As an example, from the values $V_x N_x$, $V_x N_y$, $V_x N_z$, we derive

$$\hat{N}_{x,y,z} = \frac{V_x N_{x,y,z}}{\sqrt{(V_x N_x)^2 + (V_x N_y)^2 + (V_x N_z)^2}} \ . \tag{6.10}$$

The other roots, if different from the middle root, actually give rise to complex motion fields, but nonetheless their values can be used to estimate the product of the magnitudes of V and N, (VN), and their scalar product $V \cdot N$. The latter is useful as it is the reciprocal of the *time-to-contact* — the time it would take the camera to collide with the plane (Longuet-Higgins 1984).

6.2.2   Ambiguities of V and N

We have already noted that β in equation (6.8) contains only products of V and N and that the best we can infer are their directions. This point deserves closer attention however.

Since we can interchange V and N without affecting the β, these equations permit four interpretations. Let us denote the true scene values by V_{true} and N_{true} and let V and N just be computed vectors, without physical significance. The analysis permits the true scene vectors to be associated with any of the four combinations given in the following table:

V_{true}	N_{true}
V	N
N	V
−V	−N
−N	−V

However, for any given situation, *certainly* two and *possibly* three of these represent *invisible* surfaces and can therefore be eliminated. Recalling that N points out of the surface, the visibility condition is (see Figure 6.2):

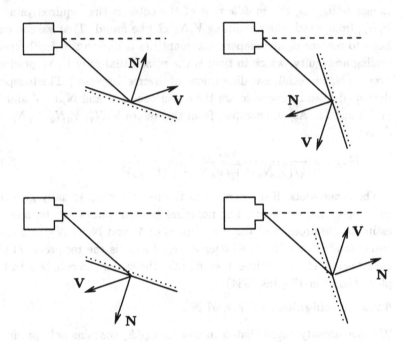

Figure 6.2: The visibility conditions for the planar facet. One pair (here the lower pair) of solutions is always invisible. (The dashed line is inside the solid surface.)

$$\forall i : \mathbf{r}_i \cdot \mathbf{N}_{true} > 0 . \tag{6.11}$$

This must eliminate two of the possibilities, because if $\mathbf{N}_{true} = \mathbf{V}$ satisfies it, $\mathbf{N}_{true} = -\mathbf{V}$ certainly cannot, and similarly for $\pm\mathbf{N}$.

The remaining twofold ambiguity can be resolved when for some data i and j

$$(\mathbf{r}_i \cdot \mathbf{V}_{true})(\mathbf{r}_j \cdot \mathbf{V}_{true}) < 0 , \tag{6.12}$$

or, in other words, points are in view which lie both in front of and behind the plane perpendicular to the *true* direction of translation, as illustrated in Figure 6.3.

Up to now we have discussed the ambiguity between the interchange of $\mathbf{V}$ and $\mathbf{N}$ without reference to the angular velocity $\mathbf{\Omega}$. However, it is

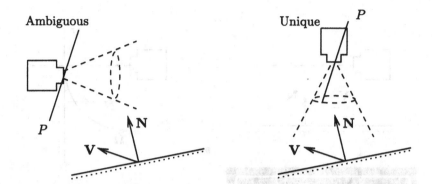

Figure 6.3: Resolving the twofold ambiguity. If the camera views points which lie both sides of a plane P perpendicular to $\mathbf{V}$, as on the right, then the pairwise ambiguity is broken. Note that for this to happen P must intersect the viewing cone.

apparent from equation (6.8) that $\mathbf{\Omega}$ will be different in the two cases and, in cases where the veridical angular velocity can be estimated by other means, this may be used to disambiguate solutions. Specifically, if one solution yields an angular velocity $\mathbf{\Omega}$, the alternative solution will have an angular velocity $\mathbf{\Omega}'$ of:

$$\mathbf{\Omega}' = (\beta_8 - \beta_6, \beta_3 - \beta_7, \beta_4 - \beta_2)^T - \mathbf{\Omega} . \tag{6.13}$$

By way of example, consider an aircraft carrying a camera coming in to land on a flat planar airstrip, as sketched in the top left of Figure 6.4, and suppose that $\mathbf{V} = (0,0,-1)^T$, $\mathbf{N} = (0,1,0)^T$ and $\mathbf{\Omega} = (0,0,0)^T$. Suppose the camera is looking forward, so there is a twofold ambiguity, with the ambiguous dual having $\mathbf{V} = (0,1,0)^T$, $\mathbf{N} = (0,0,-1)^T$ and $\mathbf{\Omega} = (1,0,0)^T$. This solution corresponds to a frontal plane swinging towards the camera (Longuet-Higgins 1984). Clearly, a conservative expectation for a landing aircraft is that it is not wildly gyrating in this way. The lower part of this figure shows the recovery of the two solutions experimentally.

6.2.3 The least squares fit

A least squares solution for β from equation (6.9) is probably best found directly using Householder transformations, but it instructive to develop

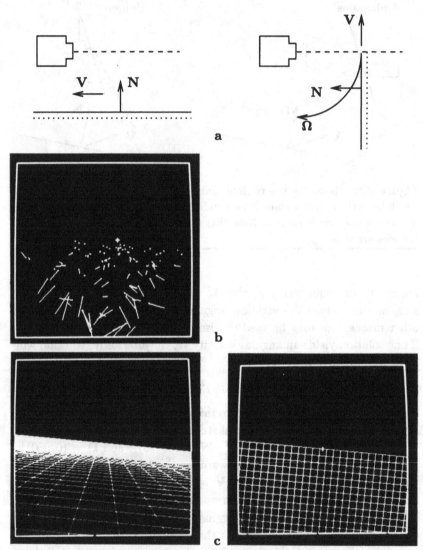

Figure 6.4: The dual solutions for an aircraft flying over flat textured ground carrying a forward directed camera (a). The visual motion components (b) are from the veridical physical situation, and the ambiguous planar orientations recovered shown in (c) are the results from a computer experiment.

the "classical" least squares solution here. This is found by writing

$$[\mathbf{J}^T][\Lambda]\tilde{\mathbf{v}} = [\mathbf{J}^T][\Lambda][\mathbf{J}]\boldsymbol{\beta} , \tag{6.14}$$

where $[\Lambda]$ is the diagonal matrix of weights, a system which can be solved for $\boldsymbol{\beta}$ using, for example, Gauss-Jordan elimination with pivoting.

The weights may be taken directly as the confidences derived during the visual motion computation. However, an examination of the probability distribution of the magnitude of the visual motion component $\mathbf{v}$ given the projected motion $\dot{\mathbf{r}}$ shows that the weights are improved if multiplied by an extra term involving the edge-tangential component of the full visual motion at that point (see Figure 6.5). Obviously this is not available initially and so the weights can only be improved iteratively. The initial unmodified weights $[\Lambda^0]$ are used to compute a first guess at the $\boldsymbol{\beta}$ parameters, and these are used to predict the full motion field, as described in §6.6.1. The improved weighting at each point i for the next iteration is

$$\Lambda^1_{ii} = \frac{1}{\sqrt{|\dot{\mathbf{r}}^{pred} - \mathbf{v}^{pred}|^2 + (\Delta v_i)^2}}\Lambda^0_{ii} , \tag{6.15}$$

and so on, where Δv_i is the expected noise in the measured visual motion components $\mathbf{v}_i$. In experiment, we find that two or three iterations produce useful improvements.

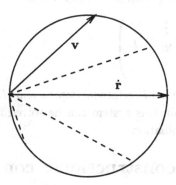

Figure 6.5: The probability distribution for $\mathbf{v}$ is affected by the fact that for a given full visual motion, $\dot{\mathbf{r}}$, $\mathbf{v}$ must lie on the circle with $\dot{\mathbf{r}}$ as diameter.

6.3 Planar facets with known motion

In this section we consider the recovery of the disposition of planes with
known motion. We discussed the known motion constraint fully in Chapter 3, but it is useful to consider the case of planes here, because the
stability analysis of the algorithm will assist our understanding where
the scene motion is unknown.

If the relative motion between scene and camera is known, equation (3.6) is easily rearranged to give an equation for Z, or rather the
reciprocal depth, equation (3.7):

$$\zeta = \frac{\hat{\mathbf{v}} \cdot [\mathbf{\Omega} \times \mathbf{r} + \mathbf{r}(\mathbf{\Omega} \times \mathbf{r}) \cdot \hat{\mathbf{z}}/l] - v}{\hat{\mathbf{v}} \cdot [\mathbf{V}l + \mathbf{r}(\mathbf{V} \cdot \hat{\mathbf{z}})]} \; .$$

Now, although we are not obliged to assume a particular surface to
recover the depths (as we illustrated more fully in Chapter 3), we can
fit a plane to the data if we have three or more points. At each image
point where there are motion data we can write

$$\mathbf{r} \cdot \mathbf{N} = l\zeta \tag{6.16}$$

and for three or more measurements of ζ we can derive a least-squares
solution for $\mathbf{N}$ from

$$[r^T][\Lambda][r]\mathbf{N} = l[r^T][\Lambda]\zeta \tag{6.17}$$

where $[r]$ is an $m \times 3$ matrix of image vectors

$$[r] = \begin{pmatrix} \vdots & \vdots & \vdots \\ x_i & y_i & -l \\ \vdots & \vdots & \vdots \end{pmatrix} , \tag{6.18}$$

ζ is an $m \times 1$ vector of reciprocal depths and $[\Lambda]$ is the $m \times m$ weight
matrix. Once again this system can be solved for $\mathbf{N}$ by, for example,
Gauss-Jordan elimination.

6.4 3D reconstructions: computer experiments

In this section we discuss some computational experiments with the
planar facet algorithms we have described. We first consider the known
motion case.

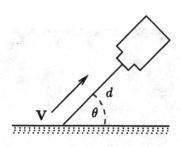

Figure 6.6: The camera/desk geometry recovered from the visual motion sequence of Chapter 2 where the camera translates towards the planar desk surface. The veridical orientation and displacement were $\theta = 24°$ and $d = 800$mm, and those reconstructed using the planar facet algorithm were $\theta = 21 \pm 3°$ and $d = 830 \pm 90$mm.

6.4.1 The known motion algorithm

We show first experiments using real imagery captured from an EEV Photon CCD camera fitted with a 16mm focal length lens subtending a half angle at the image of $7.5°$.

Camera approaching desk. In Figure 6.6 we show again the visual motion computed from the sequence (Figure 2.8) where the camera translated towards a cluttered desk top scene along the optic axis with $V = (0, 0, 20)$mm per frame. The visual motion was input to the known motion planar facet algorithm, and the recovered disposition of the desk top with respect to the camera compared with physical measurements (ie using a tape measure!) (Figure 6.6). The scene is recovered accurately to within experimental error.

Translating camera viewing ceiling. In a further experiment the camera translated sideways while gazing at the ceiling. Figure 6.7 shows two images from the sequence when V was $(-40, 0, 0)$mm per frame, the computed visual motion, and compares the veridical and reconstructed scenes.

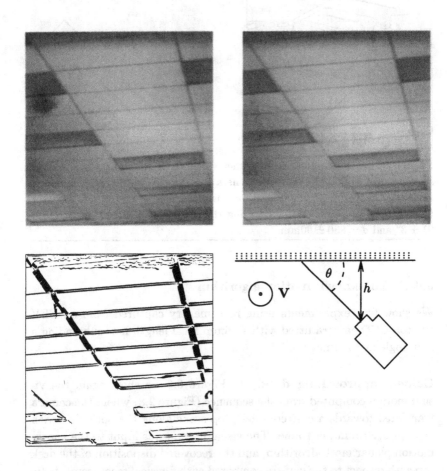

Figure 6.7: The images, visual motion, and the recovered camera/ceiling geometry. The veridical orientation and displacement were $\theta = 17°$ and $h = 2.05$m, and those reconstructed using the planar facet algorithm were $\theta = 14 \pm 3°$ and $h = 1.93 \pm 0.15$m.

Camera translating past desk. In Figure 6.8 we show visual motion and structure from motion computed for a second desk sequence. The motion here is lateral translation with $\mathbf{V} = (40, 0, 0)$mm per frame. Again the veridical scene and its reconstruction agree to within experimental error.

6.4.2   Stability of the algorithm

Tests of the stability of the known motion algorithm against noise were carried out by simulating edge-normal visual motion at random points in the image having random edge orientations, viewed with a camera with half cone angle 45°. The visual motion was predicted as that from a randomly oriented plane with random motion. Three hundred data points were used. Increasing levels of random noise were added to the visual motion and the error in the reconstructed scene parameters assessed. The averaged results of a large number of trials indicated that the known motion algorithm amplified noise by a factor of around four. That is, for example, if the fractional noise in the input vectors was 1%, the fractional noise in the output scene vectors ($\delta V_x / V_x$ and so on) could be expected to be around 4%. Above around 7% input noise, the method began to break down.

Given the large number of data (around 7000) used in the experiments with *real* imagery (eg Figure 6.6) one might have expected more accurate results. The limiting factor in those experiments however is the maximum angle subtended by the scene at the lens. Figure 6.9 shows the variation in certainty with which the components of $\mathbf{N}$ can be recovered as the cone half-angle α is reduced from its maximum of 90°. Remarkably, the recovery quality of N_z is maintained, but that of N_x and N_y decreases rapidly. The problem is ill-conditioning of $[r^T r]$, the matrix whose pseudo-inverse is computed to recover $\mathbf{N}$.

As $\alpha \approx x/l \approx y/l$ becomes limitingly small,

$$[r^T r]_{\alpha \to 0} \to \begin{pmatrix} 0 & 0 & 0 \\ 0 & 0 & 0 \\ 0 & 0 & l^2 m \end{pmatrix} \tag{6.19}$$

where m is the number of data. The singular values of the matrix are thus approximately zero (twice) and $l\sqrt{m}$: thus $[r^T r]$ is indeed ill-conditioned. The singular vector is $(0, 0, 1)^T$ and thus only N_z can be found with certainty. When $\alpha = 7.5°$, as in our experiments with real

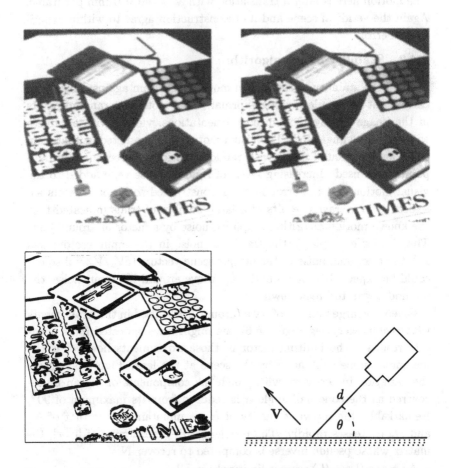

Figure 6.8: Two images and visual motion from a second desk sequence and the recovered camera–desk geometry. The veridical orientation and displacement were $\theta = 39°$ and $d = 885$mm, and those reconstructed using the planar facet algorithm were $\theta = 39 \pm 4°$ and $d = 890 \pm 80$mm.

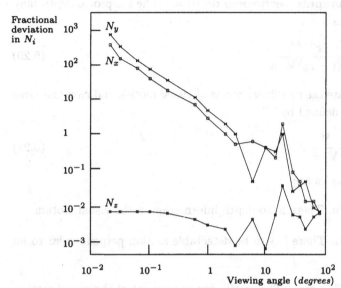

Figure 6.9: As the camera cone half angle is reduced from its maximum of $90°$, the component N_z is obtained more reliably than N_x and N_y.

imagery, the noise amplification is almost intolerable. Faced with such difficulties, we did not carry out systematic experiments on real imagery using the unknown motion, 8-point algorithm described in §6.2. In particular, computer experiments of the kind described in §6.6 (Buxton, Buxton, Murray and Williams 1985) indicated that the noise amplification is larger than that for the known motion algorithm. For example, under the conditions quoted earlier with a camera half field of view of $45°$, the noise amplification factor was ten as opposed to approximately four for the known motion algorithm.

6.5 Failures of the planar facet algorithms

6.5.1 Failure in the known motion case

The known motion algorithm will fail for two principal reasons:

Failure to compute reciprocal depths.   The reciprocal depth may be rewritten as

$$\zeta = \frac{\hat{\mathbf{v}} \cdot \dot{\mathbf{r}}^{trans}}{\hat{\mathbf{v}} \cdot (\mathbf{r} - \mathbf{r}_0)\mathbf{V} \cdot \hat{\mathbf{z}}} \tag{6.20}$$

where $\dot{\mathbf{r}}^{trans}$ are the rectilinear terms of visual motion and $\mathbf{r}_0$ is the focus of expansion, defined by

$$\mathbf{r}_0 = -l\frac{\mathbf{V}}{\mathbf{V} \cdot \hat{\mathbf{z}}} \ . \tag{6.21}$$

The failure modes are

- $\mathbf{V}$ is zero. There is no depth information in the visual motion

- $\mathbf{v}$ is zero. There has to be detectable motion perpendicular to an edge.

- $\mathbf{v} \cdot \dot{\mathbf{r}}^{trans}$ is zero. The rectilinear component of the visual motion happens to be parallel to the edge direction

- $\hat{\mathbf{v}} \cdot (\mathbf{r} - \mathbf{r}_0)$ is zero. Either the point is at the focus of expansion, or $\mathbf{v}$ is located on a edge which runs through the focus of expansion.

Failure to invert.   If $[r]$ is rank deficient there is a linear relationship between the columns of the matrix and attempts to invert $[r^T r]$ will fail. The linear relationship is

$$\forall i : a_1 x_i + a_2 y_i - a_3 l = 0 \ . \tag{6.22}$$

This merely says that the three image points lie on the same line in the image. Thus either the three points lie on a straight line in space, for which there is an infinity of possible planes, or (most unlikely) they lie on a plane viewed edge on.

Thus failures of the known motion algorithm can be fully understood.

6.5.2   Failure in the unknown motion case

As not knowing the motion can hardly improve matters we should expect the unknown case to suffer all the pitfalls of the known motion algorithm together with some of its own.

Failure to compute scene parameters. In the case of unknown motion, once we have obtained the parameter set β, a solution for the Ω is guaranteed. The recovery of the remaining scene parameters is also certain unless $\mathbf{V}$ or $\mathbf{N}$ vanishes. These conditions are easy enough to interpret. If the rectilinear velocity vanishes then we lose all depth information, and there is no possibility of recovering surface orientation. If $\mathbf{N}$ vanishes then the scene is infinitely far away.

Failure to invert. The much more common source of failure is that the set of equations to determine β is rank deficient. Again this happens whenever there is a linear relationship between the columns of the $m \times 8$ matrix $[\mathbf{J}]$: that is, for all data there is a linear relationship

$$a_1 cx + a_2 sx - a_3 lc + a_4 cy + a_5 sy -$$
$$a_6 ls + a_7 (cx + sy)x/l + a_8 (cx + sy)y/l = 0 \qquad (6.23)$$

where the $(c, s) = (\cos, \sin)\theta$ and θ is the edge orientation. It is satisfied whatever the orientation of the edge features if

$$a_7 = a_8 = 0 \qquad (6.24)$$
$$a_1 x + a_4 y = a_3 l$$
$$a_2 x + a_5 y = a_6 l$$

which implies that

$$a_1/a_2 = a_4/a_5 = a_3/a_6 . \qquad (6.25)$$

Thus the algorithm fails as the known motion one did when the image points are collinear, whatever the orientation of the edge features, as sketched in Figure 6.10.

The unknown motion algorithm also fails if all the edge features have the same orientation, whatever their position. This can be seen by choosing

$$a_7 = a_8 = 0 \qquad (6.26)$$
$$a_1/a_2 = a_4/a_5 = a_3/a_6 = -\tan\theta .$$

This failure is not shared by the known motion case.

In addition the unknown motion algorithm fails when the image points lie on certain curves. This problem was studied by Waxman and Wohn

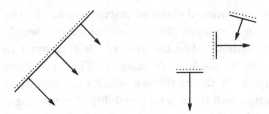

Figure 6.10: The algorithms fails whenever the image points are collinear, irrespective of whether the edge feature is straight.

(1985) for an algorithm similar to ours, but described from a different standpoint. They concluded that the algorithm fails if the points lie on conics in the image. We can obtain similar failure modes as follows. First note that if there is a smooth edge contour $f(x, y) = 0$, then the orientation at each point is $(c, s) \propto (-dy, dx)$, as shown in Figure 6.11. Equation (6.23) is then equivalent to the differential equation

$$(a_2 x + a_5 y - a_6 l + a_7 xy/l + a_8 y^2/l)dx -$$
$$(a_1 x + a_4 y - a_3 l + a_7 x^2/l + a_8 xy/l)dy = 0 \qquad (6.27)$$

which expresses the most general condition that a smooth contour must satisfy if the algorithm is to fail. The equation is easy to solve in some special cases. For example, if $a_7 = a_8 = 0$ and $a_5 + a_1 = 0$ it is exact and

$$a_2 x^2 - 2a_1 xy - a_4 y^2 - 2a_6 lx + 2a_3 ly = \text{constant} . \qquad (6.28)$$

So the algorithm does indeed fail for conics, but we note that there are more general solutions to equation (6.27) that are not conics, but for

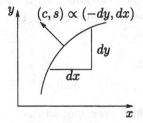

Figure 6.11: The orientation of a smooth contour.

which the unknown motion planar facet algorithm still fails.

6.6 Reconstructing full visual motion: image and scene based approaches

It was noted in Chapter 3 that a considerable amount of effort has been expended in solving the aperture problem using 2D constraints in the image. The foundation for such constraints although plausible is not always absolutely secure. It is interesting to compare this sort of approach with the 3D solutions to the aperture problem we propose here, and specifically we will compare computer simulations of full visual motion recovery based on the planar facet algorithm for unknown motion, with full visual motion recovery using the contour smoothness constraint of Hildreth and Ullman (1982).

6.6.1 Full visual motion from planar facets

Having reconstructed the 3D scene using the planar facet algorithm, it would be a trivial matter to predict the full motion anywhere in the image. However, it is not necessary to reconstruct the scene explicitly, for it turns out that the β parameters alone suffice for this task. Thus there is no need to get involved with the business of solving cubic equations and resolving ambiguities.

The predicted full visual motion is found from equations (1.5) and (6.4) as

$$\dot{\mathbf{r}}^{pred} \cdot \hat{\mathbf{x}} = \beta_1 x + \beta_2 y - \beta_3 l + \frac{\beta_7 x^2 + \beta_8 xy}{l} \qquad (6.29)$$

$$\dot{\mathbf{r}}^{pred} \cdot \hat{\mathbf{y}} = \beta_4 x + \beta_5 y - \beta_6 l + \frac{\beta_7 xy + \beta_8 y^2}{l} \ .$$

from which we can further predict an edge-normal component of visual motion using

$$\mathbf{v}^{pred} = (\dot{\mathbf{r}}^{pred} \cdot \hat{\mathbf{v}})\hat{\mathbf{v}} \ . \qquad (6.30)$$

In Figure 6.12(a) we show a synthesized full visual motion field from a plane which is translating towards the camera and rotating. The horizon is visible. In (b) we project the full visual motion onto randomly chosen directions to create visual motion components. Random noise of 10% was added to these vectors to create the input data to the unknown

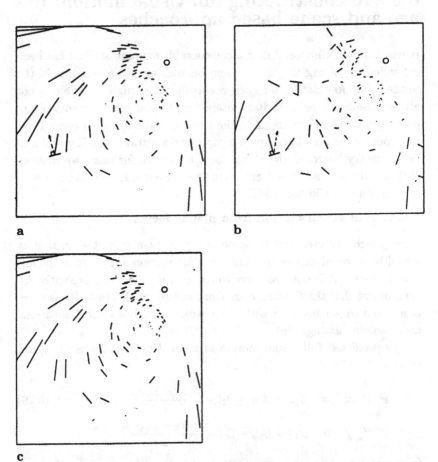

a

b

c

Figure 6.12: The (unobserved) veridical full visual motion (a) and observed edge normal components (b) for random points on a random plane. The components were corrupted with 10% noise and supplied to the 8-point algorithm which reconstructed the full visual motion in (c).

motion planar facet algorithm. From the computed β parameters we are able to reconstruct the full visual motion in (c), which may be compared with (a). It is interesting to note that although the β values are very sensitive to such high noise, the reconstructed 2D visual motion is not. This is not surprising: as the inverse mapping is ill-posed, it implies that the forward mapping itself is insensitive to noise.

6.6.2 Full visual motion from contour smoothness

As outlined in Chapter 3, Hildreth and Ullman (1982) recovered an approximation to the full visual motion along an edge contour by minimizing the measure:

$$I = \int \left(n^2 + k \left| \frac{\partial \dot{\mathbf{r}}}{\partial s} \right|^2 \right) ds \qquad (6.31)$$

where s is the arc length along the contour and where

$$n^2 = |\mathbf{v} - (\dot{\mathbf{r}} \cdot \hat{\mathbf{v}})\hat{\mathbf{v}}|^2 . \qquad (6.32)$$

Given the edge-normal components $\mathbf{v}$, Hildreth further suggested that, in orthographic projection, the values of $\dot{\mathbf{r}}$ that minimize I, and which make $\dot{\mathbf{r}} \cdot \hat{\mathbf{v}} = v$, correspond to a plausible full visual motion field. Yuille (1983) has shown this to be true if

$$\mathbf{T} \cdot \frac{\partial^2 \dot{\mathbf{r}}}{\partial s^2} = 0 \qquad (6.33)$$

where $\mathbf{T}$ is the tangent to the contour. This condition holds (for orthographic projection) trivially for rectilinear motion and for any motion of straight edges in space. In general the condition is violated, but Hildreth suggests that the full visual motion is still plausible, and is close to that perceived by the human visual system, for example in the barber's pole illusion.

The minimization can be effected by standard numerical techniques. For each measured edge-normal component $\mathbf{v}_i$ we express the full visual motion as

$$\dot{\mathbf{r}}_i = v_{xi}\hat{\mathbf{x}} + v_{yi}\hat{\mathbf{y}} + w_{xi}\hat{\mathbf{x}} + w_{yi}\hat{\mathbf{y}} \qquad (6.34)$$

so that the tangential components w_{xi} and w_{yi} become variables in the minimization. Thus for m vectors around the contour there are $2m$ variables U_i:

$$U_i = \begin{cases} w_{x[\frac{i+1}{2}]} & \text{if } i \text{ odd} \\ w_{y[\frac{i}{2}]} & \text{if } i \text{ even.} \end{cases} \tag{6.35}$$

The integral is performed by discrete summation along the contour, assuming linear segments between adjacent points, and by interpolating the integrand at the midpoint of a segment. Suppose we measure $\mathbf{v}_i$ at positions $\mathbf{r}_i$ around the contour and let the ith contour segment run from $\mathbf{r}_i$ to $\mathbf{r}_{i+1}$. The integral is

$$I \approx \sum_i \left[n_i^2 + k \left(\frac{\Delta \dot{\mathbf{r}}}{\Delta s} \right)_i^2 \right] \tag{6.36}$$

where

$$\left(\frac{\Delta \dot{\mathbf{r}}}{\Delta s} \right)_i^2 = \frac{(\Delta_{v_{xi}} + \Delta_{w_{xi}})^2 + (\Delta_{v_{yi}} + \Delta_{w_{yi}})^2}{\Delta_{s_i}^2} \tag{6.37}$$

and

$$n_i^2 = \frac{(\mu_{v_{xi}} \mu_{w_{xi}} + \mu_{v_{yi}} \mu_{w_{yi}})^2}{\mu_{v_{xi}}^2 + \mu_{v_{yi}}^2} \, . \tag{6.38}$$

The difference and mean functions are defined as

$$\Delta_{s_i} = |\mathbf{r}_{i+1} - \mathbf{r}_i| \, , \tag{6.39}$$

$$\Delta_{v_{xi}} = (v_{xi+1} - v_{xi}) \, , \tag{6.40}$$

and

$$\mu_{v_{xi}} = \frac{1}{2}(v_{xi+1} + v_{xi}) \tag{6.41}$$

and so on. (If a contour with N points is closed, index $N+1$ is of course replaced by 1.) The gradient vector $\partial I / \partial U_i$ and the Hessian $\partial^2 I / \partial U_i \partial U_j$ required for the minimization are also found at the midpoints of the contour segments.

6.6.3   Experimental comparison

In Figures 6.13 and 6.14 we compare the performance of the planar facet reconstruction with that of the smoothness constraint for a scene with translation and with translation and rotation. The planar facet reconstruction appears the more robust for the scene under rotation.

In both these comparisons the visual motion from the smoothness constraint is derived under orthographic projection, and that for the planar facet reconstruction under perspective projection. In Figure 6.15 we demonstrate that the smoothness constraint breaks down under perspective projection as an object comes close to the camera and perspective effects become important.

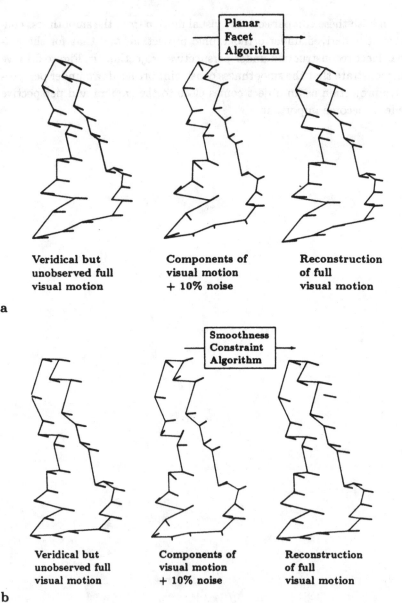

Figure 6.13: Examples of reconstruction of the full visual motion using (a) the planar facet algorithm in perspective projection and (b) the smoothness constraint of Hildreth in orthographic projection for a translating scene.

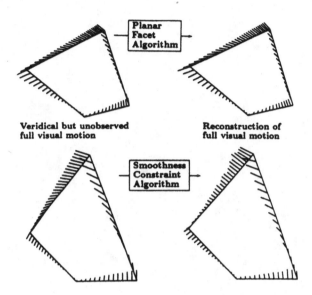

Figure 6.14: Full visual motion reconstructions for a scene with rotation.

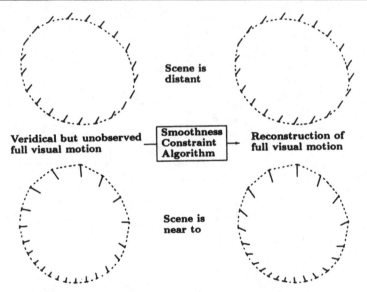

Figure 6.15: The smoothness constraint breaking down under perspective projection as the scene is brought close to the camera. The scene is translating.

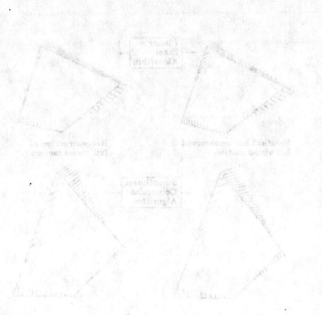

7 Visual Motion Segmentation

In Chapter 3 we saw that if the camera motion was unknown, more than one visual motion vector was required to recover the disposition and motion of a single entity in the scene. It appears then that an essential precursor to a structure from motion computation is a grouping together of visual motion vectors that we expect to arise from a moving part of the scene — in other words, we require a motion segmentation.

One can envisage several generic solutions to the problem of segmentation. The first would be to avoid the use of visual motion entirely, and to use some simpler image property such as texture or colour to segment the image, and then to apply a structure from motion computation to each segment found. This was our approach in Chapter 4, where we used the image *positions* of visual motion vectors to effect segmentation, on the assumption that the motion arose along extended straight edges.

However, this approach neglects the fact that visual motion is a very powerful cue for segmentation in many creatures. Earlier we mentioned the fly's ability to segment on the basis of motion (Reichardt and Poggio 1980). Demonstrations in our own visual system are more obvious and immediately compelling: the ease with which one sees an otherwise perfectly camouflaged creature as soon as it moves, or simple experiments with interpenetrating dot pictures. In these, the rough dotted outline of some object is superimposed (using a transparency, say) onto a randomly dotted background. When the two are stationary with respect to one another, no outline is apparent, but as soon as one is moved the outline becomes immediately and surprisingly obvious. When the motion ceases, the outline is lost immediately. This type of experiment illustrates a further aspect of motion: that it provides a powerful "fusing" influence between disparate parts of the image that are moving similarly.

So, a second approach might be to segment on the basis of some image-based property of the visual motion. For example, one might argue that vectors pointing to the left come from one moving object, and those pointing to the right come from another. This approach has been taken by several authors, eg Fennema and Thompson (1979), but is only valid if the scene structure and motion are known to be simple a priori. More recently, Thompson and Pong (1987) have given early results from a more systematic study along these lines, but they show that there are severe difficulties as soon as the motion fields involve dilation and shear.

What we really want to be able to do is to cluster visual motion vectors not on their image properties, but on their scene properties. This appears most attractive because clusters could embrace disjoint regions in the image and include the notion of fusion. It is two techniques based on this approach that we examine here.

The first computes the interpretation of the visual motion field with maximum a posteriori probability, using the assumption that the visual motion arises from several planar facets. The structure from motion computation to recover the planar facets is that discussed in Chapter 6 for the case of unknown motion. The search for the maximum is made by simulated annealing. This global method tries to capture some notion of using motion to fuse scene areas with the same motion. The second method is a compromise between the need for a global solution based on the scene, and the need to keep computational costs low. It is a technique which looks for boundaries in the visual motion field representing the boundaries between planar facets in the scene.

However, as we might expect, segmentation on the basis of the scene is difficult, because it implies a simultaneous segmentation and structure from motion computation.

7.1 Global segmentation using simulated annealing

In this section we outline, and present experimental results from, an algorithm which tries to take account of the dual aims of segmentation and fusion by taking a global view of the visual motion field. The segmentation is scene-based and occurs simultaneously with the structure from motion computation.

To achieve the segmentation, we seek the maximum a posteriori probability of an interpretation X of the visual motion data D given the data itself: that is, we seek to maximize $P(X|D)$, the probability of the interpretation X given the data D. By interpretation, we mean a collection of facts like 'this datum of visual motion arose from that planar facet in the scene'.

Now the conditional probability may be rewritten using Bayes' theorem as

$$P(X|D) = \frac{P(D|X)P(X)}{P(D)} , \tag{7.1}$$

where $P(D|X)$ is the probability of the data given the interpretation, $P(X)$ is the prior probability of the interpretation, and $P(D)$ is the prior probability of the data. Clearly $P(D)$ does not depend on X and so our problem is to find the maximum of the product

$$P(D|X)P(X) . \tag{7.2}$$

We now consider the evaluation of the two terms separately.

7.1.1 Computing $P(D|X)$ by the planar facet method

We model the visual motion data on the assumption that they arose from moving planar facets in the scene.

In a noise-free system the data D would be exactly related to the interpretation X as $D = \phi(X)$ and there would be only one interpretation for which $P(D|X)$ is non-zero. With noisy data, however, the joint probability is simply related to the noise distribution:

$$P(D|X) = P(n) . \tag{7.3}$$

Assuming that the noise is Gaussian, has zero mean, is independent at each of the m data points and has the same standard deviation σ at each datum, $P(n)$ is a univariate distribution:

$$P(n) = \frac{1}{(2\pi\sigma^2)^{m/2}} \exp\left\{-\parallel n \parallel^2 / 2\sigma^2\right\} , \tag{7.4}$$

where

$$\parallel n \parallel^2 = \sum_{i=1}^{m} n_i^2 . \tag{7.5}$$

The noise contribution for an individual datum i is

$$n_i = D_i - [\phi(X)]_i , \tag{7.6}$$

which, in the present problem, depends on how the visual motion data are distributed among the various planar facets.

We evaluate n_i as follows. At any time the interpretation X consists of a set of scene faces $\mathcal{F}$ for each member of which, $f \in \mathcal{F}$, there is a set of data $d_f \subseteq D$ which originated from the motion of face f. Provided the d_f has at least eight members, we can use the planar facet algorithm (the unknown motion '8 point' method) described in Chapter 6 to compute the eight implicit scene parameters β and thence the explicit scene descriptors, $\mathbf{V}$, Ω and $\mathbf{N}$. In fact, as we have seen earlier in equations (6.29) the parameters β alone suffice to reconstruct the predicted full visual motion $\dot{\mathbf{r}}^{pred}$ that we should observe from that surface facet. As equation (6.32) shows this enables us to derive a measure of the noise:

$$n_i^2 = |\mathbf{v}_i - (\dot{\mathbf{r}}_i^{pred} \cdot \hat{\mathbf{v}}_i)\hat{\mathbf{v}}_i|^2 \ . \tag{7.7}$$

The noise term for a complete facet f is then just the summation

$$\| \, n^2 \, \|_f = \sum_{i \in d_f} n_i^2 \ . \tag{7.8}$$

7.1.2   Computing the prior probability, $P(X)$

We choose to model our expectation for the interpretation of the visual motion field as a spatio-temporal Markov Random Field (MRF). This means that the conditional probability that a visual motion vector at some site be labelled as originating from a particular planar facet depends only on the labelling attached to the other sites within some finite spatio-temporal neighbourhood. The MRF model therefore imposes local constraints on the segmentation which, if they are to be useful, should reflect some underlying physical expectations. Two constraints suggest themselves:

- it is likely that a surface patch in the scene will be continuous or cohesive and so we should expect motion in one spatial region of the image to originate from the same surface patch.

- in a sequence of time-varying imagery we should expect the image of a particular patch to be only slightly displaced from frame to frame (provided the frame rate is commensurate with the ratio of speed to distance).

These constraints form the basis of a spatio-temporal MRF.

It may be shown that if X is an MRF with respect to some local neighbourhood, then it is also a Gibbs distribution with respect to that neighbourhood (Besag 1974) and thus $P(X)$ may be expressed in terms of a potential $U(\omega)$ as:

$$P(X = \omega) = exp\,(-U(\omega))\,/\mathcal{Z} \tag{7.9}$$

where

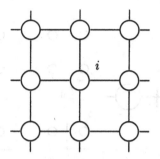

Figure 7.1: The spatial neighbourhood

$$\mathcal{Z} = \sum_{\omega} exp\left(-U(\omega)\right) \tag{7.10}$$

is the partition function. The potential U is given as the sum of local potentials, which will now be defined.

7.1.3 Local potentials

One possible neighbourhood system for the spatial part of the MRF is shown in Figure 7.1. It consists of the four nearest and four next-nearest neighbours of site i. Given such a neighbourhood, a set of cliques may be defined, each of which is a set of sites which are mutual neighbours. The total potential is then the sum over individual clique potentials:

$$U = \sum_{C} U_C(\omega) \ . \tag{7.11}$$

Because we consider only pair interactions, only cliques with two members contribute to the potential and

$$U = \sum_{i} \sum_{j} U_{2s}(i,j) \ , \tag{7.12}$$

where j runs over the neighbours of i, and i runs over the set of sites. To generate piecewise constant interpretation regions we then set

$$U_{2s}(i,j) = \begin{cases} -a_s & \text{if } X_i = X_j \\ +a_s & \text{otherwise} \ , \end{cases} \tag{7.13}$$

where X_i denotes the interpretation at site i and a_s is a positive number.

This potential favours spatial continuity of the interpretation. Geman and Geman (1984) (see also Geman and Geman (1987) and Derin, Elliot,

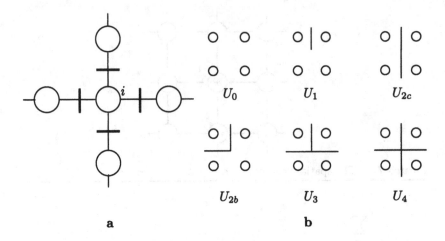

Figure 7.2: The spatial neighbourhood with line processes (a) and the line configurations (b). The associated potentials are $U_0 = 0$, $U_1 = 2.35$, $U_{2c} = 0.5$, $U_{2b} = 1.3$, $U_3 = 1.5$ and $U_4 = 2.35$.

Cristi and Geman (1984)) introduced another process in their work on image restoration, that of the discontinuity or line, which allows neighbours to have different interpretations at no extra cost other than that of the line process itself. In this way interpretation boundaries appear more naturally. The lines are introduced on an interstitial lattice L_{ij} and are Boolean variables, either on or off — active or inactive.

A new neighbourhood system incorporating the discontinuities is shown in Figure 7.2(a). For simplicity the extent of the neighbourhood has been reduced to the four nearest neighbours. The modified potentials are

$$U = \sum_i \sum_j U_{2s}(i, j, L_{ij}) + \sum_\Gamma U_\Gamma(L) \tag{7.14}$$

where

$$U_{2s}(i, j, L_{ij}) = \begin{cases} 0 & \text{if } L_{ij} \text{ is active} \\ U_{2s}(i, j) & \text{otherwise.} \end{cases} \tag{7.15}$$

The U_Γ are spatial line clique potentials, describing the cost of introducing the various line configurations, such as corners and T-junctions.

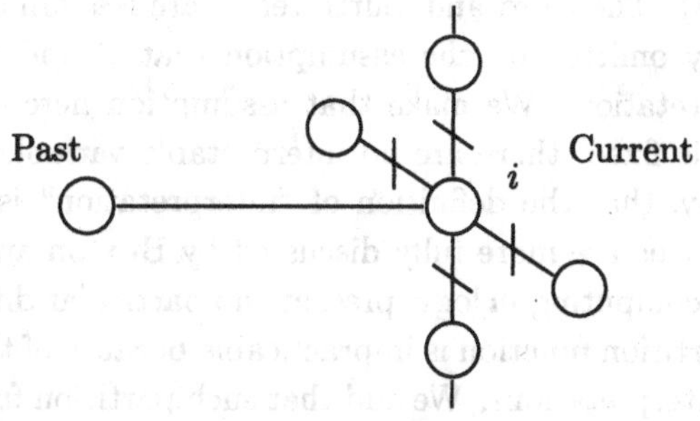

Figure 7.3: The temporal neighbourhood.

The line configurations are taken from Geman and Geman (1984), but the associated potentials differ somewhat. They are shown in Figure 7.2(b).

Finally, we consider the spatio-temporal MRF neighbourhood shown in Figure 7.3. The potential of equation (7.14) is augmented by the extra term

$$U_t = \sum_i \sum_k U_{2t}(i, k) \tag{7.16}$$

where k runs over the temporal neighbours of i (just one here), and where

$$U_{2t}(i, k) = \begin{cases} -a_t & \text{if } X_i = X_k \\ +a_t & \text{otherwise.} \end{cases} \tag{7.17}$$

The parameter a_t is positive and its size relative to a_s controls the strength of the temporal memory. It is not unreasonable to make $a_t \approx a_s$.

7.1.4   The optimization

Taking the logarithm of expression (7.2), and inserting equations (7.4) and (7.9), we see that our optimization problem becomes one of *minimizing* the function:

$$U(\omega) + \| n \|^2 / 2\sigma^2 + m \log \sigma + \log \mathcal{Z} . \tag{7.18}$$

The second term expresses the familiar least squares condition, and the first is like a regularizer for an ill-posed problem (Poggio, Torre and

Koch 1985). The third and fourth terms are less familiar, because they are usually omitted on the assumption that Z and σ are not part of the interpretation. We make that assumption here. This means that the noise is fixed, there are no interpretable variables in the potential and, finally, that the definition of "interpretation" is fixed. The rôles of these terms are more fully discussed by Buxton and Murray (1985). Although computing $m \log \sigma$ presents no particular difficulties, computing the partition function is impracticable because of the vast number of possible interpretations. We add that such partition functions are either very difficult or, more usually, impossible to derive analytically.

So the cost function we shall minimize is then

$$C = U(\omega) + \kappa \parallel n \parallel^2 / 2\sigma^2 . \tag{7.19}$$

Recall that the first term represents how well the interpretation meets our expectations, and the second represents how well the interpretation fits the data. The constant κ has been introduced merely to allow us to choose potentials near unity, $\kappa/2\sigma^2$ being a measure of the signal-to-noise ratio of the system.

The cost function C is far from convex and contains many local minima. We therefore perform the optimization using the method of stochastic optimization known as simulated annealing (Kirkpatrick, Gellatt and Vecchi 1983), which is based on the Metropolis algorithm (Metropolis, Rosenbluth, Rosenbluth, Teller and Teller 1953).

Starting at a high "temperature" T, sites are visited in random order and at each a random change in interpretation is suggested, say from surface facet f to f'. The local change in potential ΔU is computed from equation (7.14) (or (7.14) with (7.16) if the temporal site is included) and the change in noise contribution derived using the planar facet algorithm:

$$\Delta \left(\parallel n \parallel^2 \right) = \Delta \left(\parallel n \parallel_f^2 \right) + \Delta \left(\parallel n \parallel_{f'}^2 \right) . \tag{7.20}$$

The total change in cost is then just

$$\Delta C = \Delta U + \kappa \Delta \left(\parallel n \parallel^2 \right) / 2\sigma^2 \tag{7.21}$$

If ΔC is negative or zero the proposed change is accepted immediately, but if ΔC is positive it is accepted with a probability equal to $\exp(-\Delta C/T)$. After each cycle of site visits the temperature is lowered according to the schedule of Geman and Geman (1984):

$$T = \tau / \log(K + 1) \qquad\qquad (7.22)$$

where K is the iteration cycle and $\tau / \log 2$ is the initial temperature. The addition of line processes introduces another set of changes at each temperature. The line sites are visited at random, the change in cost computed from $\Delta C = \Delta U$, and the line status altered probabilistically. In addition we use an ergodicity theorem (Geman and Geman 1984) to predict the line site status. An average line status is recorded over a number of cycles, and if the line is active more than 50% of the time it is turned active, and otherwise set inactive.

7.1.5 Results from computer experiments

Figure 7.4 shows the performance of the segmentation algorithm on a synthetic motion field of 16×16 sites. The field was produced by the motion of three planes, each with different orientation and motion. Figure 7.4(a) shows the veridical interpretation, where the grey levels indicate which plane was visible at that point in the image, and so indicate from which plane the motion at that site arose. Notice that the background (dark) plane was visible in two disjoint parts of the image. The initial guessed segmentation was random (b), and the segmentation after annealing without and with the line process is shown in (c) and (d), respectively. The computed line processes are shown in (e). (The annealing was carried out over 1200 cycles, with $\tau = 8.5$, $a_s = 1$, $\kappa = 0.008$, 0.5% noise in input.)

The performance of the full spatio-temporal annealing is shown in Figure 7.5. In (a) we show the veridical interpretation for the next frame, obtained by allowing the scene facets to execute their motions for a time. The initial guess is now the annealed interpretation for the previous frame, and (b) shows the resulting annealed interpretation for the second frame. Because the starting point is now far more ordered than the initial random guess, the starting temperature was reduced to $\tau = 4.5$. The memory potential was $a_t = 0.4$. The process converged after 600 cycles.

Figure 7.6 shows the segmentation computed for surfaces which differ in orientation but have the same motion, and are at broadly similar depths from the camera. The configuration is that of the back wall, floor and side wall of a room, with the camera gazing at a corner. The visual motion components are shown in Figure 7.6(a) and the veridical

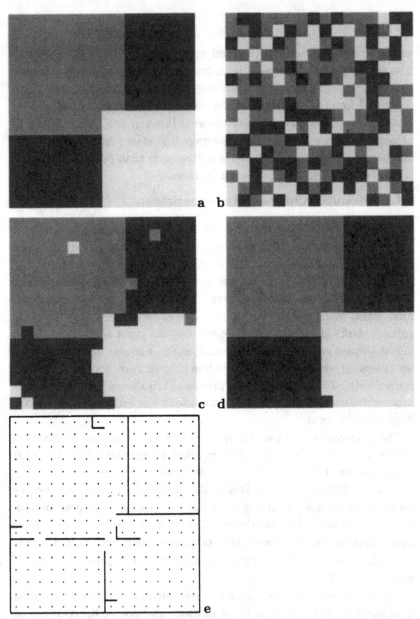

Figure 7.4: The veridical (unobserved) segmentation (a), the initial random guess (b) and the final annealed segmentation (c) without line processes. When line processes were introduced, the final annealed result was that of (d), with the active lines shown in (e).

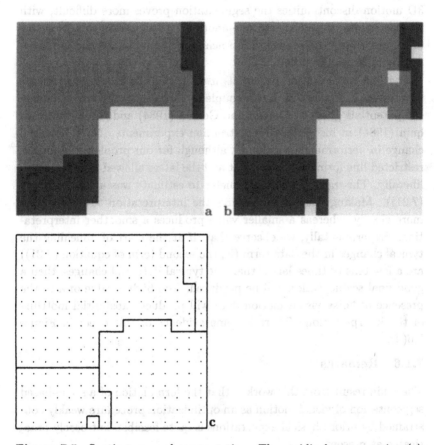

Figure 7.5: Spatio-temporal segmentation. The veridical segmentation (a) for the second frame of the sequence. The initial guess was the annealed segmentation of the first frame. The final segmentation and line processes are shown in (b) and (c).

configuration in (b). The segmentation after spatial annealing of the first
frame and spatio-temporal annealing of the second frame (over 2500 and
1000 cycles, respectively) is shown in (c). The cost function parameters
used were the same as in earlier experiments. Because of the absence of
3D motion discontinuities the segmentation proves more difficult, with
regions tending to bleed into one another. To illustrate this, we show
in Figure 7.6(d) the segmentation achieved if the 'back wall' is moved
differently from the others.

The line configuration potentials used in the illustrated experiments
were given in Figure 7.2, but a couple of variations were tried, namely
the potentials given by Geman and Geman (1984) and those of Marroquin (1984) in his surface reconstruction experiments. No substantial
change in performance was found, although for our problem the former
restricted line formation somewhat and the latter allowed it to occur too
liberally. The most difficult parameter to estimate was κ (see equation
(7.21)). Making this larger requires the interpretation to fit the data
more closely, whereas a smaller value produces a smoother interpretation. Experimentally, we observe that, if at the start of annealing the
typical changes in the data term (ie, the second term of equation (7.21))
are a few tens of times larger than the typical potential changes, then a
good final segmentation will be produced. Too high a value of κ in the
presence of noisy visual motion data will produce substantial mottling
of the interpretation. There is some evidence of this effect in Figure
7.6(d).

7.1.6   Remarks

The main result from this work is that the formulation of a scene-based
segmentation of visual motion as an optimization procedure weakly constrained by prior physical expectations is quite feasible, but barely practicable at present.

The approach to convergence has been found to be much less pre-
dictable than in the picture restoration algorithm of Geman and Geman
where there is fairly inexorable drive towards a global or near global
minimum (Geman and Geman 1984; Murray and Buxton 1987). We
believe this difference in behaviour is a result of the non-local nature
of the noise term in the segmentation process. If a site changes facet
membership, this can alter the noise contributed by all sites which were
members of the old and new facets (see equation (7.20)), possibly quite

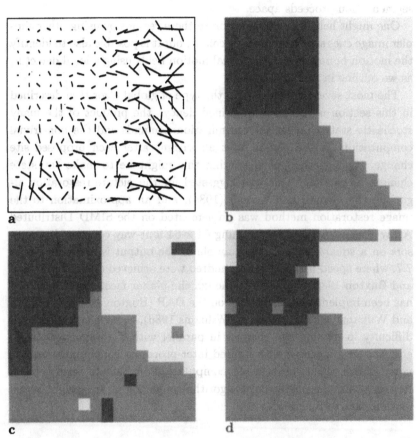

Figure 7.6: Segmention of differently oriented surfaces with the same 3D motion. The visual motion (a) and the veridical (unobserved) interpretation (b). The orientation segmentation achieved after spatio-temporal annealing with line processes (c). For comparison in (d) we show the segmentation achieved when there is a motion and orientation boundary.

drastically. Thus one can envisage in state space very many high energy states, with only relatively few low energy regions where *most* of
the visual motion is correctly segmented. Once in these regions, the
segmentation proceeds apace.

One might help the segmentation to these regions by using other simpler image cues such as texture or colour, but it is possible also to identify
the motion boundaries in the visual motion fields using a local detector,
as we outline in the next section.

The most severe difficulty with the type of global algorithm described
in this section is computational inefficiency: the product of the many
stochastic state changes the optimization demands and the non-trivial
computation (ie the planar facet algorithm) after each proposed site
change. One method of alleviating this might be to make the state
changes in parallel. This was suggested for the picture restoration algorithm by Geman and Geman (1984), and an approximation to the
image restoration method was implemented on the SIMD Distributed
Array Processor (DAP) containing 64 × 64 four-way connected processors on a square lattice. An example of the output is given in Figure
7.7, where speed-ups of order a hundred were achieved (Murray, Kashko
and Buxton 1986). However, although the planar facet algorithm itself
has been implemented in parallel on the DAP (Buxton, Murray, Buxton
and Williams 1985; Buxton and Williams 1986), there is a fundamental
difficulty in making site changes in parallel with the segmentation algorithm on a machine with limited inter-processor communication. As
noted above, this is because the computation of the data term is not a
local process, the planar facet algorithm requiring at least eight visual
motion data to function at all.

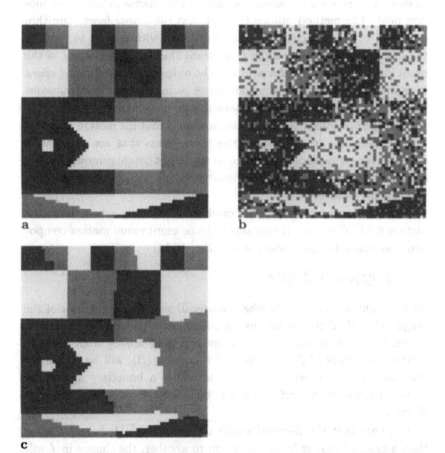

Figure 7.7: Parallel image restoration. Unobserved original (a), corrupted start (b), and final annealed interpretation (c). The restoration on the DAP took 30s as compared with 4000s on a 1Mip serial machine.

7.2   Local segmentation

Our second method for segmentation (Murray and Williams 1986) tries to exploit more local constraints to detect boundaries in the visual motion field. The method utilizes the fact that the planar facet algorithm described in the last chapter is ill-conditioned with respect to noise in the input. In the popular sense this means that small deviations in the input data result in large deviations in the output. Ill-conditioning arises in many vision problems, the root cause being that the instantaneous mapping from the scene to the image has no unique inverse.

As in the previous method, an assumption is that the motion at points that are adjacent in the image arise from points that are adjacent in space on the same planar facet, and so we do not consider interpenetrating motion fields, as might arise from viewing a scene through another transparent surface.

Consider now running a spatial mask systematically across the visual motion field. Whenever it contains eight or more visual motion components we can solve the system of equation (6.14)

$$[\mathbf{J}^T][\Lambda]\tilde{\mathbf{v}} = [\mathbf{J}^T][\Lambda][\mathbf{J}]\boldsymbol{\beta}$$

for the eight members of $\boldsymbol{\beta}$, where we recall that $\tilde{\mathbf{v}}$ is the vector of the magnitudes of all the visual motion components included in the mask. When the mask moves within the motion field arising from a single surface the values of $\boldsymbol{\beta}$, and also any function $f(\boldsymbol{\beta})$, will be notionally constant. However, when the mask straddles a boundary and visual motion from another surface facet is included the value of $f(\boldsymbol{\beta})$ must change.

It is here that the ill-conditioning of $[\mathbf{J}]$ and $[\mathbf{J}^T][\mathbf{J}]$ helps. Rather than a gradual change from one region to another, the change in f will in general be very large across a boundary. Any motion vector from a neighbouring facet included in the mask can be regarded as noise. If we consider just perturbations $\Delta\tilde{\mathbf{v}}$ in $\tilde{\mathbf{v}}$, then (Wilkinson 1965)

$$\| \Delta\boldsymbol{\beta} \| = c_J \| \boldsymbol{\beta} \| \left(\frac{\| \Delta\tilde{\mathbf{v}} \|}{\| \tilde{\mathbf{v}} \|} \right) , \tag{7.23}$$

where c_J is the spectral condition number of $[\mathbf{J}]$, which for an ill-conditioned system is large.

7.2.1   Test experiments

In our experiments we set the function of the β parameters to

$$f = \sum_{n=1}^{8} \beta_n^2 . \tag{7.24}$$

Figure 7.8 shows part of a dense visual motion field comprising 64×64 sites. The visual motion was derived from the motion of five different moving planar facets in the scene, and the visual motion components were projected perpendicular to random edge directions, simulating randomly oriented edge features or random texture on the scene surface. Although the portion shown in the figure contains motion boundaries, they are not at all obvious, and it is clear that segmentation methods based on simple properties of the visual motion in the image, alluded to in the introduction to this chapter, would have difficulty working here. In Figure 7.9(a) we plot as a relief map the absolute value of β_1 computed within the mask as it was moved over the field. The motion boundaries become immediately apparent, delineating the five image regions. All the $|\beta_n|$ have similar appearance and when combined give the function f of Figure 7.9(b). The problem of picking out the boundaries is now one of conventional image processing.

The spectral condition number of $[\mathbf{J}^T][\mathbf{J}]$, given by the ratios of the largest to smallest singular values of the matrix, was found to be typically around 10^7 for this example. The on-boundary values are all at least 10^3 larger than those off-boundary, and crude thresholding is sufficient to recover the boundaries.

In the presence of noise in the visual motion (ie intrinsic image noise rather than boundary noise) the very ill-conditioning that helps us find the boundaries with such ease also amplifies the noise in the function f in the non-boundary planar regions. In Figure 7.10(a) and (b) we show the function f for the cases of 3% and 6% noise added to the visual motion components. (The noise process at $p\%$ adds Gaussian random components with zero mean and half width $p\%$ of the vector magnitude to both x and y components of the edge-normal motion.) Although the boundaries are still clear, some more care is required to recover them. We used a simple ridge detector to produce the Boolean boundary maps of Figure 7.10(c) and (d).

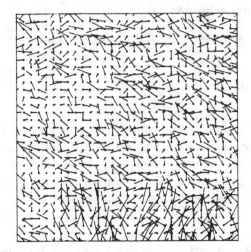

Figure 7.8: Part of a field of visual motion components in which there are three motion boundaries. The boundaries are not obvious, and the subfields have no immediately apparent global properties.

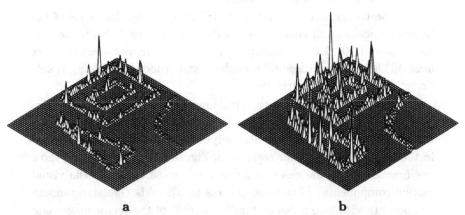

a   b

Figure 7.9: Maps of the values of (a) β_1 and (b) the function f. For the function f, the off-boundary values are all near unity, whereas the largest on-boundary value is $\sim 10^5$.

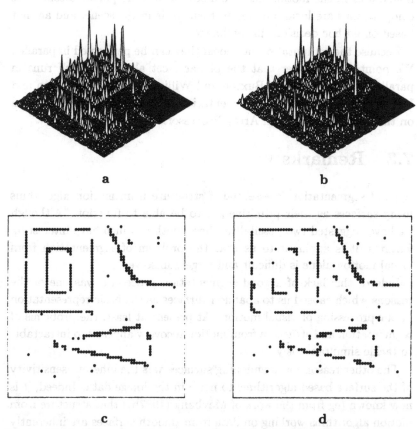

Figure 7.10: The map of function f after adding (a) 3% and (b) 6% noise to the visual motion. (c) and (d) show the respective outputs of a ridge detector.

7.2.2 Summary

It has been shown that the ill-conditioning inherent in the algorithm to recover planar surface disposition and motion can be exploited to locate boundaries in the motion field from several moving planar facets. The computations are local, but retain their basis in the scene, and are not based on ad hoc decisions in the image.

Because the computations are local they can be performed in parallel. We pointed out earlier that the planar facet algorithm itself runs in parallel (Buxton, Murray, Buxton and Williams 1985) and Buxton and Williams (1986) report an implementation of the segmentation algorithm on the 64 × 64 Distributed Array Processor.

7.3 Remarks

A good segmentation is essential if structure from motion algorithms using surfaces as their primitive are to be able to function. Although we have suggested two possibilities here, both of which have interesting features, it is apparent to us that the problem of segmentation from visual motion alone is difficult and largely unsolved.

Indeed, this lack of a good segmentation procedure was one of the reasons which caused us to abandon surfaces as the basic representation in our processing of visual motion. At present at least, the problems of segmentation and structure from motion recovery appear too intractable to tackle simultaneously.

The other reason for abandoning surfaces was the inherent sensitivity of the surface based algorithms to noise in the image data. Indeed, it is now known (eg from the work of Maybank (1987b)) that structure from motion algorithms working on data from smooth surfaces are inherently unstable and that planar surfaces cause the gravest instabilities. The most stable reconstructions are obtained from "rough" objects which have a depth change commensurate with their lateral extent. A dihedral (an object presenting two planar surfaces intersecting at a reasonable, finite angle) is a good example of such a "rough" object and gives a stable reconstruction. For similar reasons, polyhedral objects such as those used in the experiments reported in Chapters 4 and 5 give usable, stable reconstructions. However, it should be stressed that, as discussed in the opening paragraphs of this chapter, the polyhedral objects themselves had to be segmented from the rest of the scene on the basis of other information.

Automatic grouping of the edges and surfaces of a rigid body on the basis of their common scene motion and thereby obtaining a stable reconstruction thus remains as a tantalizing but as yet unimplemented prospect, although some theoretical ideas are discussed in Buxton and Murray (1985).

8 Matching to Edge Models

In previous chapters we have described several methods of recovering 3D descriptions of the scene from visual motion.

In this and the following chapter we discuss the matching of those scene descriptions to simple models described in terms of (i) 3D straight edges and (ii) surface normals.

By discussing the recognition of structure from motion, we do not intend to suggest that the vision processing we have described thus far should be regarded as a realistic stand-alone system. Our aim in pursuing processing to the recognition stage is primarily to test the quality of the structure from motion processing. Indeed it is surely a worthwhile test of any vision process to ensure that it can supply usable input further up the visual processing hierarchy. Notwithstanding the primary aim, the recognition stage is of interest itself. As we have pointed out many times, the structure recovered from visual motion suffers a depth/speed scaling ambiguity. The matching therefore has to use only shape, not size. It is interesting to see how well or badly matching fares without absolute size to guide it. Furthermore, if matching is performed to models with unique size, it is possible to resolve the ambiguity, enabling size and speed to be recovered absolutely.

Grimson and Lozano-Pérez (1984) introduced constraints for matching surface normals as part of their RAF recognition system. They described constraints which utilized size and shape (so-called *extended* constraints) and suggested that by normalizing any vector involving size (ie, making it a unit vector), the constraints could be used straightforwardly for shape alone (as so-called *simple* constraints). Although that is almost true, in fact the use of unit vectors makes evaluation of the range limits of the simple constraints rather more involved than those for the extended constraints, as noted by Murray (1987). Grimson and Lozano-Pérez (1985b) also described constraints to handle 2D edge matching. Here we extend this approach to 3D edges and introduce extra power in the form of a director-vector disambiguator.

The structure from motion algorithm of Chapter 4 recovers the disposition of 3D edges. Here we will not assume that complete edges are available and will generalize the data to be edge *fragments*. The fragments could be sensed by any means, and we will give an example using data obtained by stereo processing before discussing application to our data obtained from visual motion processing. This will highlight the fact that data from visual motion processing introduces an extra complication in the generation of constraints. This is that the *absolute* depths and lengths of the edge fragments are not available, a consequence of the depth/speed scaling ambiguity. We can say that one sensed edge is twice as long as another but, without introducing extra information, we have no idea whether its absolute length is measured in millimetres or furlongs.

Thus the constraints we develop involve only *shape* not *size*. In fact, the use of shape alone can be useful even when absolute sensed distances *are* available, for it allows the description of several objects of different size but the same shape by just one model entry in the database. For the sake of completeness, we will also describe the additional constraint required to exploit absolute size where it is available. If nothing else, this permits a comparison of the performance of the matching procedure with and without absolute size.

In the next section we specify what information is explicit in the models and sensed data and in §8.2 we introduce the matching algorithm, a variant of the Grimson and Lozano-Pérez (1984) "hypothesize and test" paradigm, and outline the constraint geometry. The remaining sections contain details of the matching and experimental examples.

8.1   Model and data specification

The models are specified by the list of the model space (μ-space) coordinates of the n model edge terminators $\mathbf{T}$, and an ordered pair of terminator indices for each of the g model edges $\mathbf{M}$, so that

$$\mathbf{M}_i = \mathbf{T}_{i2} - \mathbf{T}_{i1} \ . \tag{8.1}$$

The model edges need not actually be connected in any way. This raw model information is compiled once off-line and stored as several two-dimensional look-up tables (LUTs) to save computation during matching. This is described later.

Notice that by specifying the start and end terminators as an ordered pair, we define edge directions on the model — in other words the edges are vectors rather than directors. The choice of direction is quite arbitrary but, once made, is fixed. One of the aims of the matching is then to determine *consistent* directions among the sensed data edges. Establishing this consistency requires extra computation early on, but leads to much more rapid determination of inconsistent matches at the later stages of matching.

The sensed data comprise straight edge fragments in 3D sensor space (σ-space). A sensed edge fragment a is defined by its start and end points, $\mathbf{E}_{a1}$ and $\mathbf{E}_{a2}$. Its direction is thus

$$\hat{\mathbf{e}}_a = \frac{\mathbf{E}_{a2} - \mathbf{E}_{a1}}{|\mathbf{E}_{a2} - \mathbf{E}_{a1}|} \qquad (8.2)$$

Notice here that we again make an arbitrary choice of start and end labels even though before matching the actual direction of the edge is unknown — that is, it may be $\pm\hat{\mathbf{e}}_a$. As we indicated above, it is possible during matching to assign unambiguous signs to the sensed edges such that they are consistent with the corresponding model edge directions. At that stage, if the assignment of start and end labels is wrong, we will not reverse them, but rather prefix $\hat{\mathbf{e}}_a$ by an explicit sign. Thus anywhere $\hat{\mathbf{e}}_a$ appears, its definition is that of equation (8.2). There are in fact five possible states for the sign label of an edge fragment:

$$(U) \quad (+) \quad (-) \quad (+b) \quad (-b) \ .$$

(U) means that the sign is uncertain. The symbol $(+)$ means that the choice of start and end labels for the edge datum is consistent with the model edge. The label $(-)$ indicates that it is not. The symbol $(+b)$ means that the sign is the same as that of another edge fragment b, and $(-b)$ the opposite. It also implies that the sign of b itself is (U). However, if at a later stage the sign of b is disambiguated, then the sign of a can be disambiguated. For example, if a is labelled $(-b)$ and b is later labelled $(-)$, a may be relabelled as $(-)(-) = (+)$. We stress now that the signs only have scope within the current *active interpretation*, the potential set of matches being explored at that time. If at some point the matcher concludes that this interpretation is not viable, then the signs must be re-evaluated. A more detailed explanation of the process is given later.

Inevitably, there will be sensing errors in the positions of $\mathbf{E}_{a1}$ and $\mathbf{E}_{a2}$. We assume that the uncertainty in position is an ellipsoid around the endpoint with radii $r^\perp$ and $r^\parallel$ as shown in Figure 8.1. The direction of $\hat{\mathbf{e}}_a$ will be uncertain within a cone of error with half angle α_a which can be as large as

$$\alpha_a = \tan^{-1}\left(\frac{r_{a1}^\perp + r_{a2}^\perp}{\max[0, \ (|\mathbf{E}_{a2} - \mathbf{E}_{a1}| - r_{a1}^\parallel - r_{a2}^\parallel)]}\right) \ . \qquad (8.3)$$

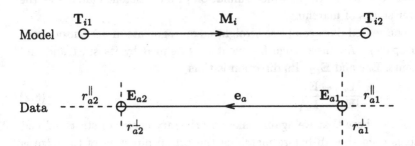

Figure 8.1: The vectors describing a model edge (above) and sensed edge fragment (below).

8.2   Matching in overview

The crucial task in the search for a match between sensed data and object models is to quench the potential combinatorial explosion in the size of the search space. Grimson (1984) has given a succinct description of the ways that have been used to control the combinatorics. The method we use here is based on matching partial data to complete model descriptions, an approach typified by the work of Gaston and Lozano-Pérez (1984), Grimson and Lozano-Pérez (1984, 1985a, 1985b), Grimson (1984, 1987) and Faugeras and co-workers (Faugeras and Hébert 1983; Faugeras, Hébert, Ponce and Pauchon 1983).

Given k sensed data all arising from a model of g edges, there are naïvely g^k ways of assigning the data to the model. The set of potential matches can be represented by an interpretation tree, the early part of which is sketched in Figure 8.2 for a model with three edges. Even for the problem of matching twelve data fragments to a cuboid wireframe the potential number of leaves on the tree is $g^k \sim 10^{13}$ and so the pruning of interpretation trees must be drastic and efficient. Grimson and Lozano-Pérez (1984) demonstrated that simple pairwise geometrical constraints are highly effective pruners for problems of matching sensed oriented patches to surface models and they have also shown that a similar approach is possible for 2D edge matching (Grimson and

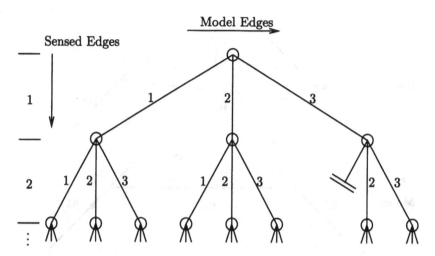

Figure 8.2: The root part of an interpretation tree for a model with $g = 3$ edges. Without pruning there are g^k branches at data level k. An entire subtree can be removed by establishing, for example, that if sensed fragment 1 is matched with model edge 3, then sensed fragment 2 cannot be matched with model edge 1.

Lozano-Pérez 1985b). Here, we establish geometrical constraints which are appropriate to 3D edge matching.

The pairwise constraints establish facts like

>   *if* edge fragment a is matched to model edge i,
>   *then* edge fragment b (can/cannot) be matched with model
>   edge j

by demanding consistency between the following metrics on the data and model:

Data:	$\hat{\mathbf{e}}_a \cdot \hat{\mathbf{e}}_b$	$\hat{\mathbf{e}}_a \cdot \hat{\mathbf{p}}_{ab}$	$\hat{\mathbf{e}}_b \cdot \hat{\mathbf{p}}_{ab}$	$\hat{\mathbf{e}}_{ab} \cdot \hat{\mathbf{p}}_{ab}$
	$\updownarrow$	$\updownarrow$	$\updownarrow$	$\updownarrow$
Model:	$\hat{\mathbf{M}}_i \cdot \hat{\mathbf{M}}_j$	$\hat{\mathbf{M}}_i \cdot \hat{\mathbf{q}}_{ij}$	$\hat{\mathbf{M}}_j \cdot \hat{\mathbf{q}}_{ij}$	$\hat{\mathbf{M}}_{ij} \cdot \hat{\mathbf{q}}_{ij}$

Note that because we wish to apply the matcher to structure obtained from visual motion processing, absolute size is unavailable and so the above constraints involve only scalar products of *unit* vectors — ie only

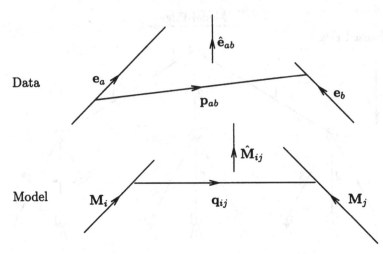

Figure 8.3: The geometry for the metrics on the data and on the model. Note that the geometry is 3D and $\hat{e}_a$, $\hat{e}_b$ and so on are not necessarily coplanar.

involve angles. We shall refer to these as the angle constraint and direction constraints 1,2 and 3, respectively. The various vectors involved are illustrated in Figure 8.3. In particular, $\hat{p}_{ab}$ is a unit vector in the direction between any two points on the sensed edge fragments a and b and $\hat{e}_{ab}$ is a unit vector in the direction of $\hat{e}_a \times \hat{e}_b$, and similarly for the model vectors.

By establishing "cannot" facts (such as that illustrated in Figure 8.2) whole subsections of the interpretation tree need never be explored. Notice too that it becomes harder to grow a new branch at deeper levels of the tree; to establish a new branch at data level K requires $K - 1$ "can" facts ($[K, K - 1], [K, K - 2], \ldots, [K, 1]$) to ensure an unblemished pairwise ancestry back to the root.

The choice of constraints is suggested by the criteria of Grimson (1984) and also Marr (1982):

- They are independent of any global coordinate frame.

- They are simple but effective in reducing the size of the search space.

- The constraints can be made to degrade gracefully in the presence of noise.

- They are independent of the specific sensing mode.

The constraints are similar to those used to assign surface patches to model faces (Grimson and Lozano-Pérez 1984) (and see Chapter 9), although for each constraint we have the extra complication of various subcases depending on whether the signs of the sensed edge fragments have been determined or not. In this respect an interesting distinction occurs between the angle and third direction constraints on the one hand and direction constraints 1 and 2 on the other. Because the former involve a product of two edge vectors they are unable to determine edge signs absolutely if both signs are uncertain. The latter two constraints involve only one edge vector, and thus can determine an edge sign absolutely. Thus the latter *determine* signs and the former *propagate* them.

The aim of the pruning stage then is to deliver (or hypothesize) all the interpretations of the data that are *feasible* under the constraints. Typically there will be a mere handful of these which are then further reduced in number by demanding that they are consistent with a single transformation between sensor and model spaces as described in §8.5. However it is the pruning that is the decisive factor in reducing the search space size and its effectiveness depends on the power of the constraints we now detail.

8.3 The constraints in detail

8.3.1 The angle constraint

This constraint requires that if edge fragments a and b are assigned to model edges i and j, respectively, then the range of possible angles between the sensed fragments must embrace the angle between the model edges.

Model geometry. On the model all edges have an arbitrarily chosen but unambiguous sign. If $\hat{\mathbf{M}}_i$ and $\hat{\mathbf{M}}_j$ are unit vectors in the direction of the model edges, then the angle between them is

$$A_{ij} = \cos^{-1}(\hat{\mathbf{M}}_i \cdot \hat{\mathbf{M}}_j) \ . \tag{8.4}$$

These values need be computed once only for a particular model and stored in a LUT for on-line comparison with the sensed data. The A_{ij}

occupy one triangle of a $g \times g$ matrix: because $A_{ji} = A_{ij}$ and $A_{ii} = 0$ these need not be stored explicitly.

Data geometry. There are two possibilities for the angle between the sensed fragments a and b. If the fragments have the same sign, then the angle is

$$\gamma_{ab} = \cos^{-1}(\hat{\mathbf{e}}_a \cdot \hat{\mathbf{e}}_b) \ . \tag{8.5}$$

Otherwise it is

$$\gamma_{ab}{}^* = \cos^{-1}(-\hat{\mathbf{e}}_a \cdot \hat{\mathbf{e}}_b) = \pi - \gamma_{ab} \ . \tag{8.6}$$

Satisfaction conditions. Including the error angles α_a and α_b, for a valid pairing the following logical expression must be true

$$l_s \vee l_d \tag{8.7}$$

where

$$l_s = \max[(\gamma_{ab} - \alpha_a - \alpha_b), 0] \le A_{ij} \le \min[(\gamma_{ab} + \alpha_a + \alpha_b), \pi] \tag{8.8}$$

$$l_d = \max[(\gamma_{ab}{}^* - \alpha_a - \alpha_b), 0] \le A_{ij} \le \min[(\gamma_{ab}{}^* + \alpha_a + \alpha_b), \pi]. \tag{8.9}$$

The subscripts s and d here denote that these are the satisfaction conditions if fragments a and b have the same or different signs. However, it is important to appreciate that because of measurement uncertainties the logical OR ($\vee$) is not exclusive — that is, both conditions can be true.

There are several outcomes to consider, depending on the signs of the fragments on entry to the constraint test.

1. Suppose on entry the signs of a and b are both uncertain (U). If l_s is true and l_d false, then the pairing is valid and the two edges a and b must have the same sign for that interpretation, and can be relabelled ($+b$) and ($+a$), respectively. Conversely, if l_d is true and l_s false, then the signs are different, and the edges can be relabelled ($-b$) and ($-a$), respectively. If both tests succeed, then the pairing is valid, but nothing is learned about the signs. If both tests fail, then the pairing is invalid and the search backtracks to the most recent unexplored branch, in the usual depth-first search pattern.

2. Suppose that the sign of one of the fragments is known on entry
   to the test. For example, let a be signed $(-)$. Now, if l_s is true
   and l_d false, fragment b must have the same sign as a, ie, $(+a) =$
   $(+)(-) = (-)$. Conversely, if l_d is true and l_s false, b must be $(+)$.
   If both conditions are true, the sign of b remains (U); and if both
   are false, the search backtracks.

3. Suppose that both signs are known on entry. If the signs of a and b
   are identical, then for a valid pairing l_s must be shown to be true,
   otherwise the search backtracks. Conversely, if the signs differ, l_d
   must be shown to be true for a valid pairing.

8.3.2   Direction constraint 1

Direction constraint 1 requires that if an interpretation pairs sensed edge
fragments a and b with model edges i and j, then the range of angles
between *any* vector $\mathbf{p}_{ab}$ from a point on a to a point on b and the edge
a itself must be wholly included in the angle between *any* vector $\mathbf{q}_{ij}$
between points on model edges i and j and the direction of model edge
i itself.

The model geometry.   On the model, the angle between $\mathbf{q}_{ij}$ and edge
i is given by

$$D_{ij} = \cos^{-1}(\hat{\mathbf{M}}_i \cdot \hat{\mathbf{q}}_{ij}) \qquad (8.10)$$

where $\hat{\mathbf{q}}_{ij}$ is a unit vector in the direction of $\mathbf{q}_{ij}$. This will have a range
of values from $D_{ij}{}^{min}$ to $D_{ij}{}^{max}$ as the vector $\mathbf{q}_{ij}$ joins different points
along the model edges i and j. We shall return to consider how to
compute these extremes below. The values will be stored in two $g \times g$
LUTs as $D_{ij}{}^{min}$ and $D_{ij}{}^{max}$ for all i and j.

The data geometry.   The angle between any vector $\mathbf{p}_{ab}$ and the edge
fragment a is either

$$\omega_{ab} = \cos^{-1}(\hat{\mathbf{e}}_a \cdot \hat{\mathbf{p}}_{ab}) \qquad (8.11)$$

or

$$\omega_{ab}{}^* = \cos^{-1}(-\hat{\mathbf{e}}_a \cdot \hat{\mathbf{p}}_{ab}) = \pi - \omega_{ab} \ , \qquad (8.12)$$

depending on the sign affixed to fragment a. As $\hat{\mathbf{p}}_{ab}$ varies, these angles will sweep out ranges R and R^*

$$R: \qquad \omega_{ab}{}^{min} \rightarrow \omega_{ab}{}^{max} \tag{8.13}$$
$$R^*: \quad \pi - \omega_{ab}{}^{max} \rightarrow \pi - \omega_{ab}{}^{min}$$

The method to determine $\omega_{ab}{}^{min,max}$ is deferred until the end of this subsection.

The satisfaction conditions.   For a valid pairing we require that one or other of these ranges be included within the model range. Incorporating the uncertainty angle in the direction of fragment a, the satisfaction condition becomes:

$$l_s \vee l_d \tag{8.14}$$

where

$$l_s \; = \; ((D_{ij}{}^{min} \le \omega_{ab}{}^{min} + \alpha_a) \wedge \tag{8.15}$$
$$(\omega_{ab}{}^{max} - \alpha_a \le D_{ij}{}^{max}))$$

$$l_d \; = \; ((D_{ij}{}^{min} \le \pi - \omega_{ab}{}^{max} + \alpha_a) \wedge \tag{8.16}$$
$$(\pi - \omega_{ab}{}^{min} - \alpha_a \le D_{ij}{}^{max})).$$

Here $\wedge$ denotes AND and, as for the angle constraint, the logical OR is not exclusive. There are, however, two cases to consider:

1. If on entry to the test the sign of fragment a is uncertain and l_s is true and l_d false, then the pairing is valid and a must be signed $(+)$. If, however, l_d is true and l_s false, a is signed $(-)$. Thus this constraint can determine absolute signs. If both l_s and l_d are true, then the sign remains uncertain. If both are false, the search backtracks.

2. If on entry the sign of a is known to be $(+)$ or $(-)$, the appropriate condition, l_s or l_d respectively, must be shown to be true for a valid pairing.

The range of angle D_{ij}.   Writing

$$d = \cos D_{ij} = \hat{\mathbf{M}}_i \cdot \hat{\mathbf{q}}_{ij} \tag{8.17}$$

and recalling that $\hat{\mathbf{M}}_i = \mathbf{T}_{i2} - \mathbf{T}_{i1}$, and similarly for j, we may write

$$d(\rho, \eta) = \hat{\mathbf{M}}_i \cdot \left(\frac{\mathbf{T}_{j1} - \mathbf{T}_{i1} + \eta \mathbf{M}_j - \rho \mathbf{M}_i}{|\mathbf{T}_{j1} - \mathbf{T}_{i1} + \eta \mathbf{M}_j - \rho \mathbf{M}_i|} \right) \tag{8.18}$$

where ρ and η are parameters in the range $(0, 1)$ inclusive. For skew edges, an appreciation of the behaviour of this function may be obtained by noting that if the parameter ranges are extended to $(-\infty, +\infty)$ then $\hat{\mathbf{q}}_{ij}$ can point anywhere in the half-space defined by the plane containing $\hat{\mathbf{M}}_i$ whose normal is the mutual perpendicular to $\hat{\mathbf{M}}_i$ and $\hat{\mathbf{M}}_j$. (The half space is obviously that containing $\hat{\mathbf{M}}_j$.) It is easily seen that $d(\rho, \eta)$ only reaches its analytic extrema of ± 1 as $\rho \rightarrow \mp \infty$ with η remaining finite. Also it can easily be shown that for a fixed value of ρ there is a turning point in d with respect to changes in η; but that for a fixed value of η there is *no* turning point in d with respect to ρ. Now, we are looking for the smallest and largest values of d in the parameter window $(\rho, \eta) = ([0, 1], [0, 1])$. This *certainly* excludes the 2D analytic extrema, and so the maximum and minimum values of d we require will be in the set

$$\{ \ d(0,0) \ d(0,1) \ d(1,0) \ d(1,1) \ d(0,\eta_0) \ d(1,\eta_1) \ \} \ .$$

The members must be evaluated explicitly, except that the penultimate member is included only if $0 \leq \eta_0 \leq 1$ where η_0 is the solution of

$$\frac{\partial}{\partial \eta} d(0, \eta) = 0 \ . \tag{8.19}$$

Similarly, the final member is included only if $0 \leq \eta_1 \leq 1$ where η_1 is the solution of

$$\frac{\partial}{\partial \eta} d(1, \eta) = 0 \ . \tag{8.20}$$

The range of angle ω_{ab}. Values $\omega_{ab}{}^{min}$ to $\omega_{ab}{}^{max}$ are found in a similar way to the range of D_{ij}, but with $\hat{\mathbf{M}}_i$, $\hat{\mathbf{M}}_j$ and $\hat{\mathbf{q}}_{ij}$ replaced by $\hat{\mathbf{e}}_a$, $\hat{\mathbf{e}}_b$ and $\hat{\mathbf{p}}_{ab}$. However, to take account of sensing errors, the $\mathbf{T}_{i1}$ are not replaced with $\mathbf{E}_{a1}$ etc. Instead the range is pinched inwards by using $\mathbf{E}_{a1} + r_{a1}^{\parallel} \hat{\mathbf{e}}_a$ and $\mathbf{E}_{a2} - r_{a2}^{\parallel} \hat{\mathbf{e}}_a$ as the effective endpoints of the fragment a.

8.3.3   Direction constraint 2

Direction constraint 2 requires that if an interpretation pairs sensed edge fragments a and b with model edges i and j, then the range of angles between *any* vector $\mathbf{p}_{ab}$ from a point on a to a point on b, and the edge b itself must be wholly included in the angle between *any* vector $\mathbf{q}_{ij}$ between points on model edges i and j and the direction of model edge j itself.

If we exchange labels a,b and i,j but keep the actual data fixed, it is easy to see that this constraint is the same as direction constraint 1, but applied from the point of view of the other edge. It therefore uses information held in D_{ji}^{min} and D_{ji}^{max} and follows the method already described for constraint 1.

8.3.4   Direction constraint 3

Direction constraint 3 requires that if an interpretation pairs sensed edge fragments a and b with model edges i and j, then the range of angles between *any* vector $\mathbf{p}_{ab}$ from a point on a to a point on b and the unit vector mutually perpendicular to both sensed edges must be wholly included in the angle between *any* vector $\mathbf{q}_{ij}$ between points on model edges i and j and the unit vector mutually perpendicular to the model edges.

The model geometry.   On the model, the unit vector along the mutual perpendicular is

$$\hat{\mathbf{M}}_{ij} = \frac{\hat{\mathbf{M}}_i \times \hat{\mathbf{M}}_j}{|\hat{\mathbf{M}}_i \times \hat{\mathbf{M}}_j|} \ . \tag{8.21}$$

The angle required is

$$F_{ij} = \cos^{-1}(\hat{\mathbf{M}}_{ij} \cdot \hat{\mathbf{q}}_{ij}) \tag{8.22}$$

which will have a range $F_{ij}{}^{min}$ to $F_{ij}{}^{max}$. Noting that F_{ij} and F_{ji} are identical and that the F_{ii} are undefined, the range limits can be held within a single $g \times g$ LUT. We discuss how to find the range of F below.

The data geometry.   The angle between the cross product and any vector $\mathbf{p}_{ab}$ is

$$\lambda_{ab} = \cos^{-1}(\hat{\mathbf{e}}_{ab} \cdot \hat{\mathbf{p}}_{ab}) \tag{8.23}$$

when the signs of a and b are the same or

$$\lambda_{ab}{}^* = \pi - \lambda_{ab} \ , \tag{8.24}$$

when different.

There are thus two ranges of values:

$$R: \qquad \lambda_{ab}{}^{min} \to \lambda_{ab}{}^{max} \tag{8.25}$$
$$R^*: \quad \pi - \lambda_{ab}{}^{max} \to \pi - \lambda_{ab}{}^{min} \ .$$

The method to determine $\lambda_{ab}{}^{min,max}$ is deferred to the end of this section.

The satisfaction conditions. For direction constraint 3 there are, again, two parts to the satisfaction condition:

$$l_s \vee l_d \tag{8.26}$$

with

$$
\begin{aligned}
l_s \ = \ & ((F_{ij}{}^{min} \leq \lambda_{ab}{}^{min} + \alpha_{ab}) \wedge \\
& (\lambda_{ab}{}^{max} - \alpha_{ab} \leq F_{ij}{}^{max}))
\end{aligned}
\tag{8.27}
$$

$$
\begin{aligned}
l_d \ = \ & ((F_{ij}{}^{min} \leq \pi - \lambda_{ab}{}^{max} + \alpha_{ab}{}^*) \wedge \\
& (\pi - \lambda_{ab}{}^{min} - \alpha_{ab}{}^* \leq F_{ij}{}^{max}))
\end{aligned}
\tag{8.28}
$$

Here, the angles α_{ab} and $\alpha_{ab}{}^*$ are the effective half angles of the error cones surrounding $\hat{\mathbf{e}}_{ab}$ when a and b have the same or different signs respectively. Their derivation is given in the Appendix to this chapter.

Again, the logical OR is not exclusive. The argument as to validity of pairing proceeds exactly as in the three cases for the angle constraint.

The range of F_{ij}. Let

$$f = \cos F_{ij} = \hat{\mathbf{M}}_{ij} \cdot \hat{\mathbf{q}}_{ij} \ . \tag{8.29}$$

Again using parameters ρ, η we have thence

$$f(\rho, \eta) = \hat{\mathbf{M}}_{ij} \cdot \left(\frac{\mathbf{T}_{j1} - \mathbf{T}_{i1} + \eta \mathbf{M}_j - \rho \mathbf{M}_i}{|\mathbf{T}_{j1} - \mathbf{T}_{i1} + \eta \mathbf{M}_j - \rho \mathbf{M}_i|} \right) \tag{8.30}$$

Insight into this function can be obtained by noting that for skew lines $f \to 0$ as ρ and/or $\eta \to \pm\infty$. Also there is a two dimensional analytic extremum when $\hat{\mathbf{q}}_{ij}$ lies along the direction of $\hat{\mathbf{M}}_{ij}$. Suppose that (ρ_e, η_e) are the parameter values for this extremum. If both are in the range $(0,1)$ inclusive, then one range limit (ie f^{max} or f^{min}) will be $f(\rho_e, \eta_e) = +1$ or -1, and the other range limit will be in the set

$$\{ \, f(0,0) \; f(0,1) \; f(1,0) \; f(1,1) \, \} \; .$$

If however the analytic extremum is outside the parameter window, then f^{min} and f^{max} will be members of the set

$$\{ \, f(0,0) \; f(0,1) \; f(1,0) \; f(1,1) \; f(0,\eta_0) \; f(1,\eta_1) \; f(\rho_0,0) \; f(\rho_1,1) \, \}$$

where each of the last four members is included only if the value of η_0, η_1, ρ_0, ρ_1, respectively, is in the range $(0, 1)$ inclusive. These parameter values are obtained, respectively, as solutions of

$$\frac{\partial}{\partial\eta} f(0,\eta) \;=\; 0 \qquad\qquad\qquad (8.31)$$

$$\frac{\partial}{\partial\eta} f(1,\eta) \;=\; 0$$

$$\frac{\partial}{\partial\rho} f(\rho,0) \;=\; 0$$

$$\frac{\partial}{\partial\rho} f(\rho,1) \;=\; 0 \; .$$

(Note that if the either of the first two terms is included, the last two will be excluded and vice versa.)

The range of λ_{ab}. Values $\lambda_{ab}{}^{min}$ to $\lambda_{ab}{}^{max}$ are found in a similar way to the range of F_{ij}, but with $\hat{\mathbf{M}}_i$, $\hat{\mathbf{M}}_j$ and $\hat{\mathbf{q}}_{ij}$ replaced by $\hat{\mathbf{e}}_a$, $\hat{\mathbf{e}}_b$ and $\hat{\mathbf{p}}_{ab}$. As previously, to take account of sensing errors the sensed fragments are pinched inwards by using $\mathbf{E}_{a1} + r_{a1}^{\parallel}\hat{\mathbf{e}}_a$ and $\mathbf{E}_{a2} - r_{a2}^{\parallel}\hat{\mathbf{e}}_a$ as the effective endpoints of the fragment a, and similarly for b.

8.3.5   Using absolute distances

Our main concern here is to develop matching constraints for structure from motion, which therefore cannot include size. However, if size is available it can be incorporated in two obvious ways. First, rather than use unit vectors in the constraint metrics, we can use full displacement vectors $\mathbf{p}_{ab}$ and $\mathbf{q}_{ij}$. All this does is simplify the tests to find extrema. For example, as d no longer requires normalization, its extrema must be found in the set

$$\{ \ d(0,0) \ \ d(0,1) \ \ d(1,0) \ \ d(1,1) \ \} \ .$$

The second and more direct way of using absolute size is in an edge length constraint. This has the advantage that it does not operate in a pairwise fashion, but rather uses one sensed fragment and one model edge. The constraint demands that if fragment a is paired with model edge i then the length of the fragment cannot be greater than that of the model edge. Hence, for a valid pairing:

$$|\mathbf{E}_{a2} - \mathbf{E}_{a1}| - r_{a1}^{\|} - r_{a2}^{\|} \le |\mathbf{T}_{i2} - \mathbf{T}_{i1}| \ . \tag{8.32}$$

8.4 Sign management within search

The interpretation tree is explored quasi-exhaustively using a depth first recursive search. Whenever a "cannot" constraint holds or a tree leaf is reached, the search backtracks. The management of the edge sign labels within this search framework is less straightforward however.

First we stress that a sign label only has meaning within the active interpretation — that is, the data–model pairings indicated by the current branch-to-root path in the interpretation tree. When the search algorithm considers an edge fragment, b say, for the first time in the active interpretation it will of course label its sign as (U). Suppose that in the course of applying the constraints we establish the sign of fragment b as $(+)$, for example. There are two quite different ways we could treat that information:

1. Following the depth first search strategy exactly, information about the sign of data fragment b should be allowed to affect only the assignment of data fragments $b' > b$, ie to propagate deeper into the tree. Then, if at any stage backtracking occurs to a higher level only assignments below that new higher level have to be reset to (U).

2. Knowledge about the datum b might be allowed to propagate in both directions. An example is given step by step in Figure 8.4. The search is verifying the ancestry of a branch at level b which

is putatively matched with model edge 7. In other words, we are performing the $b-1$ constraint checks between $[b, b-1]$, $[b, b-2]$, ..., $[b, 1]$ which for the example are answering questions such as: with datum $b-1$ matched with model edge 3 can or cannot datum b be matched with model edge 7, and so on. Suppose that while checking the $[b, n]$ pairwise constraint, the sign of b is established as $(+)$. Now, when making the remaining checks, $[b, n-1]$, ..., $[b, 1]$, we could use the newly found sign of b to establish the signs of fragments $n-1, \ldots, 1$ if these were not known. Thus knowledge is travelling back up the tree. If we allow this, to maintain consistency when backtracking we must either keep a detailed chart of sign labels' origins and dependencies or, whenever backtracking occurs, cause *all* the assignments on that root-to-branch path to be reset to (U).

If we follow plan (1) there is no inefficiency when backtracking, but sign ambiguities are more common in the early levels in the tree and the collective pruning power of the constraints is weakened. On the other hand, if we follow plan (2), the back-propagation of knowledge means that the constraints become tighter and pruning is more efficient early on, but there is either (a) an inefficiency when backtracking or (b) a computational overhead in maintaining the chart of sign dependencies. In practice we find that the back-propagation of sign information occurs rapidly and thus pruning efficiency is high early in the tree. As a consequence, we find so few paths in existence deeper in the tree that the opportunity for gross backtracking inefficiency under (a) above is low. Hence we adopt plan (2) but do not run a sign dependency chart.

In summary then, the tree is grown by depth-first search. Information about the sign of a fragment is allowed to move both ways in the tree, but when backtracking occurs all signs in the active interpretation are set to (U). In addition, whenever the sign of an edge fragment is determined absolutely, a search is instigated for any edge fragments whose signs depend on it and these are updated recursively.

Finally, we note that because of the movement of information both ways, a root-to-leaf interpretation delivered by the algorithm might not completely satisfy the constraints and the latest fragment signs. For example, when adding the final data edge to an interpretation, we might determine the sign of the first. With its newly found sign, the first datum

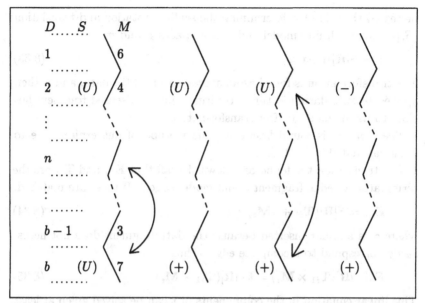

Figure 8.4: Four steps showing an example of back-propagation of sign information. D, M, S denote the data and model edge indices and the data edge sign. The pairwise ancestry of a tentative match of datum b with model edge 7 is being checked. While checking the validity of the $[b, n]$ pairwise matching (step 1) the sign of b is established as $(+)$ as shown in step 2. In step 3, when checking the pairing of $[b, 2]$, the newly found sign of b is used to determine datum 2's sign as $(-)$. Thus sign information has moved rootwards.

might not be compatible with the second, thus invalidating the entire interpretation. Thus each root-to-leaf interpretation is refiltered through the constraints. (Strictly this should be done iteratively; empirically, in numerous tests we have never required more than one refiltering step.)

8.5 Location stage and testing global validity

Because the constraints are applied successively to pairs of data there is no guarantee that the complete interpretations delivered or hypothesized by the search algorithm are consistent with a single global transformation between model and sensor spaces. The feasible interpretations must be tested therefore by determining the scaling, rotation and translation $(S, [\mathbf{R}], \mathbf{t})$ which link model and sensor spaces μ and σ:

$$\sigma = S[\mathbf{R}]\mu + \mathbf{t} \ . \tag{8.33}$$

The transformation is found as an average over all the data, and is then applied to each datum in turn, requiring that each sensed fragment lies close to its model edge after transformation.

The rotation is found first using the method of quaternions due to Faugeras and Hébert (1983).

The translation $\mathbf{t}$ is found as follows. Recall that $\mathbf{E}_{a1}$ and $\mathbf{T}_{i1}$ are the terminators of edge fragment a and model edge i. If these are matched:

$$\mathbf{E}_{a1} = S[\mathbf{R}](\mathbf{T}_{i1} + \gamma \mathbf{M}_i) + \mathbf{t} \tag{8.34}$$

where γ is a scalar inserted because the data fragment does not necessarily correspond to a complete edge. Thus

$$\mathbf{E}_{a1} \cdot [\mathbf{R}](\mathbf{T}_{i1} \times \mathbf{M}_i) = \mathbf{t} \cdot [\mathbf{R}](\mathbf{T}_{i1} \times \mathbf{M}_i) \ . \tag{8.35}$$

This linear equation in the components of $\mathbf{t}$ can be solved given at least three matched pairs with independent directions. Note that using two endpoints of one edge adds no information because

$$\mathbf{T}_{i2} \times \mathbf{M}_i = (\mathbf{T}_{i1} + \gamma \mathbf{M}_i) \times \mathbf{M}_i = \mathbf{T}_{i1} \times \mathbf{M}_i \ . \tag{8.36}$$

The scaling factor is found by eliminating $\mathbf{M}_i$ but not $\mathbf{T}_{i1}$ from equation (8.34) by using the fact that $\mathbf{M}_i \times (\mathbf{T}_{i1} \times \mathbf{T}_{i2})$ is certainly perpendicular to $\mathbf{M}_i$ but not necessarily perpendicular to $\mathbf{T}_{i1}$. Thus we find S from the average:

$$S = \left\langle \frac{(\mathbf{E}_{a1} - \mathbf{t}) \cdot [\mathbf{R}](\mathbf{M}_i \times (\mathbf{T}_{i1} \times \mathbf{T}_{i2}))}{[\mathbf{R}]\mathbf{T}_{i1} \cdot [\mathbf{R}](\mathbf{M}_i \times (\mathbf{T}_{i1} \times \mathbf{T}_{i2}))} \right\rangle \ . \tag{8.37}$$

8.5.1 Resolving the depth/speed scaling ambiguity

The edge data produced by visual motion processing suffer the depth/speed scaling ambiguity and we cannot use size when matching. We can regard the position vectors relating to the sensed fragments – the $\mathbf{E}$ – as being supplied to the matcher and locator using an assumed speed of $V_{assumed}$. Let us denote a supplied datum by $\mathbf{E}_{assumed}$.

Now, suppose S is computed as greater than unity: that means that we have oversized the data, and over-estimated the speed. Similarly for $S < 1$. Thus, it becomes obvious that to resolve the scaling uncertainty, the real or absolute position vectors should be

$$\mathbf{E}_{absolute} = \mathbf{E}_{assumed}/S \qquad\qquad (8.38)$$

and the absolute speed should be

$$V_{absolute} = V_{assumed}/S \ . \qquad\qquad (8.39)$$

It is worth noting that the unique resolution of the ambiguity relies on the model database containing uniquely sized objects. For example if it were to contain three cubes of different sizes, there would be three possible resolutions of the scaling.

8.6   Computer experiments

8.6.1   Performance tests

To test the performance of the constraints as a function of increasing uncertainty in the sensed data we use the simple model with thirty edges shown in Figure 8.5(a). Twenty-one of these model edges were visible in the views used for tests in which the sensed edge orientations were synthesized with increasing orientation and location error. Examples are given in Figure 8.5(b) where the orientation error is distributed about 15° and 30°.

In Figure 8.6 we show the relative computational effort required as a function of error angle, both with and without the absolute length constraint. It is seen that the computational effort rises slowly at first with increasing angle until some critical point where confusion sets in rapidly. The critical angle is of course model and data dependent, but the trend is typical. The other trend is that matching without absolute size is obviously less efficient, but not disastrously so.

8.6.2   Matching 3D edges from stereo

Although our main application of the matcher is to data from Chapter 4's motion processing algorithm, to indicate its generality we describe a test on data obtained from stereo processing. Figure 8.7 shows the wireframe model of a chipped block (with edges arrowed with their arbitrarily chosen directions) from which a stereo-pair is created and processed using the PMF stereo algorithm of Pollard, Mayhew and Frisby (1985) and the CONNECT algorithm (Pridmore, Bowen and Mayhew 1986) from the University of Sheffield's stereo system TINA (Porrill, Pollard,

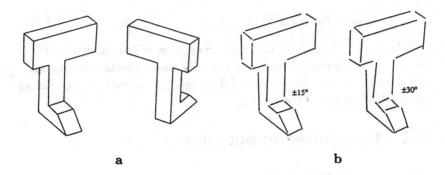

a   b

Figure 8.5: Front and back views of a wireframe object with 30 edges (a). In (b) are views of the data edges synthesized when the model edges are clipped and skewed by around 15° and 30°.

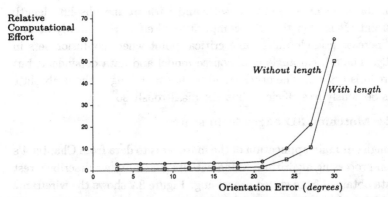

Figure 8.6: The relative computational effort expended during matching to the wireframe object with and without the edge length constraint for various orientation errors.

Pridmore, Bowen, Mayhew and Frisby 1987; Frisby and Mayhew 1990). The substantial 3D edge fragments are shown in Figure 8.7(c) along with their labels and arbitrarily chosen directions before matching.

From the 15^{12} ($\approx 10^{14}$) combinatorial possibilities, only one feasible interpretation was found after the pruning stage, which was run without the length constraint. The search time was around 3 seconds on a 3 Mips Sun 3/160. The data–model match and associated sign labels deduced are shown in Figure 8.7(e). The testing stage confirmed this feasible interpretation as geometrically valid, and the veridical and computed transformations are shown in Table 8.1.

Table 8.1: The computed transformation between model and sensor spaces derived from stereo processing compared with the veridical one derived a priori from the CSG body modeller.

Quantity	Computed			Veridical		
Rotation [R]	−0.68	0.01	−0.73	−0.71	0	−0.71
	0.38	0.85	−0.34	0.35	0.87	−0.35
	0.62	−0.51	−0.59	0.61	−0.50	−0.61
Scale S	8.77			8.96		
Translation t	(−41.6	−78.8	2485)	(−38.0	−81.7	2618)

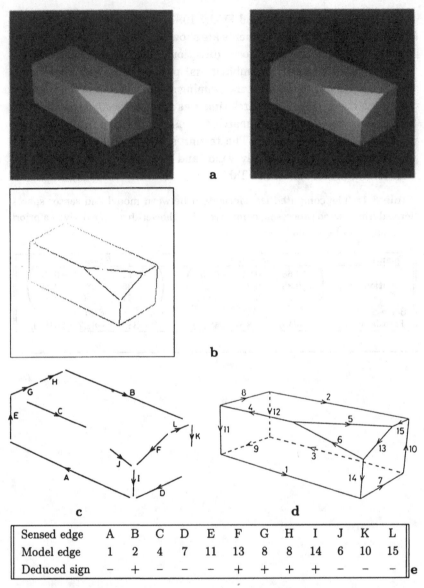

Sensed edge	A	B	C	D	E	F	G	H	I	J	K	L
Model edge	1	2	4	7	11	13	8	8	14	6	10	15
Deduced sign	−	+	−	−	−	+	+	+	+	−	−	−

Figure 8.7: Matching from stereo data. The stereo pair (a), the stereo depth map (b) (lighter is further away) and a view of the processed 3D edge fragments (c). The original model is in (d). The matching of data to model edges and the deduced sign compatibilities are shown in (e).

8.6.3 Matching 3D edges from motion

CSG house. The results of matching the reconstructed 3D partial wireframe of the CSG house, views of which were shown in Figure 4.6, to a small library of models are shown in Figure 8.8. One feasible interpretation is found during the search stage. Figure 8.9 shows other models to which no feasible match was found. The one feasible interpretation was verified and located, and the resulting transformation from model space to sensor space shown in Figure 8.10 applied to the house *model*. The model is moved into sensor space and reprojected onto the image. (The grey-scale relating to the image itself has been compressed and moved into mid-range for display purposes.)

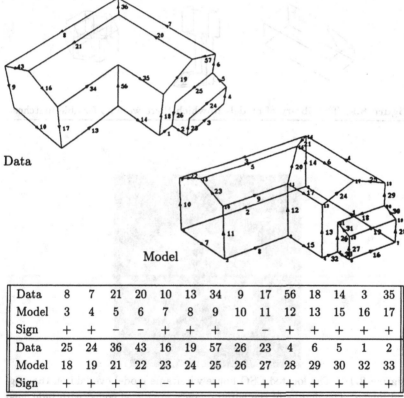

Data	8	7	21	20	10	13	34	9	17	56	18	14	3	35
Model	3	4	5	6	7	8	9	10	11	12	13	15	16	17
Sign	+	+	−	−	+	+	+	−	−	+	+	+	+	+
Data	25	24	36	43	16	19	57	26	23	4	6	5	1	2
Model	18	19	21	22	23	24	25	26	27	28	29	30	32	33
Sign	+	+	+	+	−	+	+	−	+	+	+	+	+	+

Figure 8.8: The data to model match for the CSG house.

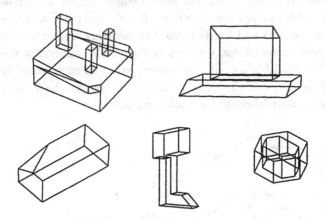

Figure 8.9: The library of models to which there were no feasible matches.

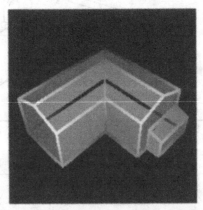

Figure 8.10: The located CSG house wireframe model overlaid on the original image. The depths of the wireframe are grey-level coded with light near to, dark far off.

Chipped block. The next example, in Figure 8.11, matches the data recovered in the structure from motion experiment described in Figure 4.8.

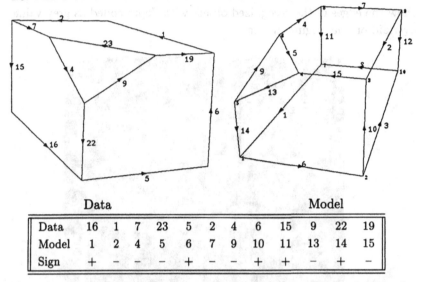

Data	16	1	7	23	5	2	4	6	15	9	22	19
Model	1	2	4	5	6	7	9	10	11	13	14	15
Sign	+	−	−	−	+	−	−	+	+	−	+	−

Figure 8.11: The sole feasible match for the block data (upper left) to the block model (upper right). No other match was found in the library of models.

The toy truck. The final example shows matching to the toy truck reconstruction of Figure 4.11. The detailed depth and motion values recovered have been given already in Table 4.4 but in Figure 8.12 we show the edges of the recognized object with depth coded as grey value overlaid on the original image.

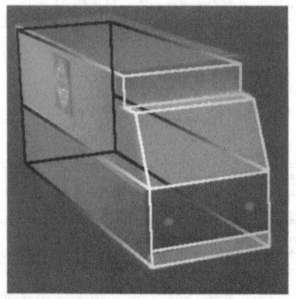

Figure 8.12: The located truck model overlaid onto the original image. The depths of the wireframe are grey-level coded.

8.7   Remarks

This chapter has described constraints which impose consistency between model edge and sensed edge fragment geometries in order to collapse the search space in model matching. The constraints have been successfully applied to synthetic edge data (which included errors), on data from stereo processing, and on data from visual motion processing. An important feature of the matching is the ability to attach sign labels to the data enforcing consistency with the model. This progressively increases the power of the constraints and assists in finding the transformation between model and sensor spaces. The constraints appear to satisfy the criteria suggested by Grimson (1984), being both effective and efficient, able to tolerate large errors and able to accept input from a wide variety of sensing modes.

The constraints have been demonstrated using the matching paradigm of Grimson and Lozano-Pérez in its simplest form. Although this works well on fully segmented scenes, the time required for quasi-exhaustive search becomes prohibitive when the data include edge fragments from other objects. To include data from other objects, each data edge must be given the opportunity to withdraw from the matching processing, effectively by matching to a wildcard model edge. The growth of the tree with wildcard matches can be limited only by pruning the search if more than a threshold number of wildcards have been included. To mitigate this effect Pollard, Porrill, Mayhew and Frisby (1987) have proposed a hybrid matcher which introduces a "feature-focus" stage (Bolles, Horaud and Hannah 1983) prior to the tree search. The longest data edges in a region of the image are chosen as feature-foci, and sub-tree searches are initiated for each focus edge and a small number of the longer edges in its neighbourhood. The model to sensor space transformation is found for each of these matched cliques, and those with consistent transformations are amalgamated.

Finally, recalling our primary aim stated at the start of the chapter, the reconstructions yielded by the method discussed in Chapter 4 certainly are capable of driving a higher level process.

8.8 Appendix

Here we determine the effective error-cone half angles α_{ab} and α_{ab}^{*} around the direction of $\hat{\mathbf{e}}_{ab}$. The former is the error when the signs of the fragments a and b are the same and the latter when they differ. If the signs are the same then

$$\hat{\mathbf{e}}_{ab} = \frac{\hat{\mathbf{e}}_a \times \hat{\mathbf{e}}_b}{\sin \gamma_{ab}} \tag{8.40}$$

and if different

$$\hat{\mathbf{e}}_{ab} = \frac{-\hat{\mathbf{e}}_a \times \hat{\mathbf{e}}_b}{\sin \gamma_{ab}^{*}} . \tag{8.41}$$

Here we pursue only the derivation of α_{ab}; that for α_{ab}^* is obviously similar. Recall that the values of $\hat{e}_a$ and $\hat{e}_b$ lie within cones of error with half angles α_a and α_b. That is, the possible sensed directions are $\hat{u}_a$ and $\hat{u}_b$ where

$$\cos \alpha_a \;\leq\; \hat{u}_a \cdot \hat{e}_a \leq 1 \tag{8.42}$$
$$\cos \alpha_b \;\leq\; \hat{u}_b \cdot \hat{e}_b \leq 1$$

The possible sensed directions of $\hat{e}_{ab}$ are therefore

$$\hat{u}_{ab} = \frac{\hat{u}_a \times \hat{u}_b}{|\hat{u}_a \times \hat{u}_b|} \; . \tag{8.43}$$

The extremal locus of $\hat{u}_{ab}$ is somewhat complicated, and for error analysis we conservatively adopt the error cone that everywhere encloses the extremal locus. This cone has half angle of

$$\alpha_{ab} = \max \left[\cos^{-1} \left(\hat{u}_{ab} \cdot \hat{e}_{ab} \right) \right] \; . \tag{8.44}$$

One caveat is that the angle γ_{ab} between fragments a and b must be less than $\alpha_a + \alpha_b$, else the error cones overlap, $\alpha_{ab} = \pi$ and direction constraint 3 is of no value.

The maximum value of the angle α_{ab} will be achieved at some point when $\hat{u}_a$ and $\hat{u}_b$ describe their extremal loci, as shown in Figure 8.13. A description of these loci in terms of parameters $\theta_{a,b}$ is

$$\hat{u}_a \;=\; \cos \alpha_a \hat{e}_a + \sin \alpha_a (\cos \theta_a (\hat{e}_{ab} \times \hat{e}_a) + \sin \theta_a \hat{e}_{ab}) \tag{8.45}$$
$$\hat{u}_b \;=\; \cos \alpha_b \hat{e}_b + \sin \alpha_b (\cos \theta_b (\hat{e}_{ab} \times \hat{e}_b) + \sin \theta_b \hat{e}_{ab}).$$

As shown in Figure 8.13, geometrical considerations indicate that the maximum angle α_{ab} is obtained when $\hat{u}_a$ and $\hat{u}_b$ lie in a plane tangential to both cones, where the plane lies above one cone and below the other so that θ_a and θ_b lie in different quadrants.

Looking along this plane it is clear that in this special situation the vector $(\hat{u}_a - \hat{u}_b)$ is orthogonal to both $(\hat{u}_a - \hat{e}_a / \cos \alpha_a)$ and $(\hat{u}_b - \hat{e}_b / \cos \alpha_b)$. Hence we find the two equalities:

$$\hat{u}_a \cdot \hat{u}_b = \frac{\hat{u}_b \cdot \hat{e}_a}{\cos \alpha_a} = \frac{\hat{u}_a \cdot \hat{e}_b}{\cos \alpha_b} \; . \tag{8.46}$$

Now, in the basis system $(\hat{e}_a, \hat{e}_b, \hat{e}_{ab})$, the scalar product of two vectors is

$$(p_1 q_1 r_1)(p_2 q_2 r_2)^T = p_1 p_2 + q_1 q_2 + r_1 r_2 + \cos\gamma_{ab}(p_1 q_2 + p_2 q_1). \quad (8.47)$$

Hence we find the following identities for the items in equation (8.46):

$$\hat{u}_a \cdot \hat{u}_b = (c_\gamma c_a c_b + s_\gamma c_b s_a \cos\theta_a - s_\gamma c_a s_b \cos\theta_b + \quad (8.48)$$
$$c_\gamma s_a s_b \cos\theta_a \cos\theta_b + s_a s_b \sin\theta_a \sin\theta_b)$$

$$\frac{\hat{u}_b \cdot \hat{e}_a}{\cos\alpha_a} = \frac{c_\gamma c_b - s_\gamma s_b \cos\theta_b}{c_a} \quad (8.49)$$

$$\frac{\hat{u}_a \cdot \hat{e}_b}{\cos\alpha_b} = \frac{c_\gamma c_a + s_\gamma s_a \cos\theta_a}{c_b} \quad (8.50)$$

where $c, s_\gamma = \cos, \sin\gamma_{ab}$; $c, s_a = \cos, \sin\alpha_a$; and $c, s_b = \cos, \sin\alpha_b$.

The equality of the right hand sides of these equations could supply two simultaneous equations in functions of θ_a and θ_b, from which α_{ab} could be derived. To simplify matters though, we continue the analysis conservatively assuming that both angular errors are equal to the larger of α_a and α_b.

Let us set $C = c_a = c_b$ and $S = s_a = s_b$. Then from the equality of each item in equations (8.49) and (8.50)

$$\frac{c_\gamma c_b - s_\gamma s_b \cos\theta_b}{c_a} = \frac{c_\gamma c_a + s_\gamma s_a \cos\theta_a}{c_b} \quad (8.51)$$

we see that $\cos\theta_b = -\cos\theta_a$ and, as θ_a and θ_b are in opposite quadrants, $\sin\theta_a = -\sin\theta_b$. Substituting in equations (8.48) and (8.50) we find a quadratic equation in $\cos\theta_a$:

$$\cos^2\theta_a S(1 - c_\gamma) + \cos\theta_a s_\gamma(2C^2 - 1)/C - S(1 + c_\gamma) = 0 . \quad (8.52)$$

The solution is

$$\cos\theta_a = (-y + (y^2 - 4xz)^{1/2})/2x \quad (8.53)$$

where $x = S(1 - c_\gamma)$, $y = s_\gamma(2C^2 - 1)/C$ and $z = -S(1 + c_\gamma)$. (The "minus square root" solution always gives an impossible value for $\cos\theta_a$.) From this equation we obtain a value for θ_a. We use this and $\theta_b = \pi + \theta_a$ in equations (8.45) to give $\hat{u}_a$ and $\hat{u}_b$ and then obtain α_{ab} from equation (8.44).

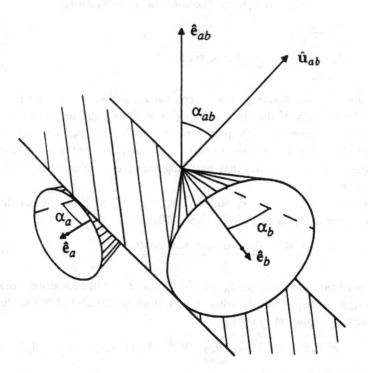

Figure 8.13: Cone geometry for error analysis.

9 Matching to Planar Surfaces

In the preceding chapter, we described in some detail a method for matching sensed edge data to wireframe models and applied it to the data obtained from the structure from motion algorithms described in Chapter 4. In this chapter we describe a method of matching surface normal data that can be applied to the polyhedral models obtained from the algorithms discussed in Chapter 5. Murray (1987) has described a method of matching surface normal and relative position data to CAD-type models. The method is based on the search strategy of Grimson and Lozano-Pérez (1984) and on their scaleless constraints, but corrects a slight defect in the development of the constraints.

9.1 The matching constraints

Following the method of the previous chapter, a data–model match is established by considering the compatibility of the following metrics between pairs of data patches (a and b) and pairs of model faces (i and j):

Data	$\hat{N}_a \cdot \hat{N}_b$	$\hat{N}_a \cdot \hat{D}_{ab}$	$\hat{N}_b \cdot \hat{D}_{ab}$	$\hat{N}_{ab} \cdot \hat{D}_{ab}$
	$\updownarrow$	$\updownarrow$	$\updownarrow$	$\updownarrow$
Model	$\hat{n}_i \cdot \hat{n}_j$	$\hat{n}_i \cdot \hat{d}_{ij}$	$\hat{n}_j \cdot \hat{d}_{ij}$	$\hat{n}_{ij} \cdot \hat{d}_{ij}$

The vector $\hat{N}_a$ is the unit normal to data patch a, $\hat{D}_{ab}$ is the unit vector in the direction between patches a and b, and

$$\hat{N}_{ab} = \frac{\hat{N}_a \times \hat{N}_b}{|\hat{N}_a \times \hat{N}_b|} \tag{9.1}$$

and similarly for the model metrics. The various vectors are illustrated in Figure 9.1. As with the edge matcher of Chapter 8, because the data normals have sensing errors, and because the model faces have finite extent, both sets of metrics exhibit *ranges* of validity, which must overlap for consistency.

The pairwise constraints have obvious similarities to those used for edge matching in Chapter 8, but are simpler to apply because there is no ambiguity in the direction of a surface normal as there is with the

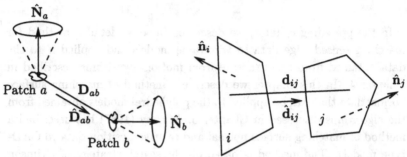

Figure 9.1: The vectors used for matching between the data (left) and model (right).

direction of an edge. The normal always sticks out of the surface into free space.

In each case we assume that sensed data patches a and b are being matched putatively with model faces i and j, respectively.

9.1.1   The angle constraint

This requires that the range of angles between the sensed surface normals of a and b embraces the angle between the normals of i and j on the model.

The model angle is

$$A_{ij} = \cos^{-1}(\hat{\mathbf{n}}_i \cdot \hat{\mathbf{n}}_j) \tag{9.2}$$

which, as in Chapter 8 earlier, may be computed once and stored off-line in a look-up table. The angle between the sensed normals is

$$\gamma_{ab} = \cos^{-1}(\hat{\mathbf{N}}_a \cdot \hat{\mathbf{N}}_b) \tag{9.3}$$

and, if the sensed surface normal $\mathbf{N}_a$ is surrounded by an error cone with half angle α_a and similarly for b, the condition for a valid pairing is:

$$\max[\gamma_{ab} - \alpha_a - \alpha_b, 0] \leq A_{ij} \leq \min[\gamma_{ab} + \alpha_a + \alpha_b, \pi] \ . \tag{9.4}$$

9.1.2   Direction constraints 1 and 2

Direction constraint 1 requires that for a valid match of data patches a and b with model faces i and j, respectively, the range of angles between the sensed surface normal at a and the direction of a vector joining the sensed data patches a and b must overlap the angle between the normal of model face i and the direction of any possible vector between a point on face i and a point on face j.

On the model we need to compute the range of $D_{ij} = \cos^{-1}(\hat{\mathbf{n}}_i \cdot \hat{\mathbf{d}}_{ij})$. The normal is fixed, but to be sure of covering the range swept out by $\hat{\mathbf{d}}_{ij}$ we must carry out an edge-edge test and a vertex-face test.

In the edge-edge test, $\hat{\mathbf{d}}_{ij}$ lies in the direction between any pair of points, one on any edge of face i, the other on any edge of face j. Using the notation of Chapter 8 we have

$$\mathbf{d}_{ij} = \mathbf{T}_{p1} - \mathbf{T}_{m1} - \rho\mathbf{M}_p + \eta\mathbf{M}_m \ , \tag{9.5}$$

for all edges m around model face i and all edges p around model face j, where ρ and η are in the range $(0,1)$ inclusive. For a given pair of edges,

$$\hat{\mathbf{n}}_i \cdot \hat{\mathbf{d}}_{ij} = c(\rho,\eta) = \hat{\mathbf{n}}_i \cdot \frac{\mathbf{T}_{p1} - \mathbf{T}_{m1} - \rho\mathbf{M}_p + \eta\mathbf{M}_m}{|\mathbf{T}_{p1} - \mathbf{T}_{m1} - \rho\mathbf{M}_p + \eta\mathbf{M}_m|} \ . \tag{9.6}$$

This function c has a form similar to that of the function f derived for the problem of matching edges in Chapter 8, although it does not tend to zero as ρ or η tend to infinity. If the 2D analytic extremum, $c(\rho_e, \eta_e) = +1$ or -1, found from solving $\partial c/\partial \rho = \partial c/\partial \eta = 0$, is inside the parameter window, then the other extremum (c_{min} or c_{max}, respectively) will be in the set of values

$$\{c(0,0) \ c(0,1) \ c(1,0) \ c(1,1)\} \ .$$

If however the analytic extremum is outside the window, then $c_{min,max}$ will be found in

$$\{c(0,0) \ c(0,1) \ c(1,0) \ c(1,1) \ c(0,\eta_0) \ c(1,\eta_1) \ c(\rho_0,0) \ c(\rho_1,1)\}$$

where the last four values are found from $\partial c(0,\eta)/\partial \eta = 0$ and so on, and only included if $0 \le \eta_0 \le 1$ and so on.

The extreme angles $D = \cos^{-1}c$ from the edge-edge test above must be compared with those from the vertex-face test. This accounts for the situations depicted in Figure 9.2 by testing whether any vertex of i can be joined to face j (or vice versa) by a vector $\mathbf{d}_{ij}$ of non-zero length along $\pm\hat{\mathbf{n}}_i$. If successful it means that one of the extreme angles is 0 or

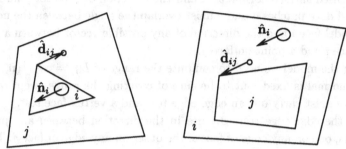

Figure 9.2: The vertex-face test for planar face matching accounts for cases where one face, j say, is wholly enclosed in the volume created by sweeping the other face i along its normal, $\hat{n}_i$, as in the right hand example.

π, depending on whether $\hat{d}_{ij}$ is along $+\hat{n}_i$ or $-\hat{n}_i$. The model data can again be precomputed and stored in a LUT.

Turning to the sensed data, the range of possible angles is

$$\max[\omega_{ab} - \alpha_a, 0] \rightarrow \min[\omega_{ab} + \alpha_b, \pi] \tag{9.7}$$

where $\omega_{ab} = \cos^{-1}(\hat{N}_a \cdot \hat{D}_{ab})$. For a valid pairing the sensed data and model ranges of angles must overlap.

Direction constraint 2 is similar to constraint 1, but viewed from data face b rather than a. It therefore requires no further explanation.

9.1.3   Direction constraint 3

This requires that the range of angles between the vector in the direction between the sensed data patches a and b and the mutual perpendicular to the sensed normals at a and b must overlap the range of angles measured from the model.

The model vector $\hat{n}_{ij}$ is

$$\hat{n}_{ij} = (\hat{n}_i \times \hat{n}_j)/|\hat{n}_i \times \hat{n}_j| \tag{9.8}$$

and so this constraint cannot be applied to model faces where the faces are parallel. On the model $\hat{n}_{ij}$ is fixed, but $\hat{d}_{ij}$ can vary. The extreme angles can be found using the method described for direction constraint 1. (There is however no need to perform the vertex-face test. Because $\hat{n}_{ij}$ is perpendicular to both normals, if there is a vector which joins the faces and lies along its direction, the faces must lie in the same plane, and thus the vector must intersect edges on both planes. Thus the vertex-face test is subsumed by the edge-edge test.) The maximum and minimum values of the angle are stored in the lower and upper triangles of a $g \times g$ LUT, F.

Turning to the data, the actual sensed value of the vector product is

$$\hat{\mathbf{N}}_{ab} = \hat{\mathbf{N}}_a \times \hat{\mathbf{N}}_b / \sin \gamma_{ab} \ . \tag{9.9}$$

We assume that it is surrounded by an error cone with half angle α_{ab} which is computed in precisely the same way as that for edge matching. If the angle $\lambda_{ab} = \cos^{-1}(\hat{\mathbf{N}}_{ab} \cdot \hat{\mathbf{D}}_{ab})$ then the range of sensed angles is

$$\max[\lambda_{ab} - \alpha_{ab}, 0] \to \min[\lambda_{ab} + \alpha_{ab}, \pi] \ . \tag{9.10}$$

For a valid pairing this range must overlap the range of angles in F.

9.2 Location stage

The search space is explored using plain depth-first search, here without the complications of maintaining sign consistency which were a feature of the edge matching.

However, just as in the case of matching with edges an interpretation which is feasible under the local pairwise constraints does not necessarily possess a valid global transformation $(S, [\mathbf{R}], \mathbf{t})$ relating model and sensor spaces, μ and σ, as:

$$\sigma = S[\mathbf{R}]\mu + \mathbf{t} \tag{9.11}$$

where $[\mathbf{R}]$ is a rotation matrix, $\mathbf{t}$ is a translation and S is a scaling factor. The transformation is derived in much the same way as in the previous chapter using first the technique of quaternions to obtain a least squares solution for the rotation and only then finding the translation and scaling.

9.3 An experimental example

Several examples of matching to synthesized data were given in (Murray 1987) where experiments were performed to evaluate various geometrical effects such as the positions of sensed patches within a planar face. Here we confine discussion to the recognition of the toy truck surface structure

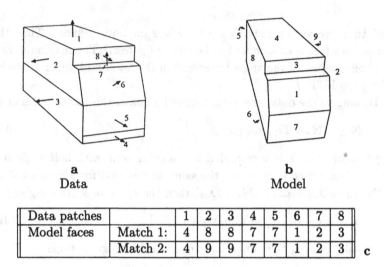

	Data patches		1	2	3	4	5	6	7	8	
	Model faces	Match 1:	4	8	8	7	7	1	2	3	
		Match 2:	4	9	9	7	7	1	2	3	

c

Figure 9.3: The surface patch data labelling (a) and model face labelling (b) used in planar surface matching, and the table (c) showing the two feasible matches found. The second of these is found globally invalid by transformation.

computed in Chapter 5 from a real image sequence taken with the camera approaching the truck.

Recall from that chapter that the first $3m$ components of η, the vector describing the various scene parameters, contain the surface normals of the m planar faces of the reconstructed object. The surface normals from η were normalized and placed at the centre of each reconstructed face, as shown in Figure 9.3(a). Figure 9.3(b) shows the labelling of faces of the surface model.

We find that there are two feasible matches — that is, feasible under the constraints — and these are shown in Figure 9.3(c). The two solutions arise because of the reflection symmetry of the truck; there is no difference between the angle between the surface normal of model face 8 and another model face and model face 9 and that model face. Thus data normals 2 and 3 are able to be matched (both) either to model face 8 or 9. However, running the location stage tells us that the second solution does not represent a valid global transformation, whereas the first does.

The scale factor derived for the globally valid interpretation finally

Table 9.1: The absolute 3D motion and depths recovered after matching and location. Rectilinear and angular velocities in mm per frame and radians per frame, positions in mm.

3D Motion	x	y	z
V	0.3	0.1	-17.9
Ω	2.10^{-4}	-5.10^{-4}	-2.10^{-4}
3D Structure	x	y	z
R_{19}	4.4	-26.2	534.6
R_1	-60.4	-17.5	561.2
R_8	89.6	20.7	719.2
R_7	93.5	71.0	719.5
R_6	18.1	32.3	555.6
R_{23}	18.5	14.8	559.6
R_{20}	-47.6	24.2	588.6
R_2	-52.6	19.9	571.2
R_{15}	11.7	11.2	544.7
R_{12}	-46.9	41.5	584.1
R_{13}	32.1	80.2	748.7
R_9	90.4	-17.0	736.3
R_{21}	2.9	-66.9	547.7
R_3	-62.4	-57.7	574.5
R_4	-62.6	-49.3	571.8
R_{22}	3.2	-58.4	544.8

resolves the depth/speed scaling ambiguity, enabling the recovery of *absolute* depths and translation velocity. These are given in Table 9.1. For comparison, the veridical width of the toy truck was 76mm and that recovered is 71.1mm; the veridical rectilinear velocity was $\mathbf{V} = (0, 0, -20)$mm per frame and that computed is $(0.3, 0.1, -17.9)$mm per frame.

10 Commentary

Our closing chapter draws together the strands of our work and, in a short essay on the current state of motion understanding, provides a context for future research. First, we discuss the importance of sensing and perception to the development of intelligently acting robot systems.

10.1 Sensing, perception and action

Perception is an essential precursor to intelligent action. Without it, actions can only be programmed, and robots are then little more than martinets able to give flawless displays in flawless environments. Whilst such perfection can be aspired to in the most basic robotic tasks, the need to create and maintain perfect surroundings, free from the uncertain and the unexpected, is a severe impediment to the deployment of robots in our everyday world. Certainly then, two key long term goals in robotics research must be first to enable robots to sense their environment, and secondly to enable them to make sense of the sensory data.

Because of inevitable imperfections in even strictly engineered worlds, even the most basic robotic systems incorporate some degree of simple sensing and some adaptive control mechanism. However, such primitive "perception" is not the issue addressed here. Rather, the issue is the exploitation of sensory data which are much richer in information, but in which the *useful* information is highly implicit — in the case of passive vision, implicit in the spatial and temporal correlations of the light received by the sensor. Making use of such data usually entails building perceptual models of the environment, models which become the basis for planned actions.

In our everyday world, awash with photon information, vision has a demonstrably crucial rôle to play in both sensing and perception, making it worthwhile — arguably imperative — to solve its formidable engineering and scientific problems. Principally and respectively these are the prodigious computational resources required (several hundred Mops for continuous operation) and the fact that, as mentioned above, information about the world is only implicit in the images captured. As Marr (1982) pointed out, vision is an information processing task. Moreover, it is an information processing problem that is compounded by the mathematical difficulties arising from the projection of the three spatial dimensions of the world onto the two dimensions of the imaging surface[1].

Making the information in an image or image sequence explicit as a perceptual model of the environment entails decoding correlations within the images and overcoming the loss of information which results from the projection from the world to the image. *Both* processes require constraints to be applied if they are to be carried out reliably and robustly. Exposing useful constraints has been the taxing and often elusive problem in computational vision of the last decade. The good news is that there has been considerable success in demonstrating the possibility of recovering high quality perceptual information through the application of sensible physical and geometrical constraints in data-driven processes.

The work we have described here is part, we believe, of the good news for motion understanding in computer vision. Our aim was to answer, with an appropriate emphasis on empiricism, questions about the sufficiency of information in visual motion for the task of building useful perceptual models, where the notion of "useful" was tested by seeing if visual motion could drive a complete interpretation chain from images to objects. It was not our aim to build motion processing systems per se. To have done so would have been to suggest, wholly misguidedly, that one sensory and perceptual mode alone is sufficient to effect robotic action in complex environments. Our purpose has been to demonstrate a visual competence rather than system performance.

The visual motion algorithm of Chapter 2, the segmentation and structure from motion algorithms of Chapter 4 and the matcher and locator of Chapter 8 comprise a complete processing chain from 2D images, through 2D and 3D edge representations, to 3D objects. This sequence is shown as a flow chart in Figure 10.1, where the columns embrace the principal tasks of computing visual motion, segmentation, structure from motion, and model matching.

A similar chart can also be drawn for the structure from motion method in which strictly polyhedral reconstructions are imposed (Chapter 5), with the edge matching and location stages replaced by those for planar surfaces described in Chapter 9. However, for the structure from motion techniques which recover planar surfaces directly, the process-

---

1) The reader needing to be convinced by this statement should consult the early German work on photogrammetry (eg (Kruppa 1913)) or recent work in machine vision (Maybank and Faugeras 1990; Maybank 1990) and algebraic geometry (Demazure 1988) on the reconstruction or "relative orientation" problem, masquerading in this book in its instantaneous form as the structure from motion problem.

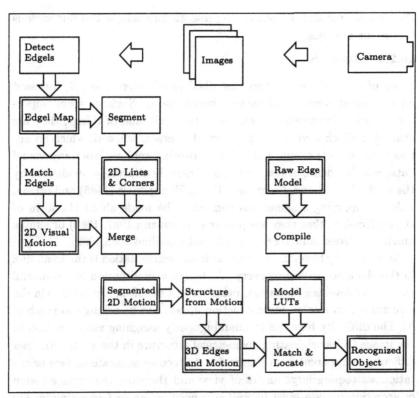

Figure 10.1: An overview of the entire edge structure from motion processing and recognition scheme.

ing chain from images to objects could not be completed. The weak link was the segmentation, which had to determine which visual motion data arose from which surface. We return to this problem later.

10.2 Representation

Here we review and discuss the representations adopted in our various processing schemes.

10.2.1 Surfaces

Much of our early work, here described in Chapters 6 and 7, focussed on the direct recovery of surface information. Surfaces seem important — they demarcate the extent of the solid stuff of things, they are that with which a robot gripper should interact, but with which an autonomous vehicle should not. But recovering surfaces from any visual data, whether dense or not, proves surprisingly difficult, as evidenced by the work of Blake and Zisserman (1987), Terzopoulos (1986) and others, unless simplifying assumptions can safely be made about the form of the surfaces, eg that they are planar (Grossmann 1987, 1989) or simple quadrics (Grossmann 1988; Mangili and Cassilino 1988,1989).

As we noted above, in our work at least, segmentation is the weak link in the chain to surface recovery. Although visual motion is a powerful cue for low-level segmentation, performing a simultaneous fusion via the structure from motion reconstruction appears to be asking too much of it. The difficulty here lies in unambiguously assigning visual motion in the image to its originating geometrical structure in the scene. Another difficulty is apparent from Figure 6.9: to recover accurate surface orientation we require large angles of view and therefore the surface fusion or accretion process must be well advanced before surface estimates are reliable — but at the same time we require good surface estimates to reliably segment and fuse the data. The process is obviously co-operative and highly nonlinear.

Experience shows that it is much easier to handle representations based on points and edges. We discuss these now.

10.2.2 Points

Point or corner features have the advantage of generality — they can be detected reliably in images from either indoor scenes containing mainly man-made objects or outdoor scenes dominated by natural features and vegetation. Moreover, their mapping onto the underlying scene geometry is usually unambiguous, point representations are easy to integrate over time and, using techniques such as Delaunay triangulation, it appears quite straightforward to make a surface representation explicit.

Indeed, Brady (1987) has argued that point or corner features are the most fundamental representation in machine vision: certainly in motion work Harris and colleagues (Harris and Pike 1988; Harris 1987; Charnley and Blisset 1989) have developed a most impressive 3D vision system (DROID) by integrating the motion of corner features over time in a long sequence. On the other hand, corners are sparse. More significantly, unless steps are taken to develop a combined corner and edge detector (Harris and Stephens 1988), corner features are isolated and therefore cannot be ascribed to a single object without the application of some underlying fusion principle such as consistent motion over time. In fact, this is precisely what good motion systems based on point features do. For example, in the application of Harris' system to vehicle navigation (Charnley and Blisset 1989), points not consistent with the motion of the vehicle through a rigid environment are rejected as outliers.

10.2.3 Edgels and linked edge segments

Edgels — the pixels marked as belonging to an edge feature by a detector such as Canny's and carrying orientation, strength and geometrical offset (sub-pixel acuity) information — are only slightly less general than point features. They are, however, far more plentiful in most images (especially those taken from scenes containing man-made objects) and, if a good edge detector is used, can be linked so that an attempt can be made to delineate geometrical objects. Some simple linking algorithms that can be used on the output of the Canny edge detector were described in §4.1. These performed satisfactorily for our experiments although it is likely that better algorithms could be devised if more modern edge detectors designed to preserve topology and geometrical information (eg (Fleck 1988a,b, 1989; Noble 1988a,b)) were used. As described in Chapter 4, our linking process was based on techniques from standard texts such as (Ballard and Brown 1982). Another linker which performs satisfactorily on Canny data has been designed by Giraudon and Garnesson (1987a,b) — a linker that has found favour as the first step in producing the straight edge segments used in the stereo work of Faugeras and colleagues at INRIA (eg (Ayache and Lustman 1987)) and that has been implemented as a finite state automaton in the DMA hardware suite (Faugeras, Deriche, Ayache, Lustman and Guiliano 1988).

10.2.4   The vertex-edge graph

Following linking of the edgels, the next step in our motion processing and recognition scheme (Figure 10.1) was to form the vertex-edge graph by coalescing linked edges and refining the position of vertices which had two or more edges entering them. Although not apparent in Chapter 4, our vertex-edge graphs suffer from a weakness that is also shared by systems based on corner features: problems are caused by T-junctions which are image features that do not arise from a single, well defined entity in the scene, but from the interaction of two edge features where one surface occludes another.

Such features are termed "multilocal phenomena" by those studying the details of object representations (Rieger 1987a,b) and can only be reliably distinguished from local phenomena such as distorted Y-junctions by reference to stereo data. This is indeed the route adopted in the Sheffield TINA stereo system (Porrill, Pollard, Pridmore, Bowen, Mayhew and Frisby 1987; Frisby and Mayhew 1990). Where stereo information is not available (for example, because it only becomes explicit later in the processing chain as in our systems), additional rules should be incorporated in the formation of the vertex-edge graph to break its connectivity at junctions that may be T's. In fact, our experimental examples were chosen so as to avoid T-junctions altogether since, for example in the work of Chapter 4, they would have left dangling edge segments whose depth could not be assigned.

Since T-junctions do not correspond to well defined features in the scene, it is interesting to note that the DROID motion system mentioned above has to adopt a strategy for ignoring all order three vertices that do not correspond to consistent structures in the scene (Stephens and Harris 1988)[2]. Furthermore, in the stereo and motion systems of Faugeras and colleagues (Faugeras, Lustman and Toscani 1987; Faugeras, Deriche and Navab 1989) the edge segments are deliberately not linked to vertices, although they are treated as belonging to one or more rigid objects.

---

2) Order one vertices — those with only a single incident edge fragment — are also ignored because of the intrinsic instability of edge detectors in locating where edges end.

10.3   Computing motion and depth

Computing image motion and scene depth (structure from motion) are
two problems that have received much attention in the vision literature
and a wide variety of approaches to each problem can be found. Many
of these enjoy considerable detailed mathematical support, though few
seem to have been tested to see if they can function as part of a larger
system, a test which, in our experience, is crucial.

10.3.1   Image motion estimation

Image motion estimation algorithms range from the very simple, dependent essentially on some form of grey-level differencing, to the complex,
incorporating a detailed model of the motion field, often a Markov random field model, and some maximum a posteriori probability measure.
Of course, the particular form of the algorithm depends on the image
representation to which it is applied, but both the above types of algorithm can be applied to the estimation of edgel motion and we and
our colleagues have done so (Buxton and Buxton 1984; Kashko, Buxton,
Buxton and Castelow 1988).

Unfortunately, simple differential schemes, even with considerable spatial and temporal smoothing, did not provide us with the required accuracy and reliability (the smoothing required to reduce noise causes
systematic errors). Furthermore, the more complex schemes proved too
fickle (there are several parameters that have to be correctly tuned) and,
even with access to a large scale parallel machine (Kashko, Buxton, Buxton and Castelow 1988), they were too computationally demanding to be
useful. The remaining candidates in the middle-ground were algorithms
based on cross-correlation and on matching of distinctive features, which
suffered the problem of sparseness outlined above.

It was into this scenario that the pixel patch matcher of Scott
(1987a,b) made its appearance. This algorithm almost worked well
enough for our purposes and treated the aperture problem in the estimation of edge motion in a very natural and elegant way. However,
as outlined in §2.1.1, the pixel patch sampling produced coarse-grained
results that were not quite accurate enough for our purposes. The solution we found was to sharpen the probability surface by using image
features more distinctive than pixels (ie Canny edgels) and by using a
Gaussian function in assigning the initial probabilities. These sharpen-

ing tricks (which are actually quite old — see for example the comments by Nishihara (1984) on the development of a stereo vision system) gave us the accuracy required and, with a few other ingredients to reduce systematic errors, we arrived at the edgel matching algorithm described in Chapter 2.

This algorithm has now been tested on many sets of images (including some taken not from the visible spectrum but from magnetic resonance images of parts of the body) and has rarely failed. The major drawback of the algorithm is its computational cost. However, as pointed out at the end of Chapter 2, the algorithm is inherently parallel (indeed, the original Scott pixel patch matcher has been implemented on a parallel machine (Kashko, Buxton, Buxton and Castelow 1988)) and the computational load can be reduced by windowing the search for matches and by utilizing results computed in previous frames. In fact, these measures could be most fully exploited if the algorithm were implemented as part of a Kalman filter to estimate the edgel motion, which would enable the complete predict-match-update cycle to be utilized. As pointed out at the end of Chapter 2, McIvor (1988) has made valiant efforts in this direction though with the intention of improving edge detection rather than motion estimation. The success of Kalman filters in estimating the motion of line segments (Crowley, Stelmaszyk and Discours 1988; Stelmaszyk, Discours and Chehikian 1988; Deriche and Faugeras 1990; Crowley and Stelmaszyk 1990) indicates that this is the way forward. Indeed, on-going estimates are essential: the perceptive reader will have noted that, unless a prediction of the expected rotation of edgels between frames is available, such rotation is limited to the few degrees $\pm\sigma_a$ around the default value of zero.

10.3.2   Depth estimation

The situation here was not dissimilar to that for motion estimation. Again, a great many algorithms of widely varying sophistication could be found in the literature on structure from motion. We, together with colleagues, had contributed to both ends of the spectrum — to straightforward depth estimation algorithms under particular simplifying assumptions (Buxton and Buxton 1984) and to more sophisticated algorithms (Buxton, Buxton, Murray and Williams 1984; Buxton, Murray, Buxton and Williams 1985) that had been analyzed mathematically in some detail.

Our experience then was that despite the notorious instability of structure from motion algorithms (this was already appreciated back in 1984) we were able to obtain encouraging results and, *given enough data*, at least one algorithm, the planar facet algorithm, could work with relatively crude motion estimates from a simple gradient-based scheme (for an example see (Buxton and Williams 1986)). In this respect our findings were similar to those of Waxman and colleagues who, at about the same time, were investigating an approximate algorithm to compute the structure and motion of curved surface patches (Waxman and Wohn 1985; Waxman, Kamgar-Parsi and Subbarao 1987) (and for later work along same lines see (Subbarao 1988)).

The major problem in this case was that, except in some specialized navigation tasks, one could not assume a simple global form for the surface in view. In particular, it was necessary to segment the scene, ie group the data into sets belonging to different surfaces, especially as we wished to perform object recognition in order to test our algorithms objectively. Our attempts to surmount the segmentation problem were described in Chapter 7. Once again, the reader will notice that we tried techniques at either end of the complexity spectrum — one based on Markov random field models of high complexity that aimed to achieve an optimal, global segmentation (§7.1) and the other a very simple scheme based on familiar image processing operations (§7.2) that aimed at local segmentation. Both worked on computer simulations, but neither could be used successfully on the real visual motion data we had available to us. Unfortunately, in this case, we were unable to come up with a satisfactory algorithm which lay between the two extremes.

So, although the planar facet structure from motion algorithms were extensively tested as described in Chapter 6, and are now attractive candidates for incorporation into a Kalman filter for navigation tasks, we could not use them to complete a chain to object recognition. For this purpose we chose to adopt a more conventional segmentation based on the image vertex-edge graph and developed new structure from motion algorithms tailored to this representation.

The algorithms so obtained were described in Chapters 4 and 5. Both depend on a partial wireframe representation of the object and both treat the depths of the vertices of the object as the quantities to be estimated. In Chapter 4, these depths were independent variables (apart from an overall depth/speed scaling) whereas in Chapter 5 polyhedral constraints of the kind introduced by Sugihara (1984) for the interpretation of line drawings were imposed. The algorithm described in Chapter 4 generally left the faces of an object somewhat distorted and twisted, while the constrained algorithm of Chapter 5 yielded flat faces, but at the expense of some loss of generality and of the computational effort required to determine an independent set of vertex depths.

More notable in the present context was that both algorithms exhibited an instability associated with the bas-relief ambiguity and that, this apart, both algorithms were gratifyingly stable.

The instability arises because is it is difficult to distinguish the effects of a translation across the image plane (V_x say) from a rotation about an axis in the plane (Ω_y). Their distinction requires reliable data on the second order deformations of the flow field (Koenderink and van Doorn 1975; Maybank 1986, 1987a,b; Scott 1987b), which in turn demands wide viewing angles with strong perspective effects. In our experiments, the instability manifested itself as incorrect estimates of V and Ω and, consequently, as a slight distortion of the object's shape. However, the results obtained were good enough to enable the subsequent geometric model matching and location algorithms to work, and the problem could be, and was, alleviated by supplying prior knowledge of the rotation.

The surprisingly good performance of the algorithms has already been mentioned in the discussion on visual motion segmentation at the end of Chapter 7. It depends on the fact that the most stable reconstructions in a structure from motion calculation are obtained from objects which have a depth change commensurate with their lateral extent (Maybank 1986). This condition is fulfilled by the polyhedral objects we used in Chapters 4 and 5.

10.4   Object recognition and location

Our motives for including object recognition in this work were twofold. First, we were interested in recognition without using absolute size, where our conclusion is that this is possible without disastrous loss of efficiency. Secondly, as we have stressed several times, we needed some objective measure of the quality of the structure from motion reconstructions.

Since, from the work of Chapters 4 and 5, we had two successful structure from motion reconstructions available, the first yielding data related to object edges and the second yielding data on object surfaces, two recognition and location algorithms were required. These were described in Chapters 8 and 9 for matching to edges and planar surfaces respectively. Both match the partial object descriptions obtained from the structure from motion algorithms to complete CAD-type models. Both use the pairwise constraint pruning strategy developed by Grimson and Lozano-Pérez (1984) to control the search for a correct match of object features to model features. Also, because of the depth/speed scaling ambiguity in structure from motion calculations, neither matcher utilizes absolute distance or size. In this sense, they are primitive *shape* recognition algorithms.

Both of the matching algorithms are followed by a least squares location and verification algorithm which, if necessary, determines the best global match between models in the database and the object and the best estimates for the object's position, orientation and size. These location and verification algorithms contain little that is novel once familiarity is established with quaternions or some other method of efficiently determining rotations, such as using matrix exponentials or singular value decompositions. Of greater interest are the matching algorithms, in particular the edge matcher described in Chapter 8.

10.4.1 The edge matcher

The major problem confronting the edge matcher is that edges, unlike surface normals, are directors not vectors. This means that, whereas we always know which way a surface normal is pointing (outwards because only the outside of a surface is visible [3]), we cannot infer the direction of an edge fragment locally. It can be either way round, as shown in Figure 10.2.

Since, in the CAD-type models we use, edges are represented by their end points chosen in some arbitrary order, they are actually represented as vectors whose signs, though arbitrary, are fixed. The same is true of the sensed object edges, and the relationship between the two choices has to be determined during the matching. Handling this introduces an additional labelling problem in the search for a match between object and model, in the course of which a consistent set of directions amongst

---

3) This is strictly true even when inside a box; although the situation can become complicated in an origami world of infinitesimally thin paper (Kanade 1981).

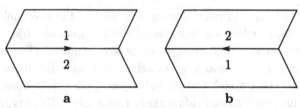

Figure 10.2: The direction of an edge fragment can be either way round, with surface 1 above surface 2 as in (a) or vice versa as in (b).

the set of sensed object edges is established. The details were given in Chapter 8, but two points are noteworthy. First, two of the so-called pairwise direction constraints *determine* the sign of an edge direction whilst the third direction constraint and the angle constraint *propagate* signs consistently through the overall interpretation. Secondly, it was found to be efficient to allow edge sign information to propagate both down and *up* an active branch of the interpretation tree. Although propagation of sign information back up the tree causes an inefficiency when backtracking occurs in the depth first search, this is more than compensated for by the tightening of the pairwise constraints which results from being able to use vectors rather than directors as the matching moves deeper into the search tree.

The edge matcher worked well in practice and, with the final location and verification algorithm, enabled us to *quantitatively* test the performance of our algorithms and of a complete processing chain from image sequences to recognized objects (Murray, Castelow and Buxton 1989).

10.4.2   The planar surface matcher

Since there is no ambiguity in the direction of a surface normal, the planar surface matcher described in Chapter 9 is much simpler to apply than the edge matcher. For this reason and the fact that the number of surface facets on an object is always less than the number of edges, surface matching would generally be preferred. Unfortunately, as mentioned in §10.2.1, reliable surface data are much harder to acquire than edge data, so that in practice edge matching is often more appropriate. This is generally true, whether data are acquired by motion or by stereo, or by a combination of the two via the fusion of multiple views, although recent work on grouping edge segments into simple surfaces (Grossmann

1987, 1988, 1989) may be tipping the balance back in favour of surface matching.

In our work, data appropriate to surface matching could be obtained from the structure from motion calculation by imposing Sugihara's polyhedral constraints (although a number of simpler, less rigorous options could also have been used) at the expense of some loss of generality. Like the edge matcher, the surface matcher worked well in practice and similarly, after location and verification, enabled us to test quantitatively the constrained structure from motion algorithm. Given that the surface matcher is fed data which are more constrained than those fed to the edge matcher (it utilizes more prior knowledge) and that the search space is simpler, its good performance is only to be expected.

10.5 What next?

Of course this can't be the end of the story. In our own work, in seeking the shortest path towards object recognition, we have to an extent diverted ourselves from current issues in motion research which include: the development of qualitative descriptions of shape and motion, the pursuit of time evolving systems, integration of sensory and perceptual modes, and the study of control within vision. It is fitting to close with a brief foray into some of these areas and, in particular, to speculate on future lines of research.

10.6 Perception begets action

Our work has addressed the two goals of robotics mentioned early in this chapter, those of sensing and perception. But to the engineer, machine perception as an end in itself is somewhat sterile, smacking perhaps of 'machine philosophy'. As we noted earlier, perception should beget the third goal in robotics, action.

A criticism that can be levelled at most work in motion understanding in the 1980s, ours included, is that, because of the scientific and engineering difficulties (particularly the latter), the interdependencies of perception and pursuant action have barely been touched upon. Most work to date has been carried out in the static or near static regime, with scant regard to what came before or what went after. For some time researchers involved with motion processing have been acutely aware of the limitations of this and, indeed, of the overall paucity of knowledge of the behaviour of 3D vision outside a time span of a few interframe periods. The need to introduce dynamic processes is increasingly evident in areas which were formerly regarded as static domains, such as edge detection, segmentation, stereo and so on.

The lack of exploitation of the constraint of temporal continuity is unfortunate, for such continuity affords predictability which in turn enables focussing of visual computational resources or visual attention. Given the scientific and engineering challenges posed by 3D vision, predictability is a scientific imperative and focussing of resources an engineering necessity.

Moreover, just as it is impossible[4] to simulate the rich complexity of static scenes and images (using, say, constructive solid geometry), so is it impossible to simulate the complex interweaving of events which must occur when an automaton interacts with its environment. In other words, there is no substitute for doing it *for real*, and the scientific and engineering challenges have to met simultaneously. Introducing the complexity of such dynamic processing to create and maintain a central time-evolving percept of the world is like climbing to the next storey of an engineering *zikkurat*, but some of the delights of the new ground are being surveyed and explored already.

10.7 Dynamic vision

One example is the work of Porrill (1988) who has integrated multiple 3D reconstructions from a stereo sensor to reduce geometric uncertainties. The approach is similar to that of Durrant-Whyte (1987), whose primary interest lay with the integration of geometric information supplied by several different sensors rather than the temporal integration of data from a single sensor. Their work forms part of a solid body of evidence that 3D geometry is an appropriate representation for integration of multi-sensor and multi-temporal data (Kapur and Mundy 1989), though Brady (1990) suggests that more attention might be given to the integration of multi-temporal data within the image space.

---

4) Impossible, that is, without the inordinate effort devoted to some of the latest radiosity calculations in computer graphics.

The use of Kalman and extended Kalman filters in dynamic computer vision has been championed by Faugeras and co-workers. Faugeras, Lustman and Toscani (1987) and Ayache and Faugeras (1988) have demonstrated the updating of point and line matches, obtaining much improved noise tolerance over the earlier but essentially similar structure from motion results of Longuet-Higgins (1981). Their procedures have enabled an autonomous vehicle to move under visual control (Robert, Vaillant and Schmitt 1990). More recently Faugeras, Deriche and Navab (1989) have extended the previous analysis to include continuously moving lines, where they assume that the position, velocity and acceleration of the lines are available.

A most compelling example of dynamic updating in motion processing is the work of Harris and colleagues (Harris 1987; Harris and Pike 1988), which has received considerable industrial development on a mobile vehicle (Charnley and Blisset 1989). As noted in §10.2.2, in this system the positions of 2D grey-level corners are tracked and the corresponding 3D points updated using a Kalman filter. Surfaces are postulated over the points by projecting a 2D Delaunay triangulation into the scene. Navigable regions are then proposed by coalescing triangles with a similar orientation (near-horizontal) to those about to be driven over. Outdoor sequences show that corners remain reliable features even in areas (eg road surfaces) which would not at first be regarded as being dominated by such features. They demonstrate that navigable paths can be maintained over periods of tens of seconds.

A rather different approach was presented by Matthies, Szeliski and Kanade (1989) who, under the assumption of known camera motion, ascribed a best estimate of depth to each pixel in the image, and updated these values using, again, a Kalman filter. Finally we note that Pollard, Porrill and Mayhew (1990) recently outlined the modifications required to incorporate a feed-forward mechanism into stereo processing in the TINA system.

A common feature of the above examples is that they do not depend on having a detailed prior model of the scene or objects likely to be viewed. Model-based vision systems, however, do rely on such information. A notable example of dynamic model-based vision is 'The Walker' of Hogg (1983,1988) in which projected 3D generalized cylinders are fitted in image space to a walking human figure, using the representation of Marr and Nishihara (1978). Image motion and constraints on joint angles are

used to direct the search for limb positions in the next frame. Lowe
(1990) has recently reported the inclusion of temporal tracking within
his model-based system (Lowe 1985) using the viewpoint consistency
constraint. Bray (1990) has a similar system which uses visual motion
to maintain tracking. Both systems are quite robust to occlusion, though
it may be that tracking in 3D would allow a plant model with a longer
history to be maintained.

Closing the loop in dynamic vision is not restricted to 3D percepts. We
have already noted the work of Crowley, Stelmaszyk and Discours (1988)
in tracking extended 2D line segments, and that of McIvor (1988) who
used a Kalman filter to track individual edgels. A technical difficulty in
the latter is that matching cannot be one-to-one (also the case in the
edgel matching algorithm of Chapter 2). This problem is avoided by
Brint and Brady (1990) who implemented a curve matching algorithm
based on an active snake (Kass, Witkin and Terzopoulos 1987), and
Blake and Cipolla (1990) have demonstrated that snake matching can
be formulated as a dynamic process.

10.7.1   Remarks

Although the early work in dynamic vision has demonstrated some of the
advantages of temporal updating (and, equally importantly, of choosing
an appropriate representation to update), it might give the impression,
first, that dynamic vision is little more than optimal temporal filtering and, secondly, that the time-evolving percept is little more than an
updateable data structure.

There are however more powerful predictive possibilities inherent in
the time-evolving percept. These suggest that the needs of the task
in hand and the information available in the percept should be able to
direct not only the sensors, but also the sensory processing carried out by
the vision system. Prediction should enable the vision system to make
judgements about where and how to focus its attention. This possibility
is exemplified by recent work on reactive vision.

10.8   Reactive vision

One successful approach to 3D vision over the last few years, of which
our work is a part, involves data-driven processing in which operators

are applied uniformly to data at one level with the results being passed up to a higher level. This approach arose naturally enough in an attempt to validate the computational paradigm of machine vision espoused, perhaps most prominently, by Marr (1982).

However, to describe the approach as data-driven obfuscates the fact that it is largely *image*-driven. Such an approach is imperfect in three regards. First, it makes the assumption that "the more data the merrier". Although it is the case that the more intelligent sensing the merrier, the indiscriminate amassing of data is futile. It makes little sense on grounds of interpretability — a data-driven process can do nothing more than assume that there is a higher level that can and *needs* to process its output. For many vision tasks this is demonstrable nonsense. Secondly, to drive processing and thence action in the real 3D world on the basis of an impoverished 2D projection of reality alone is perverse. Finally, computational resources are wasted calculating information of doubtful utility, which is quite indefensible given the heavy computational loads inherent in visual processing.

This should be compared with the approach of reactive vision, where the credo is that if an agent interacts with the world and has active control over and percept of its own state, then many problems in sensing, perceiving, planning and acting become easier (Brown 1989b). However, as with dynamic vision, before things become easier there are significant hurdles to overcome. Perhaps the highest of these is that planning and control, which, with sensing, have formerly been treated as separate issues in robotics, now need to be integrated at a much lower level — indeed right down at that of sensory data acquisition and early processing.

10.8.1 Controlled attention

Potentially the most powerful method for achieving control of sensing and attention is by physical redirection of the sensors in gazing and converging movements, thereby fixating scene points of interest on the image. There are, or have been, several examples of such moving head/eye systems: that at MIT (Cornog 1985), at the University of Pennsylvania (Krotkov, Summers and Fuma 1986; Krotkov 1987, 1989) at Harvard (Clark and Ferrier 1988) and, currently the most advanced, that at the University of Rochester built by Ballard, Brown and co-workers (Ballard 1987; Ballard and Ozcandarli 1988; Brown 1988, 1989a, 1989b).

Cornog's early system, though now to our knowledge defunct, was interesting in that it used two electromechanical crossed-mirror devices to fixate and track moving objects. The system had six degrees of freedom, more than the three degrees of freedom actually required to track a 3D object. The emphasis of the work was on control and on a comparison of the system with the primate oculomotor system. The simple vision system was able to pursue a white sphere placed against a dark background smoothly at up to $15°s^{-1}$ (about half the rate of primates) but only over short intervals because of limitations in the camera platform mounting.

The remaining systems mentioned use steerable cameras. In the Rochester system for example, two cameras share a common tilt platform on the head, but have independent pan axes. The head platform itself is mounted on a six degree of freedom arm and is able to move quickly, at $\sim 1ms^{-1}$ for whole head translation and $300°s^{-1}$ for camera rotation. Some indication of the data throughput can be gained from the computing resources: the video output is processed by a Datacube pipeline-parallel image processing system that can do much of the low and intermediate level visual processing at video frame rate, which in turn is hosted by a BBN Butterfly Parallel Processor with twenty four nodes.

However, introducing the flexibility of moving cameras has several far reaching consequences. First, on the practical front, it makes 'conventional' advanced calibration techniques impracticable. Most recent stereo systems have cameras which converge in order to increase the working volume close to the cameras. The assumption of rigid rotation between left and right cameras was first explored by photogrammetrists many years ago (Kruppa 1913; Thompson 1959), and is now regarded as usual in computer vision (Longuet-Higgins 1981; Tsai and Huang 1981; Pollard, Mayhew and Frisby 1985; Ayache and Lustman 1987). However, to recover accurate depths, systems of this type require laborious calibration of the camera geometry (Tsai 1986; Faugeras and Toscani 1986), restricting their use to arbitrary but *fixed* angle of convergence. Current moving head/eye systems are not engineered to a degree where the calibration can be maintained during movement, and thus far have been used only for qualitative stereo measurements.

The second, and most fundamental consequence of cameras capable of controlled movements is the potential of new ways of processing visual information. Reactive vision, with its ability to shift gaze onto a region of maximal visual pertinence, can not only quicken some sorts of processing, but also *enable* new visual processing paradigms. Indeed, Ballard suggests that the primary reason for many of the difficulties experienced in 3D computer vision may be attributable to the assumption that the vision system is passive. Certainly, in reactive vision some of the degrees of freedom are under direct control: Aloimonos, Weiss and Bandyopadhyay (1987), for example, have demonstrated how this extra constraint can turn problems (such as shape from shading, texture and contour) from being ill-posed for the passive observer to being well-posed for the active observer.

But Ballard (see (Ballard and Ozcandarli 1988)) believes that the inherent advantages of reactive vision run deeper, and makes the following assertions. First, eye movements facilitate the representation of the structure of early vision with respect to an object-centred reference frame pinned to the fixation point and the eye. Next, the formulation of constraints is ameliorated around the fixated region of interest, because the mathematics involves expansions around the coordinate origin; and finally that controlled eye movements provide a mechanism for storing and accessing spatial data — because the scene is always available for re-inspection it effectively becomes part of the machine's memory.

Ballard's assertions, which are as yet barely tested, have a very different emphasis from those of Marr on viewer-centred coordinates for early and intermediate level vision. It remains to be seen what degree of overlap, reinforcement and conflict there is between the passive and reactive approaches — but in the meantime the University of Rochester group continues to produce compelling demonstrations of real-time reactive vision, so far including the kinetic depth effect, smooth pursuit, saccadic motion, active vergence and vestibular ocular reflex.

The third issue raised by permitting controlled camera movements is that of control, an issue equally relevant to dynamic vision.

10.9 Vision and control

Incorporating feedback into visual processing introduces the need for closed loop control. Unfortunately, control systems have been developed around simple scalar or low dimensional vector parameters, and not for anything as complex as the shape representations that are of concern in 3D vision.

One example of this is the work of Khatib (1986), who describes the COSMOS system architecture which supports certain cases of sensor based control. In one application, obstacle avoidance paths are computed in real-time using vision, but only on the basis of 2D position data supplied by a simple 2D vision module. Another example is the work of Andersson (1988) who has constructed a ping-pong playing robot whose skill level is quite remarkable. The system is based on a blackboard control architecture and uses special hardware for real-time computation of the motion of the ball. Low level modules find the ball as a white blob against a dark background, higher level modules compute the 3D velocity while other modules occasionally compute the trajectory, including spin and bounce, and the highest level modules compute a trajectory for the arm and bat to return the ball. Again, the system points the way forward in real-time control, but has relatively crude visual capabilities. Dickmanns and co-workers (Dickmanns and Zapp 1986; Dickmanns 1988) have developed a sensor based control system which can guide a vehicle along an autobahn at speeds up to 60km/h. The vision system picks up white lines and the edges of the road, but makes strong assumptions about the visibility of such features and the complete lack of other vehicles. Again, the visual situation is constrained and it is not obvious how the controller could be extended to cover more complex visual situations.

Introducing cameras whose motion is under visual control introduces a more fundamental change to the visual control loop. The purposive "percept-driven" vision system outlined in the credo of reactive vision cannot of itself account for all activities the visual system must perform. For example, there is no explicit mechanism for response to situations or events which are not causally linked to those already being attended to. A further requirement therefore is a reflexive response to new situations of interest. Such a response is likely to be driven from early levels of the vision system, and one idea (Ballard and Ozcandarli 1988) is that these visual units may have control strategies similar to the task hierarchies of Brooks (1986, 1989). Brown (1989b) has studied some of the control issues involved in reactive vision, simulating five responses from the Rochester head, viz: saccadic motion, smooth pursuit, vergence, vestibular ocular reflex (an open loop proportional-gain eye control which counteracts head motion with eye motion) and head compensation (which rotates the head to keep the eyes centred and away from their mechanical stops). He discovered that the critical technical issue in introducing feedback control was that of process delay, but more surprisingly, that mutual information was needed to cope with non-uniform delays, a result which runs counter to Brooks' ideal of independent reflexes which know nothing about each other.

The strong message from Brown's work is that the control paradigms required, far from being simple, are at the frontiers of current practice. Clearly, as evidenced in both dynamic and reactive vision, visual control is becoming an issue of increasing concern for machine vision.

10.10 Recognition

One of the major advantages of a rich sensory mechanism such as vision is that it enables recognition. Recognition is a nonlinear decision process: this means not only that it extends the useful signal to noise ratio; but also that processing power and speed can be traded for memory, that the overall information processing system can be made more robust, and that its performance can be enhanced by access to prior knowledge. The term recognition is most often used narrowly in computer vision to mean the detection and identification of objects in an image or scene — unfortunately so, for it is clear that many low-level image processing operations actually involve the same sort of nonlinear decision making. Edge detection is a good example, and the fitting of straight lines or circular arcs to edge pixels is another. Unfortunately, in both cases aspects of the mathematical analysis of the performance of filters, fitting algorithms and so on often obscures this fact, more especially when analysis of the pattern recognition and decision criteria is suppressed or ignored. (Devijer and Kittler 1982). However, recent work aimed at developing detectors that preserve edge topology and geometry (Fleck 1988a,b, 1989) does place more emphasis on the pattern recognition aspects.

There is a second way in which the term recognition is used narrowly in computer vision that illustrates yet again that temporal aspects of vision have received relatively little attention. This is that events, situa-

tions and phenomena are also candidates for recognition (see the work of
Nagel (1988) and many of the references therein, Neumann (1984, 1989),
Mohnhaupt and Neumann (1990) and Buxton and Walker (1988)). Recognizing such temporal phenomena in vision[5] requires a much deeper
understanding of behaviour and of goals. As Nagel wrote in 1988, these
aspects of vision are still in an exploratory phase, certainly when compared with the well developed state of geometric object recognition.

10.10.1   Higher level and improved matching

As already discussed in §10.4, our work in object recognition and location was based on the method of Grimson and Lozano-Pérez. Grimson
regards the approach as one of matching partial descriptions of the sensory data to complete descriptions of the models (Grimson 1984). By
partial data, Grimson refers to low-level tokens at the level of the $2\frac{1}{2}$D
sketch which have not been combined into high level volumetric or surface descriptions. This is very much in the mould of bottom-up vision
proposed by Marr (1982) and Barrow and Tenenbaum (1978) with an
object-centred description being computed from information in the $2\frac{1}{2}$D
sketch. The approach has had remarkable success, and other examples include work by Faugeras and Hébert (1983), Stockman and Esteva
(1984), Turney, Mudge and Volz (1985) and Pollard, Porrill, Mayhew
and Frisby (1987).

A reservation about matching low level primitives is that, despite
the work of Grimson and Lozano-Pérez (1987) on techniques to reduce
further the size of the search space, the combinatorics remain such that
one cannot conceive of using the method for matching ever more data to
ever more complex models. Other approaches, to use the classification
of Grimson (1984), are to match 'complete data to complete models',
or to match 'partial data to partial models'. In the former, 'complete'
means data which have been compiled from lower level primitives: an
example is ACRONYM (Brooks 1981) which finds the trapezoidal ribbon
projections of generalized cylinders in the image and matches these to
hierarchical models described in terms of the 3D generalized cylinders.
In the latter approach the search space is reduced by choosing only the
most salient features of the data and models for matching. Examples
are the work of Connolly, Mundy, Stenstrom and Thompson (1987) who

---

5) Indeed, in general — see (Shoham 1988).

used 2D features to recognize 3D objects, and that of Bolles, Horaud and Hannah (1983) whose 3DPO system used 3D salient data features for matching to 3D models. The success of these other approaches highlights the importance of saliency in the model and data representations and also, in the case of ACRONYM, of structured hierarchical models.

At a higher level, considerable work is needed on how to organize model databases and on how to invoke likely models for detailed matching (Fisher 1989). Progress here may derive from principled work on large databases and on optimization and content-addressable memory using networks (Hopfield and Tank 1985).

A further observation is that few established recognition algorithms have been implemented in parallel — this remark notwithstanding the work of Flynn and Harris (1985) who implemented Grimson and Lozano-Pérez's tree search on the Connection Machine (an algorithm profligate with processors) and that of Holder and Buxton (1990) who implemented a far more efficient version on the AMT DAP. Moreover, there seems to be little concerted investigation into the intrinsic parallelism in model invocation and recognition. This is in marked contrast to the large effort expended at the early levels of the visual processing hierarchy, and is perverse in that even in our work the recognition stage represents an appreciable fraction of the total computing time. As further evidence we note that the recognition stage of the TINA stereovision system (which, as described briefly in §8.7, uses a combination of Bolles' feature-focus, Grimson and Lozano-Pérez's pairwise constraints and Faugeras and Hébert's early localization strategies (Pollard, Porrill, Mayhew and Frisby 1987)) has recently been implemented in parallel on MARVIN, a coarse grained, transputer multiprocessor system being developed at the University of Sheffield (Rygol, Pollard, Brown and Kay 1990). Even using only a small library of models, the recognition stage still takes approximately 15% of the system's total computation time. Given that approximately 50% of this total is devoted to low-level image processing operations which have been implemented elsewhere on video-rate pipeline processors (see (Faugeras, Deriche, Ayache, Lustman and Guiliano 1988)), recognition is indeed one of the dominant computational processes. Object recognition seems likely to threaten as a serious computational bottleneck in the years ahead.

10.10.2 Model and data representation

Perhaps the biggest challenge in recognition, however, is what representations of model and data primitives will be effective for objects which
cannot be described in simple CAD terms?

Piecewise smooth surface patches, of the sort employed by Besl and
Jain (1985) and Fisher (1987, 1989), appear valuable where dense sensory data are available, but the number of model surfaces could become
very large. The other difficulty, which we have discussed already, is that
passive vision techniques are not particularly good at supplying dense
surface data. Another line of research is to use models which embody
the physics of their construction, thus allowing deformation over time.
So far, these dynamical models have been used for data description, both
at the image level (eg snakes for tracking edges (Kass, Witkin and Terzopoulos 1987)) and at the 3D level to describe stereo data (Terzopoulos,
Witkin and Kass 1987) as well as for graphics (Terzopoulos and Witkin
1988; Barr 1987). Such representations have only just begun to be used
for recognition (Pentland 1990), but at this stage it is not clear that
such complete physical modelling is necessary or even desirable for this
task. For example, although this approach does offer one way of trying to remedy the deficiences of the lack of recognition of phenomena
referred to earlier, it does not seem a good way of recognizing complex
phenomena such as the flow of water over a waterfall. Recognizing such
phenomena seems to require a structured representation of shape.

One structured shape representation that has been explored is the
use of characteristic views. These were used initially (but unwittingly)
by Roberts (1965) for a small set of primitive polyhedra. Chakravarty
and Freeman (1982) studied more general polyhedral objects, and more
recently the approach has been extended to generic curved objects by
several workers (Callahan and Weiss 1985; Rieger 1987a,b). This and
the use of multiple views, as in the related notion of view potential
proposed by Koenderink and van Doorn (1976b, 1979), appear to hold
most promise for future development, though there will be significant
difficulties to overcome, such as computational complexity and problems
of occluded or missing data.

10.11   Shape and motion

But the question of shape is not one which can be left until the recognition level. It is, of course, an issue which permeates every aspect of visual processing, and is one which is complicated by the issues of scale, of resolution of the sensor array, of how the images are processed, and of what is being attended to. Certainly, there has been an overemphasis on quantitative description of shape in computer vision whereas the pioneering work of Koenderink and van Doorn (1979, 1982, 1986) and Koenderink (1984b) has shown that there is considerable scope for qualitative subtlety. Furthermore, they continue to emphasize the fact that the way that shape is probed is an essential part of the theory. Motion has a key rôle here, for small movements allow the camera to explore those subtleties.

This approach is giving rise to new and exciting perspectives on motion and shape understanding which begin to erode dependency on explicit motion fields and quantitative structure from motion computations of the sort we have used in our work. At Oxford, for example Zisserman, Giblin and Blake (1989) have addressed the question of what information about a surface is available by observing the movement of specularities from the surface in an image sequence, an example of motion invading a 'traditionally' static sensing modality to give a more powerful shape probe. From observations of one specularity they found that if its motion is in the opposite sense to that of the observer then the surface is not convex; whereas if the motion of the highlight is in the same sense as that of the observer then the surface could not be concave, unless one principal curvature were below some threshold. A second example of this qualitative approach is the recent work of Blake and Cipolla (1990) who recover surface curvature by observing the motion of extremal boundaries, yielding information which would facilitate navigation round the object or indeed grasping — this without becoming embroiled in the tyranny of dense depth maps and surface fitting.

It is becoming clear — and this comment was echoed by Faugeras in his opening address at the First European Conference on Computer Vision this year — that the state of play in motion processing today says as much about inability to describe shape as it does about ability to understand motion.

References

J Aloimonos, I Weiss and A Bandyopadhyay, 1987. Active vision. In *Proceedings of the 1st International Conference on Computer Vision, London, UK*, pages 35–54, IEEE Computer Society Press, Washington DC.

P Ananden and R Weiss, 1985. Introducing a smoothness constraint in a matching approach to the computation of displacement fields. In *Proceedings of the DARPA Image Understanding Workshop*, pages 186–196.

P Ananden, 1987. A unified perspective on computational techniques for the measurement of visual motion. In *Proceedings of the 1st International Conference on Computer Vision, London, UK*, pages 219–230, IEEE Computer Society Press, Washington DC.

R Andersson, 1988. *The Design of a Ping Pong Playing Robot*. MIT Press, Cambridge MA.

H Asada and J M Brady, 1984. The curvature primal sketch. In *Proceedings of the Workshop on Computer Vision: Representation and Control, Annapolis MD*, pages 8–17, IEEE Computer Society Press, Silver Spring MD.

N Ayache and O D Faugeras, 1988. Building, registrating and fusing noisy visual maps. *International Journal of Robotics Research*, 7(6):45–65.

N Ayache and F Lustman, 1987. Fast and reliable passive trinocular stereovision. In *Proceedings of the 1st International Conference on Computer Vision, London, UK*, pages 422–427, IEEE Computer Society Press, Washington DC.

D H Ballard and C M Brown, 1982. *Computer Vision*. Prentice-Hall, New Jersey.

D H Ballard and A Ozcandarli, 1988. Eye fixation and early vision: kinetic depth. In *Proceedings of the 2nd International Conference on Computer Vision, Tampa FL*, pages 524–531, IEEE Computer Society Press, Washington DC.

D H Ballard, 1987. *Eye Movements and Spatial Cognition*. Technical Report TR-218, Department of Computer Science, University of Rochester.

P Baraldi, E De Micheli and S Uras, 1989. Motion and depth from optical flow. In *Proceedings of the 5th Alvey Vision Conference, Reading, UK, September 1989*, pages 205–208.

S T Barnard and W B Thompson, 1980. Disparity analysis of images. *IEEE Transactions on Pattern Analysis and Machine Intelligence*, PAMI-2(4):333–340.

A H Barr, 1987. Topics in physically-based modelling (SIGGRAPH'87 course notes). *Computer Graphics: Quarterly Report of ACM SIGGRAPH*, 21.

J Barron, 1984. *A Survey of Approaches for Determining Optic Flow, Environmental Layout and Egomotion*. Technical Report RBCV-TR-84-5, Department of Computer Science, University of Toronto.

H G Barrow and J M Tenenbaum, 1978. Recovering intrinsic scene characteristics from images. In A R Hanson and E M Riseman, editors, *Computer Vision Systems*, pages 3–26, Academic Press, New York.

V Berzins, 1984. Accuracy of Laplacian edge detection. *Computer Vision, Graphics and Image Processing*, 27:195–210.

J Besag, 1974. Spatial interaction and the statistical analysis of lattice systems (with discussion). *Journal of the Royal Statistical Society B*, 36:192–326.

P J Besl and R C Jain, 1985. Intrinsic and extrinsic surface characteristics. In *Proceedings of the IEEE Conference on Computer Vision and Pattern Recognition, San Francisco CA*, pages 226–233, IEEE Computer Society Press, Silver Spring MD.

P R Bevington, 1969. *Data Reduction and Error Analysis for the Physical Sciences*. McGraw-Hill, New York.

A Blake and R Cipolla, 1990. Robust estimation of surface curvature from deformation of apparent contours. In O D Faugeras, editor, *Proceedings of the 1st European Conference on Computer Vision, Antibes, France (Lecture Notes in Computer Science, Vol 427)*, pages 465–474, Springer-Verlag, Berlin.

A Blake and A Zisserman, 1987. *Visual Reconstruction*. MIT Press, Cambridge MA.

A Blake, A Zisserman and A V Papoulias, 1986. Weak continuity constraints generate uniform scale-space descriptions of plane curves. In *Proceedings of the 7th European Conference on Artificial Intelligence, Brighton, UK*, pages 518–528.

R C Bolles, R Horaud and M J Hannah, 1983. 3DPO: a three dimensional part orientation system. In *Proceedings of the 8th International Joint Conference on Artificial Intelligence, IJCAI-83, Karlsruhe, FRG*, pages 1116–1120, William Kaufmann Inc, Los Altos CA.

O J Braddick, 1974. A short-range process in apparent motion. *Vision Research*, 14:519–527.

O J Braddick, 1980. Low-level and high-level processes in apparent motion. *Phil Trans Roy Soc Lond B*, 290:137–151.

J M Brady, 1987. Seeds of perception. In *Proceedings of the 3rd Alvey Vision Conference, Cambridge, UK, September 1987*, pages 259–265.

J M Brady, 1990. Private Communication.

A J Bray, 1990. Tracking objects using image disparities. *Image and Vision Computing*, 8(1):4–9.

A T Brint and J M Brady, 1990. Stereo matching of curves. *Image and Vision Computing*, 8(1):50–56.

R A Brooks, 1981. *Model-based Computer Vision*. UMI Research Press, Ann Arbor MI.

R A Brooks, 1986. A robust layered control system for a mobile robot. *IEEE Journal on Robotics and Automation*, 2:14–23.

R A Brooks, 1989. The whole iguana. In J M Brady, editor, *Robotic Science*, pages 432–456, MIT Press, Cambridge MA.

C M Brown, 1988. *Parallel vision with the Butterfly Computer.* Technical Report, Department of Computer Science, University of Rochester.

C M Brown, 1989a. *Gaze control with interactions and delays.* Technical Report TR-278, Department of Computer Science, University of Rochester.

C M Brown, 1989b. *Prediction in robotic gaze and saccade control.* Technical Report OUEL 1771/89, Department of Engineering Science, University of Oxford.

J B Burns, A R Hanson and E M Riseman, 1986. Extracting straight lines. *IEEE Transactions on Pattern Analysis and Machine Intelligence*, PAMI-8:425–455.

P Burt and B Julesz, 1980. Modifications of the classical notion of Panum's fusion area. *Perception*, 9:671–682.

B F Buxton and H Buxton, 1983. Monocular depth perception from optical flow by space time signal processing. *Proc Roy Soc Lond B*, 218:27–47.

B F Buxton and H Buxton, 1984. Computation of optic flow from the motion of edge features in the image. *Image and Vision Computing*, 2(2):59–75.

B F Buxton and D W Murray, 1985. Optic flow segmentation as an ill-posed and maximum likelihood problem. *Image and Vision Computing*, 3(4):163–169.

H Buxton and N Walker, 1988. Query-based visual analysis: spatio-temporal reasoning in computer vision. *Image and Vision Computing*, 6(4):247–254.

H Buxton and N S Williams, 1986. Applications of a fast parallel algorithm for the extraction and interpretation of optical flow. In *Proceedings of the 7th European Conference on Artificial Intelligence, Brighton, UK*, pages 539–545.

B F Buxton, H Buxton, D W Murray and N S Williams, 1984. 3D solutions to the aperture problem. In T O'Shea, editor, *Advances in Artificial Intelligence*, pages 105–114, Elsevier, Amsterdam.

B F Buxton, H Buxton, D W Murray and N S Williams, 1985. Machine perception of visual motion. *GEC Journal of Research*, 3(3):145–161.

B F Buxton, D W Murray, H Buxton and N S Williams, 1985. Structure from motion algorithms for computer vision on a SIMD architecture. *Computer Physics Communications*, 37:273–280.

J Callahan and R Weiss, 1985. A model for describing surface shape. In *Proceedings of the IEEE Computer Vision and Pattern Recognition Conference, San Francisco CA*, pages 240–245, IEEE Computer Society Press, Silver Spring MD.

J F Canny, 1983. *Finding edges and lines in images.* Technical Report TR-720, AI Laboratory, MIT.

J F Canny, 1986. A computational approach to edge detection. *IEEE Transactions on Pattern Analysis and Machine Intelligence*, PAMI-8(6):679–698.

D A Castelow, D W Murray, G L Scott and B F Buxton, 1988. Matching Canny edgels to compute the principal axes of optic flow. *Image and Vision Computing*, 6(2):129–136.

D A Castelow, 1989. Private Communication.

I Chakravarty and H Freeman, 1982. Characteristic views as a basis for three-dimensional object recognition. *SPIE Proceedings of Conference on Robot Vision*, 336:37–45.

D Charnley and R Blisset, 1989. Surface reconstruction from outdoor image sequences. *Image and Vision Computing*, 7(1):10–16.

J J Clark and N J Ferrier, 1988. Modal control of an attentive vision system. In *Proceedings of the 2nd International Conference on Computer Vision, Tampa FL*, pages 514–523, IEEE Computer Society Press, Washington DC.

M Clowes, 1971. On seeing things. *Artificial Intelligence*, 2(1):79–116.

C I Connolly, J L Mundy, J R Stenstrom and D W Thompson, 1987. Matching from 3D range models into 2D intensity scenes. In *Proceedings of the 1st International Conference on Computer Vision, London, UK*, pages 65–72, IEEE Computer Society Press, Washington DC.

K H Cornog, 1985. *Smooth pursuit and fixation for robot vision.* Master's thesis, Department of Electrical Engineering and Computer Science, MIT.

J L Crowley and P Stelmaszyk, 1990. Measurement and integration of 3D structures by tracking edge lines. In O D Faugeras, editor, *Proceedings of the 1st European Conference on Computer Vision, Antibes, France (Lecture Notes in Computer Science, Vol 427)*, pages 269–280, Springer-Verlag, Berlin.

J L Crowley, P Stelmaszyk and C Discours, 1988. Measuring image flows by tracking edge-lines. In *Proceedings of the 2nd International Conference on Computer Vision, Tampa FL*, pages 658–664, IEEE Computer Society Press, Washington DC.

M Demazure, 1988. *Sur deux problèmes de reconstruction.* Technical Report (Rapports de Recherche) 882, INRIA, France.

R Deriche and O D Faugeras, 1990. Tracking line segments. In O D Faugeras, editor, *Proceedings of the 1st European Conference on Computer Vision, Antibes, France (Lecture Notes in Computer Science, Vol 427)*, pages 259–268, Springer-Verlag, Berlin.

H Derin, H Elliot, R Cristi and D Geman, 1984. Bayes smoothing algorithms for segmentation of binary images modeled by Markov random fields. *IEEE Transactions on Pattern Analysis and Machine Intelligence*, PAMI-6(6):707–720.

P A Devijer and J Kittler, 1982. *Pattern Recognition: A Statistical Approach.* Prentice-Hall International, Englewood Cliffs NJ.

E D Dickmanns and A Zapp, 1986. A curvature based scheme for moving road vehicle guidance. *SPIE Proceedings of Conference on Mobile Robots*, 727:161–168.

E D Dickmanns, 1988. 4D dynamic scene analysis with integral spatio-temporal models. In R Bolles and B Roth, editors, *Robotics Research: 4th International Symposium 1987*, pages 311–318, MIT Press, Cambridge MA.

L Dreschler and H-H Nagel, 1981. Volumetric model and 3-D trajectory of a moving car derived from monocular TV-frame sequences of a street scene. In *Proceedings of the 7th International Joint Conference on Artificial Intelligence, IJCAI-81*, pages 692–697, Morgan Kaufmann, Los Altos CA.

J H Duncan and T-C Chou, 1988. Temporal edges: the detection of motion and the computation of optical flow. In *Proceedings of the 2nd International Conference on Computer Vision, Tampa FL*, pages 374–382, IEEE Computer Society Press, Washington DC.

H F Durrant-Whyte, 1987. *Integration, Coordination and Control of Multisensor Robot Systems*. Kluwer, Boston MA.

O D Faugeras and M Hébert, 1983. A 3D recognition and positioning algorithm using geometric matching between primitive surfaces. In *Proceedings of the 8th International Joint Conference on Artificial Intelligence, IJCAI-83, Karlsruhe, FRG*, pages 996–1002, William Kaufmann Inc, Los Altos CA.

O D Faugeras and G Toscani, 1986. The calibration problem for stereo. In *Proceedings of the IEEE Conference on Computer Vision and Pattern Recognition, Miami Beach FL*, pages 15–20, IEEE Computer Society Press, Washington DC.

O D Faugeras, R Deriche and N Navab, 1989. From optical flow of lines to 3D motion and structure. In *Proceedings of the IEEE International Workshop on Intelligent Systems, Tsukuba, Japan*, pages 646–649.

O D Faugeras, R Deriche, N Ayache, F Lustman and E Guiliano, 1988. DMA: the machine being developed in ESPRIT Project P940. In *IAPR Workshop on Computer Vision, Special Hardware and Industrial Applications, Tokyo, October, 1988*, pages 35–44.

O D Faugeras, M Hébert, J Ponce and E Pauchon, 1983. Object representation, identification and position from range data. In J M Brady and R Paul, editors, *Proceedings of the 1st International Symposium on Robotics Research*, MIT Press, Cambridge MA.

O D Faugeras, F Lustman and G Toscani, 1987. Motion and structure from motion from point and line matches. In *Proceedings of the 1st International Conference on Computer Vision, London, UK*, pages 25–34, IEEE Computer Society Press, Washington DC.

C L Fennema and W B Thompson, 1979. Velocity determination in scenes containing several moving objects. *Computer Graphics and Image Processing*, 9:301–315.

R B Fisher, 1987. Representing three-dimensional structures for visual recognition. *Artificial Intelligence Review*, 1:183–200.

R B Fisher, 1989. *From Surfaces to Objects*. John Wiley, Chichester, UK.

M M Fleck, 1988a. *Boundaries and Topological Algorithms*. PhD thesis, Department of Electrical Engineering and Computer Science, MIT.

M M Fleck, 1988b. Representing space for practical reasoning. *Image and Vision Computing*, 6(2):75–86.

M M Fleck, 1989. Spectre: an improved phantom edge finder. In *Proceedings of the 5th Alvey Vision Conference, Reading, UK, September 1989*, pages 127–132.

A M Flynn and J G Harris, 1985. Recognition algorithms for the Connection Machine. In *Proceedings of the 9th International Joint Conference on Artificial Intelligence, IJCAI-85, Los Angeles CA*, pages 57–60, Morgan Kaufmann, Los Altos CA.

D Forsyth and A Zisserman, 1990. Shape from shading in the light of mutual illumination. *Image and Vision Computing*, 8(1):42–49.

J P Frisby and J E W Mayhew, 1990. *3D Model Recognition from Stereoscopic Cues.* MIT Press, Cambridge MA. In Press.

P C Gaston and T Lozano-Pérez, 1984. Tactile recognition and localization using object models: the case of polyhedra on a plane. *IEEE Transactions on Pattern Analysis and Machine Intelligence*, PAMI-6(3):257–266.

S Geman and D Geman, 1984. Stochastic relaxation, Gibbs distributions, and the Bayesian restoration of images. *IEEE Transactions on Pattern Analysis and Machine Intelligence*, PAMI-6(6):721–741.

D Geman and S Geman, 1987. *Relaxation and annealing with constraints.* Technical Report, Division of Applied Mathematics, Brown University.

J J Gibson and E J Gibson, 1957. Continuous perspective transformations and the perception of rigid motions. *Journal of Experimental Psychology*, 54(2):129–138.

J J Gibson, P Olum and F Rosenblatt, 1955. Parallax and perspective during aircraft landing. *American Journal of Psychology*, 68:372–384.

J J Gibson, 1950. *The Perception of the Visual World.* Houghton Mifflin, Boston MA.

J J Gibson, 1966. *The Senses Considered as Perceptual Systems.* Houghton Mifflin, Boston MA.

G Giraudon and P Garnesson, 1987. *Chainage efficace de contour.* Technical Report (Rapports de Recherche) 605, INRIA, Valbonne, France.

G Giraudon, 1987. Real-time parallel edge following in a single pass. In *Proceedings of the IEEE Computer Society Workshop on Computer Vision, Miami Beach FL, Nov-Dec 1987*, pages 228–230, IEEE Computer Society Press, Washington DC.

F Girosi, A Verri and V Torre, 1989. Constraints in the computation of optical flow. In *Proceedings of the IEEE Workshop on Visual Motion, Irvine CA*, pages 116–124, IEEE Computer Society Press, Washington DC.

S Gong, 1989a. The curve motion constraint equation and its application in parallel visual motion estimation. In *Proceedings of the IEEE Workshop on Visual Motion, Irvine CA*, IEEE Computer Society Press, Washington DC.

S Gong, 1989b. *Parallel Computation of Visual Motion.* PhD thesis, University of Oxford.

W E L Grimson and T Lozano-Pérez, 1984. Model-based recognition and localization from sparse range or tactile data. *International Journal of Robotics Research*, 3:3–35.

W E L Grimson and T Lozano-Pérez, 1985a. Recognition and localization of overlapping parts from sparse data in two and three dimensions. In *Proceedings of the IEEE International Conference on Robotics and Automation, St Louis*, pages 61–66, IEEE Computer Society Press, Silver Spring MD.

W E L Grimson and T Lozano-Pérez, 1985b. Search and sensing strategies for recognition and localization of two and three dimensional objects. In *Proceedings of the 3rd International Symposium of Robotics Research, Gouvieux, France*, pages 81–88.

W E L Grimson and T Lozano-Pérez, 1987. Localizing overlapping parts by searching the interpretation tree. *IEEE Transactions on Pattern Analysis and Machine Intelligence*, PAMI-9:469–482.

W E L Grimson, 1984. *The combinatorics of local constraints in model-based recognition and localization from sparse data*. Technical Report AI Memo 763, AI Laboratory, MIT.

W E L Grimson, 1987. Recognition of object families using parameterized models. In *Proceedings of the 1st International Conference on Computer Vision, London, UK*, pages 93–101, IEEE Computer Society Press, Washington DC.

P Grossmann, 1987. COMPACT - a 3D shape representation scheme for polyhedral scenes. In *Proceedings of the 3rd Alvey Vision Conference, Cambridge, September 1987*, pages 237–244.

P Grossmann, 1988. In *Planes and quadrics from 3D segments (Technical Report R4.1.6, ESPRIT Project P940)*.

P Grossmann, 1989. COMPACT – a surface representation scheme. *Image and Vision Computing*, 7(2):115–121.

R M Haralick, 1986. Computer vision theory: the lack thereof. *Computer Vision, Graphics and Image Processing*, 36:372–386.

C G Harris and J M Pike, 1988. 3D positional integration from 3D sequences. *Image and Vision Computing*, 6(2):87–90.

C G Harris and M J Stephens, 1988. A combined corner and edge detector. In *Proceedings of the 4th Alvey Vision Conference, Manchester, UK, August 1988*, pages 147–151.

C G Harris, M C Ibison, E P Sparkes and M Stephens, 1986. Structure and motion from optical flow. In *Proceedings of the 2nd Alvey Vision Conference, Bristol, UK*.

C G Harris, 1987. Determining ego-motion from matched points. In *Proceedings of the 3rd Alvey Vision Conference, Cambridge, UK, September 1987*, pages 189–192.

H von Helmholtz, 1896. *Treatise on physiological optics*. Translated from 3rd edition by J P C Southall (1924), republished by Dover, New York (1962).

E C Hildreth and C Koch, 1987. The analysis of visual motion: from computation theory to neuronal mechanisms. *Annual Review of Neuroscience*, 10:477–533.

E C Hildreth and S Ullman, 1982. *The measurement of visual motion*. Technical Report 699, AI Laboratory, MIT.

E C Hildreth, 1984a. Computations underlying the measurement of visual motion. *Artificial Intelligence*, 23:309–354.

E C Hildreth, 1984b. *The Measurement of Visual Motion*. MIT Press, Cambridge MA.

D C Hogg, 1983. Model-based vision: a program to see a walking person. *Image and Vision Computing*, 1(1):5–20.

D C Hogg, 1988. Finding a known object using a generate and test strategy. In I Page, editor, *Parallel Architectures and Computer Vision*, pages 119–133, Oxford University Press, Oxford.

D Holder and H Buxton, 1990. SIMD geometric matching. In O D Faugeras, editor, *Proceedings of the 1st European Conference on Computer Vision, Antibes, France (Lecture Notes in Computer Science, Vol 427)*, pages 516–520, Springer-Verlag, Berlin.

J J Hopfield and D W Tank, 1985. Neural computation of decisions in optimization problems. *Biological Cybernetics*, 52:141–152.

B K P Horn and B G Schunck, 1981. Determining optical flow. *Artificial Intelligence*, 17:185–203.

B K P Horn and R W Sjoberg, 1979. Calculating the reflectance map. *Applied Optics*, 18:1770–1779.

B K P Horn, 1986. *Robot Vision*. MIT Press, Cambridge MA.

D Huffmann, 1971. Impossible objects as nonsense sentences. In B Meltzer and D Michie, editors, *Machine Intelligence 6*, Edinburgh University Press, Edinburgh, UK.

J M Hutchinson, C Koch, J Luo and C Mead, 1988 (March). Computing motion using analog and binary resistive networks. *IEEE Computer*, 52–63.

G Johansson, 1973. Visual perception of biological motion and a model for its analysis. *Perception and Psychophysics*, 14:201–211.

T Kanade, 1981. Recovery of the three-dimensional shape of an object from a single view. *Artificial Intelligence*, 17:409–460.

D Kapur and J Mundy, editors, 1989. *Geometric Reasoning*. MIT Press, Cambridge MA.

A Kashko, H Buxton, B F Buxton and D A Castelow, 1988. Parallel matching and reconstruction algorithms in computer vision. *Parallel Computing*, 7:3–17.

M Kass, A Witkin and D Terzopoulos, 1987. Snakes: active contour models. In *Proceedings of the 1st International Conference on Computer Vision, London, UK*, pages 259–268, IEEE Computer Society Press, Washington DC.

O Khatib, 1986. Real time obstacle avoidance for manipulators and mobile robots. *International Journal of Robotics Research*, 5(1):90–98.

S Kirkpatrick, C D Gellatt and M P Vecchi, 1983. Optimisation by simulated annealing. *Science*, 220:671–680.

J J Koenderink and A J van Doorn, 1975. Invariant properties of the motion parallax field due to the movement of rigid bodies relative to an observer. *Optica Acta*, 22:773–791.

J J Koenderink and A J van Doorn, 1976a. Local structure of movement parallax of the plane. *Journal of the Optical Society of America*, 66(7):717–723.

J J Koenderink and A J van Doorn, 1976b. The singularities of the visual mapping. *Biological Cybernetics*, 24:51–59.

J J Koenderink and A J van Doorn, 1979. Internal representation of solid shape with respect to vision. *Biological Cybernetics*, 32:211–216.

J J Koenderink and A J van Doorn, 1982. The shape of smooth objects and the way contours end. *Perception*, 11:129–137.

J J Koenderink and A J van Doorn, 1986. Dynamic shape. *Biological Cybernetics*, 53:383–396.

J J Koenderink, 1984a. The structure of images. *Biological Cybernetics*, 50:363–370.

J J Koenderink, 1984b. What does occluding contour tell us about solid shape? *Perception*, 13:321–330.

J J Koenderink, 1986. Optic flow. *Vision Research*, 26(1):161–180.

E P Krotkov, 1987. *Exploratory visual sensing with an agile camera system (PhD dissertation)*. Technical Report TR-87-29, Department of Computer Science, University of Pennsylvania.

E P Krotkov, 1989. *Active Computer Vision by Cooperative Focus and Stereo*. Springer-Verlag, New York.

E P Krotkov, J F Summers and F Fuma, 1986. *The Pennsylvania Active Camera System*. Technical Report TR-86-15, Department of Computer Science, University of Pennsylvania.

E Kruppa, 1913. Zur Ermittlung eines Objektes zwei Perspektiven mit innere Orientierung. *Sitz-Ber. Akad. Wiss., Wien, math. naturw. Kl., Abt. IIa.*, 122:1939–1948.

K Levenberg, 1944. A method for the solution of certain non-linear problems in least squares. *Quart Appl Math*, 2:164–168.

J O Limb and J A Murphy, 1975. Estimating the velocity of moving images in television signals. *Computer Graphics and Image Processing*, 4:311–327.

H C Longuet-Higgins and K Prazdny, 1980. The interpretation of a moving retinal image. *Proc Roy Soc Lond B*, 208:385–397.

H C Longuet-Higgins, 1981. A computer algorithm for reconstructing a scene from two projections. *Nature*, 293:133–135.

H C Longuet-Higgins, 1984. The visual ambiguity of a moving plane. *Proc Roy Soc Lond B*, 223:165–175.

D G Lowe, 1985. *Perceptual Organization and Visual Recognition*. Kluwer, Boston MA.

D G Lowe, 1990. Reported at the 1st European Conference on Computer Vision, Antibes, France.

E Mach, 1886. *The Analysis of Sensations.* Republished by Dover, New York (1962).

F Mangili and C Cassilino, 1988a. Finding planes and cylinders from arbitrary 3D segments. In *Planes and Quadrics from 3D Segments (Technical Report R4.1.6, ESPRIT Project P940).*

F Mangili and C Cassilino, 1988b. Quadrics and planes detection from stereo using constrained Delaunay triangulation. In *Improving 3D Shape Representations (Technical Report R4.1.7, ESPRIT Project P940).*

D W Marquardt, 1963. An algorithm for the least-squares estimation of non-linear parameters. *J Soc Indust Appl Math,* 11(2):431–441.

D Marr and E C Hildreth, 1980. Theory of edge detection. *Proc Roy Soc Lond B,* 207:187–217.

D Marr and H K Nishihara, 1978. Representation and recognition of the spatial organization of 3D shapes. *Proc Roy Soc Lond B,* 200:269–294.

D Marr and S Ullman, 1981. Directional selectivity and its use in early visual processing. *Proc Roy Soc Lond B,* 211:151–180.

D Marr, 1982. *Vision.* W H Freeman, San Francisco CA.

J Marroquin, 1984. *Surface reconstruction preserving discontinuities.* Technical Report AI Memo 792, AI Laboratory, MIT.

L Matthies, R Szeliski and T Kanade, 1989. Kalman filter based algorithms for estimating depth from image sequences. *International Journal of Computer Vision,* 3:209–238.

S J Maybank and O D Faugeras, 1990. Ambiguity in reconstruction from image correspondences. In O D Faugeras, editor, *Proceedings of the 1st European Conference on Computer Vision, Antibes, France (Lecture Notes in Computer Science, Vol 427),* pages 177–186, Springer-Verlag, Berlin.

S J Maybank, 1986. Algorithm for analysing optical flow based on the least-squares method. *Image and Vision Computing,* 4:38–42.

S J Maybank, 1987a. A second look at the least-squares algorithm for recovering information from optical flow. In *Proceedings of the Third Alvey Vision Conference, Cambridge, September 1987,* pages 221–226.

S J Maybank, 1987b. *A theoretical study of optical flow.* PhD thesis, Birkbeck College, University of London.

S J Maybank, 1990. The projective geometry of ambiguous surfaces. *Phil Trans Roy Soc Lond.* To be published.

A McIvor, 1988. Edge detection in dynamic vision. In *Proceedings of the 4th Alvey Vision Conference, Manchester, UK, August 1988,* pages 141–145.

N Metropolis, A W Rosenbluth, M N Rosenbluth, A H Teller and E Teller, 1953. Equations of state calculations by fast computing machines. *Journal of Chemical Physics,* 21:1087–1091.

M Mohnhaupt and B Neumann, 1990. On the use of motion concepts for top-down control in traffic scenes. In O D Faugeras, editor, *Proceedings of the 1st European Conference on Computer Vision, Antibes, France (Lecture Notes in Computer Science, Vol 427)*, pages 598–600, Springer-Verlag, Berlin.

D W Murray and B F Buxton, 1984. Reconstructing the optic flow field from edge motion: an examination of two different approaches. In *Proceedings of the 1st IEEE Conference on Artificial Intelligence Applications, Denver CO*, pages 382–388, IEEE Computer Society Press, Silver Spring MD.

D W Murray and B F Buxton, 1987. Scene segmentation from visual motion using global optimization. *IEEE Transactions on Pattern Analysis and Machine Intelligence*, PAMI-9:220–228.

D W Murray and D B Cook, 1988. Using the orientation of fragmentary 3D edge segments for polyhedral object recognition. *International Journal of Computer Vision*, 2(2):147–163.

D W Murray and N S Williams, 1986. Detecting the image boundaries between optical flow fields from several moving planar facets. *Pattern Recognition Letters*, 4:87–92.

D W Murray, D A Castelow and B F Buxton, 1988. From an image sequence to a recognized polyhedral object. *Image and Vision Computing*, 6(2):107–120.

D W Murray, D A Castelow and B F Buxton, 1989. From image sequences to recognized moving polyhedral objects. *International Journal of Computer Vision*, 3(3):181–208.

D W Murray, A Kashko and H Buxton, 1986. A parallel approach to the picture restoration algorithm of Geman and Geman on an SIMD machine. *Image and Vision Computing*, 4(3):133–142.

D W Murray, 1987. Model-based recognition using 3D shape alone. *Computer Vision, Graphics and Image Processing*, 40:250–266.

D W Murray, 1990. Algebraic polyhedral constraints and 3D structure from motion. *Image and Vision Computing*, 8(1):24–31.

H-H Nagel, 1983. Displacement vectors derived from second-order intensity variations in image sequences. *Computer Vision, Graphics and Image Processing*, 21:85–117.

H-H Nagel, 1988. From image sequences towards conceptual descriptions. *Image and Vision Computing*, 6(2):59–74.

S Negadaripour and B K P Horn, 1985. Determining 3D motion of planar objects from image brightness patterns. In *Proceedings of the 9th International Joint Conference on Artificial Intelligence, IJCAI-85, Los Angeles CA*, pages 898–901, Morgan Kaufmann, Los Altos CA.

B Neumann, 1984. Natural language access to image sequences: event recognition and verbalization. In *Proceedings of the 1st IEEE Conference on Artificial Intelligence Applications, Denver CO*, pages 226–231, IEEE Computer Society Press, Silver Spring MD.

B Neumann, 1989. Natural language description of time varying scenes. In D L Waltz, editor, *Semantic Structures*, pages 167–207, Lawrence Erlbaum, Hillsdale NY.

H K Nishihara, 1984. Practical real-time imaging stereo matcher. *Optical Engineering*, 23(5):536–545.

J A Noble, 1988a. Finding corners. *Image and Vision Computing*, 6(2):121–128.

J A Noble, 1988b. Morphological feature detection. In *Proceedings of the 4th Alvey Vision Conference, Manchester, UK, August 1988*, pages 203–209.

A Pentland, 1990. Extraction of deformable part models. In O D Faugeras, editor, *Proceedings of the 1st European Conference on Computer Vision, Antibes, France (Lecture Notes in Computer Science, Vol 427)*, pages 397–401, Springer-Verlag, Berlin.

T Poggio, V Torre and C Koch, 1985. Computational vision and regularization theory. *Nature*, 317:314–319.

S B Pollard, J E W Mayhew and J P Frisby, 1985. PMF: a stereo correspondence algorithm using a disparity gradient limit. *Perception*, 14:449–470.

S B Pollard, J Porrill and J E W Mayhew, 1990. Experiments in vehicle control using predictive feed forward stereo. *Image and Vision Computing*, 8(1):63–70.

S B Pollard, J Porrill, J E W Mayhew and J P Frisby, 1986. *Disparity gradient, Lipschitz continuity, and computing binocular correspondences*. Technical Report AIVRU-010, Artificial Intelligence Vision Research Unit, Department of Psychology, University of Sheffield.

S B Pollard, J Porrill, J E W Mayhew and J P Frisby, 1987. Matching geometrical descriptions in three-space. *Image and Vision Computing*, 5:73–78.

J Porrill, S B Pollard, T P Pridmore, J B Bowen, J E W Mayhew and J P Frisby, 1987. TINA: the Sheffield AIVRU Vision System. In *Proceedings of the 10th International Joint Conference on Artificial Intelligence, IJCAI-87, Milan, Italy*, pages 1138–1144.

J Porrill, 1988. Optimal combination and constraints for geometrical sensor data. *International Journal of Robotics Research*, 7(6):66–77.

T P Pridmore, J B Bowen and J E W Mayhew, 1986. *Geometrical description of the CONNECT graph*. Technical Report AIVRU-012, Artificial Intelligence Vision Research Unit, Department of Psychology, University of Sheffield.

D R Proffitt and B I Bertenthal, 1984. Converging approaches to extracting structure from motion: psychophysical and computational investigations of recovering connectivity from moving point-light displays. In *Proceedings of the 1st IEEE Conference on Artificial Intelligence Applications, Denver CO*, pages 232–238, IEEE Computer Society Press, Silver Spring MD.

U Ramer, 1975. Extraction of line structures from photographs of curved objects. *Computer Graphics and Image Processing*, 4:81–103.

E S Reed, 1989. *James J Gibson and the Psychology of Perception*. Yale University Press.

W E Reichardt and T Poggio, 1980. Figure-ground discrimination by relative movement in the visual system of the fly. Part I: experimental results. *Biological Cybernetics*, 35:81–100.

J H Rieger, 1987a. *The geometry of view space of opaque objects bounded by smooth surfaces.* Technical Report, Queen Mary College, University of London.

J H Rieger, 1987b. On the classification of views of piecewise smooth objects. *Image and Vision Computing*, 5:91–97.

L Robert, R Vaillant and M Schmitt, 1990. 3D vision-based robot navigation, first steps. In O D Faugeras, editor, *Proceedings of the 1st European Conference on Computer Vision, Antibes, France (Lecture Notes in Computer Science, Vol 427)*, pages 236–240, Springer-Verlag, Berlin.

L G Roberts, 1965. Machine perception of three-dimensional objects. In *Optical and Electro-optical Information Processing*, MIT Press, Cambridge MA.

A Rosenfeld and A C Kak, 1982. *Digital Picture Processing, Volume 2.* Academic Press, New York.

M Rygol, S B Pollard, C R Brown and J Kay, 1990. MARVIN and TINA: a multiprocessor 3D vision system. Preprint.

G L Scott, 1987a. 'Four-line' method of locally estimating optic flow. *Image and Vision Computing*, 5(2):67–72.

G L Scott, 1987b. *Local and Global Interpretation of Visual Motion.* Pitman and Morgan Kaufmann, London and Los Altos CA.

Y Shoham, 1988. *Reasoning about Change: Time and Causation from the Standpoint of Artificial Intelligence.* MIT Press, Cambridge MA.

L A Spacek, 1986. Edge detection and motion detection. *Image and Vision Computing*, 4(1):43–56.

P Stelmaszyk, C Discours and A Chehikian, 1988. A fast and reliable token tracker. In *IAPR Workshop on Computer Vision, Special Hardware and Industrial Applications, Tokyo, October 1988.*

M J Stephens and C G Harris, 1988. 3D wireframe integration from image sequences. In *Proceedings of the 4th Alvey Vision Conference, Manchester, UK, August 1988*, pages 159–165.

G Stockman and J C Esteva, 1984. *Use of geometrical constraints and clustering to determine 3D object pose.* Technical Report, Department of Computer Science, Michigan State University.

M Subbarao, 1988. *Interpretation of Visual Motion: A Computational Study.* Pitman, London.

K Sugihara, 1982. Mathematical structures of line drawings of polyhedrons – toward man-machine communications by means of line drawings. *IEEE Transactions on Pattern Analysis and Machine Intelligence*, PAMI-4(5):458–469.

K Sugihara, 1984. An algebraic approach to shape-from-image problems. *Artificial Intelligence*, 23(1):59–95.

K Sugihara, 1986. *Machine Interpretation of Line Drawings*. MIT Press, Cambridge MA.

D Terzopoulos and A Witkin, 1988 (November). Physically based models with rigid and deformable components. *IEEE Computer Graphics and Applications*, 41–51.

D Terzopoulos, 1986. Regularization of inverse visual problems involving discontinuities. *IEEE Transactions on Pattern Analysis and Machine Intelligence*, PAMI-8:413–424.

D Terzopoulos, A Witkin and M Kass, 1987. *Symmetry seeking models for 3D object reconstruction*. IEEE Computer Society Press, Washington DC.

W B Thompson and S T Barnard, 1981. Lower-level estimation and interpretation of visual motion. *IEEE Computer*, 14:20–28.

W B Thompson and T-C Pong, 1987. Detecting moving objects. In *Proceedings of the 1st International Conference on Computer Vision, London, UK*, pages 201–208, IEEE Computer Society Press, Washington DC.

E H Thompson, 1959. A rational algebraic formulation of the problem of relative orientation. *Photogrammetric Record*, 3(14):152–159.

M Tistarelli and G Sandini, 1990. On the estimation of depth from motion using an anthropomorphic visual sensor. In O D Faugeras, editor, *Proceedings of the 1st European Conference on Computer Vision, Antibes, France (Lecture Notes in Computer Science, Vol 427)*, pages 211–225, Springer-Verlag, Berlin.

H P Trivedi and S A Lloyd, 1985. The role of the disparity gradient in stereo vision. *Perception*, 14:685–690.

R Y Tsai and T S Huang, 1981. Estimating three dimensional motion parameters of a rigid planar patch. *IEEE Transactions on Acoustics, Speech and Signal Processing*, ASSP-29(6):1147–1152.

R Y Tsai, 1986. An efficient and accurate calibration technique for 3D machine vision. In *Proceedings of the IEEE Conference on Computer Vision and Pattern Recognition, Miami Beach FL*, pages 364–374, IEEE Computer Society Press, Washington DC.

J L Turney, T N Mudge and R A Volz, 1985. Recognizing partially occluded objects. *IEEE Transactions on Pattern Analysis and Machine Intelligence*, PAMI-7:410–421.

S Ullman, 1979. *The Interpretation of Visual Motion*. MIT Press, Cambridge MA.

A Verri and T Poggio, 1987. Against quantitative optical flow. In *Proceedings of the 1st International Conference on Computer Vision, London, UK*, pages 171–180, IEEE Computer Society Press, Washington DC.

H Wallach and D N O'Connell, 1953. The kinetic depth effect. *Journal of Experimental Psychology*, 45:205–217.

H Wallach, 1976. On perceived identity: I. The direction and motion of straight lines. In H Wallach, editor, *On Perception*, Quadrangle, New York.

D Waltz, 1975. Understanding line drawings of scenes with shadows. In P H Winston, editor, *The Psychology of Computer Vision*, McGraw-Hill, New York.

A M Waxman and K Wohn, 1985. Contour evolution, neighbourhood deformation and global image flow: planar surfaces in motion. *International Journal of Robotics Research*, 4:95–108.

A M Waxman, B Kamgar-Parsi and M Subbarao, 1987. Closed-form solutions to image flow equations. In *Proceedings of the 1st International Conference on Computer Vision, London, UK*, pages 12–24, IEEE Computer Society Press, Washington DC.

D J A Welsh, 1976. *Matroid Theory*. Academic Press, New York.

H Westphal and H-H Nagel, 1986. Towards the derivation of three-dimensional descriptions of image sequences for nonconvex moving objects. *Computer Vision, Graphics and Image Processing*, 34:302–320.

J H Wilkinson, 1965. *The Algebraic Eigenvalue Problem*. Oxford University Press, Oxford, UK.

A Witkin, 1983. Scale space filtering. In *Proceedings of the 8th International Joint Conference on Artificial Intelligence, IJCAI-83, Karlsruhe, FRG*, pages 1019–1021, William Kaufmann Inc.

Y Yasumoto and G Medioni, 1985. Experiments in estimation of 3D motion parameters from a sequence of image frames. In *Proceedings of the IEEE Conference on Computer Vision and Pattern Recognition, San Francisco CA*, pages 89–94, IEEE Computer Society Press, Silver Spring MD.

A L Yuille and T Poggio, 1986. Scaling theorems for zero-crossings. *IEEE Transactions on Pattern Analysis and Machine Intelligence*, PAMI-8(1):15–25.

A L Yuille, 1983. *The smoothest velocity field and token matching schemes*. Technical Report AI Memo 724, AI Laboratory, MIT.

A L Yuille, 1984. *Zero crossings on lines of curvature*. Technical Report AI Memo 718, AI Laboratory, MIT.

A L Yuille, 1989. Zero-crossings on lines of curvature. *Computer Vision, Graphics and Image Processing*, 45:68–87.

A Zisserman, P Giblin and A Blake, 1989. The information available to a moving observer from specularities. *Image and Vision Computing*, 7:38–42.

Copyright acknowledgements

Several publishers have graciously permitted us to redraw figures from our papers. These are

- Kluwer Academic Publishers

    - (Murray and Cook 1988) in Chapter 8,
    - (Murray, Castelow and Buxton 1989) in Chapter 4;

- Elsevier Science (North Holland) Publishers

    - (Murray and Williams 1986) in Chapter 7;

- Academic Press

    - (Murray 1987) in Chapter 9;

- Butterworth Scientific Publishers

    - (Murray, Kashko and Buxton 1986) in Chapter 7,
    - (Murray, Castelow and Buxton 1988) in Chapter 4,
    - (Buxton and Murray 1985) in Chapter 7,
    - (Castelow, Murray, Scott and Buxton 1988) in Chapter 2,
    - (Murray 1990) in Chapter 6;

and

- The IEEE Computer Society Press

    - (Murray and Buxton 1984) in Chapter 6,
    - (Murray and Buxton 1987) in Chapter 7.

Index

Artificial Intelligence

Patrick Henry Winston and J. Michael Brady, founding editors
J. Michael Brady, Daniel G. Bobrow, and Randall Davis, current editors

AI in the 1980s and Beyond: An MIT Survey, edited by W. Eric L. Grimson and Ramesh S. Patil, 1987

Visual Reconstruction, Andrew Blake and Andrew Zisserman, 1987

Reasoning about Change: Time and Causation from the Standpoint of Artificial Intelligence, Yoav Shoham, 1988

Model-Based Control of a Robot Manipulator, Chae H. An, Christopher G. Atkeson, and John M. Hollerbach, 1988

A Robot Ping-Pong Player: Experiment in Real-Time Intelligent Control, Russell L. Andersson, 1988

Robotics Research: The Fourth International Symposium, edited by Robert C. Bolles and Bernard Roth, 1988

The Paralation Model: Architecture-Independent Parallel Programming, Gary Sabot, 1988

Concurrent System for Knowledge Processing: An Actor Perspective, edited by Carl Hewitt and Gul Agha, 1989

Automated Deduction in Nonclassical Logics: Efficient Matrix Proof Methods for Modal and Intuitionistic Logics, Lincoln Wallen, 1989

3D Model Recognition from Stereoscopic Cues, edited by John E.W. Mayhew and John P. Frisby, 1989

Shape from Shading, edited by Berthold K.P. Horn and Michael J. Brooks, 1989

Ontic: A Knowledge Representation System for Mathematics, David A. McAllester, 1989

Solid Shape, Jan J. Koenderink, 1990

Expert Systems: Human Issues, edited by Dianne Berry and Anna Hart, 1990

Artificial Intelligence: Concepts and Applications, edited by A. R. Mirzai, 1990

Robotics Research: The Fifth International Symposium, edited by Hirofumi Miura and Suguru Arimoto, 1990

Theories of Comparative Analysis, Daniel S. Weld, 1990

Artificial Intelligence at MIT: Expanding Frontiers, edited by Patrick Henry Winston and Sarah Alexandra Shellard, 1990

Experiments in the Machine Interpretation of Visual Motion, David W. Murray and Bernard F. Buxton, 1991

The MIT Press, with Peter Denning as general consulting editor, publishes computer science books in the following series:

ACM Doctoral Dissertation and Distinguished Dissertation Awards

Artificial Intelligence
Patrick Winston, founding editor
Michael Brady, Daniel Bobrow, and Randall Davis, editors

Charles Babbage Institute Reprint Series for the History of Computing
Martin Campbell-Kelly, editor

Computer Systems
Herb Schwetman, editor

The MIT Electrical Engineering and Computer Science Series

Exploring with Logo
E. Paul Goldenberg, editor

Foundations of Computing
Michael Garey and Albert Meyer, editors

History of Computing
I. Bernard Cohen and William Aspray, editors

Information Systems
Michael Lesk, editor

Logic Programming
Ehud Shapiro, editor; Koichi Furukawa, Jean-Louis Lassez, Fernando Pereira, and David H. D. Warren, associate editors

Research Monographs in Parallel and Distributed Processing
Christopher Jesshope and David Klappholz, editors

Scientific and Engineering Computation
Janusz Kowalik, editor

Technical Communications
Ed Barrett, editor

Printed in the United States
by Baker & Taylor Publisher Services

Printed in the United States
by Baker & Taylor Publisher Services